CREATIVE PROBLEM SOLVING

for Health Care Professionals

Cecelia K. Golightly, B.S.N., M.P.H.

Assistant Administrator
Eitel Hospital
Minneapolis, Minnesota

AN ASPEN PUBLICATION®
Aspen Systems Corporation
Rockville, Maryland
London
1981

Library of Congress Cataloging in Publication Data

Golightly, Cecelia K.
Creative problem solving for health care professionals.

Includes bibliographies and index.
1. Nursing service administration.
2. Hospitals — Administration.
3. Problem solving.
I. Title.

RT89.G64   001.4'2'02461   81-3631
ISBN: 0-89443-371-7   AACR2

Library of Congress Catalog Card Number: 81-3631
ISBN: 0-89443-371-7

Printed in the United States of America

1 2 3 4 5

To My Husband, *Hugh*

Table of Contents

Foreword ix
Preface xi
Acknowledgments xiii

PART I—THE PROCESS 1

Chapter 1—The PRESEARCH Process 3

    PRESEARCH—An Operational Definition 3
    PRESEARCH—The People-Centered Method 8
    Conclusion 12

Chapter 2—The Field of Uncertainty 13
    The Field of Uncertainty 13
    The Anatomy of a Conflict 17
    Simple Versus Complex Situations 22
    Conflict and the Organization's Energy 24
    Conclusion 25

Chapter 3—Data Gathering 27
    Existing Facts, Traditions, and Constraints 27
    Exploring the Field of Uncertainty 29
    Survey Methods 31
    Practical Hints from a Field Research Assistant 34
    Conclusion 37

Chapter 4—Examining Survey Responses 39
    Content Analysis 49
    Summary 51

Chapter 5—Issues Raise Questions about the Need for Change **53**

   Summary   56

Chapter 6—Data Supports Problem Statements **57**

   Formula for Defining Problems   57
   Involving the People Who Will Be Affected by Problem
      Solution   59
   Summary   62

Chapter 7—Exploring Alternatives and Arriving at Solutions **63**

   Generating Alternatives   64
   Determining Solutions   66
   Selecting the Best Acceptable Solution   69
   Summary   71

Chapter 8—The Action Plan **73**

   Management by Objectives   73
   Performance Evaluation Review Technique Charting   75
   Summary   82

Chapter 9—Evaluation and Followup **85**

   Summary   89
   Conclusion   89
   Delegating Problem-Solving Responsibilities 89

   PART II—THE APPLICATION

Chapter 10—Case Study—An Education Department Reorganized   **97**

   Identifying the Field of Uncertainty   98
   Collecting Data Systematically   99
   Analyzing the Data   102
   Stating the Problems   105
   Exploring Alternatives   109
   Charting the Action Plan   109
   Evaluating the Project   114
   Conclusion   117

Chapter 11—PRESEARCH: An Integral Part of Quality Assurance   **119**

   What Is Quality Assurance?   119

PRESEARCH'S Relevance to the JCAH Standard of
Quality Assurance in the Department of Nursing .. 123
Development of a Quality Assurance Program in a
Nursing Department 126

Chapter 12—Situational Interviewing **141**

Preparing for the Interview Process 141
Face-to-Face Interviewing 142
Situational Questionnaire 144
The Selection Process 144
Conclusion 148

Chapter 13—A Tool for Administrative Decision Making **151**

A Methods Analysis 154
Conclusion 161

Chapter 14—A Student's Nonthesis Project Paper **163**

Telephone Appointment System in the Internal
Medicine Department: Centralization Versus
Decentralization 163
Conclusion 173

Chapter 15—Interdepartmental Problem Solving **175**

Conclusion 179

PART III—THE THEORY BASE, MODELS AND CONCEPTS **187**

Chapter 16—Research within PRESEARCH **189**

Process Differentiation between Research and
Problem Solving 189
Hypothetical Case: Postoperative Respiratory
Infections 191
An Actual Research Project 193
An Anthropological Approach to the Study of
Educational Barriers of Adults at the
Postsecondary Level 193
Conclusion 207

Chapter 17—Planned Change Theory in PRESEARCH **209**

Conclusion 213

Chapter 18—The Use of Conceptual Models in Problem Solving ... **215**

   Conclusion 222

Chapter 19—A Comparison of Problem-Solving Models **223**

   Similarities and Differences in Problem-Solving
   Conceptualizations 223
   The PRESEARCH Model 227

Index **231**

Foreword

Now is the time for all levels of management, using a rational methodical process, to approach the problems and issues we face. The departmentalization of the hospital and the proliferation of technology have created a complex maze of workflow and communication patterns. The dilemma many health care industry departmental managers recognize is that while a high percentage of the management staff is primarily educated in a clinical discipline with very cursory preparation in management, the skills needed to manage the complexities of problems found in an organization such as a hospital, a health maintenance organization, or a community nursing organization are only just now being introduced into the curriculum provided to health professionals.

Managing our resources requires a systematic approach based on a solid collection of data and on the appropriate analysis of that data. The approach presented by Cecelia Golightly blends the commonly used problem-solving methodology with the infrequently used research technologies. It offers to the manager the strengths of both, since the focus is on the need for concise analysis of the problems, identification of all the parameters that influence those problems, and the determination of the most logical, effective solution.

The tool is clearly presented; it rests with the manager to use. The risk may result in improved management.

Barbara A. Donaho, R.N., M.A.

Preface

A mark of managerial excellence is the ability to solve problems and to manage change effectively. In service institutions where the work force is the single most important resource, the manager has the opportunity and obligation to tap that resource for problem solving. Participative management has nurtured numerous group problem-solving techniques. The concepts included in PRESEARCH are not basically original. In essence, it is an eclectic approach that combines research methodology, planned change theory, content analysis, methods analysis, human relations, group process, management principles, and conceptual models into a framework for systematized problem solving. The harmonious integration of theories and concepts provides a pragmatic problem-solving framework. The text relates the PRESEARCH process to each situation described. It converts a fragmented approach to complex problems into a multidisciplinary challenge. Ideally the content will stimulate an individual's synthesis of management theory into practice.

For easy reference this book is divided into three sections. Part I—*The Process* provides descriptive background information and rationale for the PRESEARCH process. The application and use of each phase of the problem-solving method is illustrated through examples, analogies, and minicase experiences.

Part II—*The Application* contains several examples of real situations and cases that illustrate the versatility of the process. The chapter that deals with a department's reorganization exemplifies each aspect of the material presented in Part I. In the chapter about quality assurance, the PRESEARCH method is a component of a comprehensive program. In the remaining chapters PRESEARCH provides a framework for approaching and dealing with multifaceted situations.

Part III—*The Theory Base, Models, and Concepts* presents the theories from which PRESEARCH was derived. This section is included for those who prefer information beyond the "why" and "how to." In this part of the book problem-solving models are compared and contrasted and the use of conceptual models is discussed. The chapter on research compares research to problem solving. It includes an actual research project that was designed and used within the PRESEARCH method.

The people-centeredness of PRESEARCH emphasizes involving those who will be affected by the outcome of their problem-solving efforts. Their inclusion, consequently, increases their acceptance of the solution and paves the way for implementation. This method has wide application in all aspects of management. Some examples are:

1. interdepartmental systems and/or relationships
2. programs that transcend organizational boundaries
3. quality assurance programs
4. problems laden with strained interpersonal relationships, and
5. academic inquiry models.

Although the process presented here grew out of hospital based experiences, the concepts are equally applicable to any organization. For years health care managers have thrived on management principles and techniques borrowed from the business world. It is therefore reasonable to believe that a problem-solving process that originated in health care has application in other work settings.

Acknowledgments

This volume exists because of a support network of colleagues who encouraged and endured its development. I am most appreciative for the opportunities afforded by Genevieve Carb, director of nursing at St. Joseph's Hospital, Chicago, Illinois, and Phyllis Crouse, patient care administrator at Mary Greeley Hospital, Ames, Iowa, both of whom allowed me to introduce "people-centered problem solving" to their nurse managers while the process was still in its infancy. Their positive feedback provided me with the stimulus to expand the original pamphlet version to a full sized volume.

I am especially grateful to my professional associates who contributed original material and personal experience to this publication. I am much indebted to Margaret Roach for her thoughts on conflict resolution. She has shared generously, for first publication, her "Anatomy of a Conflict." I am equally indebted to Catherine Marineau and Karla Klinger as well as Helen Talle, who unselfishly shared their research experiences with the readers.

In addition, a special thank you to Martyann Penberth, nurse associate of the W. L. Ganong Company who introduced PRESEARCH as an optional format for student nonthesis project papers. Adriane Weaver, R.N., one of her students at St. Joseph's College in North Windham, Maine, graciously consented to have her paper published as an example for educators and students alike. Gerard W. Frawley, president, Lawrence Seuss, hospital administrator, and Sister Dolore Rochon, assistant administrator in charge of nursing at St. Joseph's Hospital, St. Paul, Minnesota, deserve credit for providing a work environment that fostered the birth of PRESEARCH. In addition, Mary Riley, supervisor of nursing education, and the staff development coordinators at St. Joseph's deserve special recognition for their cooperative efforts in the PRESEARCH project used as the case example in Chapter 10. Francis Wiesner, hospital administrator, Eitel Hospital, Minneapolis, Minnesota, also deserves recognition for his continued support and cooperation. Numerous examples included in the book reflect the implementation of the PRESEARCH method in both organizations.

I am indebted to Ron Daline for his artistic interpretation of the models that enhance the content. I will always be grateful for the skillful secretarial services of Susan Hagen and the typing services of Judith Hamilton. Each of these ladies provided faithful and proficient assistance during the irregular hours required for the preparation of the manuscript. The encouragement, suggestions, and support from Warren and Joan Ganong were and always will be gratefully appreciated.

Part I

The Process

Chapter 1

The PRESEARCH Process

PRESEARCH—AN OPERATIONAL DEFINITION

PRESEARCH is a contemporary problem-solving process that incorporates some scientific elements of research into the art of problem solving. Contrasted to other problem-solving models that require a problem definition as one of the first steps, PRESEARCH leads the problem solver through a data collection process before defining a problem. This *pre-search* adds dimension to the original scope of immediately accessible problem-related information. Therefore, data collected through the *pre-search* phase supports and justifies problem definitions. This aspect of PRESEARCH can be of tremendous value to problem solvers when: (1) selling an idea to a boss, peers, or subordinates; (2) justifying the need for new equipment, revised procedures, department reorganization, or policy decisions; (3) determining solutions after acknowledging the circumstances surrounding the presenting situation; and (4) negotiating from strength because of having the appropriate background information available for quick reference.

Problem solving consumes a significant portion of every health care manager's workday. Within any institution, complex problems that cross departmental lines command the attention of department managers. The director of a large department often becomes the initiator of a solution-seeking process because of the number of people in the department who are affected by an interdisciplinary problem.

Usually a problem is first viewed symptomatically. Each individual symptom of a large ill-defined problem can appear as an isolated problem. The most difficult tasks are interpretation and definition in a complex situation. This is evidenced in conversations with managers about day-to-day operations when one hears, "While solving one problem we un-

3

covered three more." Problems may be so closely interrelated that a solution to only one or two produces no noticeable improvement.

The "tip of an iceberg" analogy could be used to illustrate this point; however, an example from childhood seems more descriptive. I remember my grandmother folding a newspaper and cutting out what appeared to be one-half of a paper doll. When she finished cutting, she opened up the folds and presented me with a whole string of hand-in-hand paper dolls. Each of the dolls looked alike but they originated from different parts of the newspaper. They were hand-in-hand; separate, yet joined together. In my experience a similarity exists with problems: they appear separate even though several are closely linked. Unfortunately, a great deal of time, money, and effort can be spent solving what appears to be one problem when it is actually only one component of a complex problem. How frustrating it is to spend time solving a problem and believe that it is resolved, only to discover it reappearing in a different form in the ensuing weeks or months. As a result, managers may get so tired of dealing with chronic problems that they begin to accept them as a way of life or eventually make unwise compromises. Therefore the steps leading up to problem definition are significantly associated with the solution's effectiveness.

The PRESEARCH method recognizes a "field of uncertainty" in every unbalanced situation. Within that uncertain area exists a potential for multiple, related problems. PRESEARCH provides a process framework for identifying, labeling, and dealing with as many problem components as the data-gathering phase uncovers. It does not offer a hard and fast guarantee that duplication of problem-solving efforts will be eliminated. The comprehensive approach does, however, reduce the odds of the problem's recurrence. In other words, the emphasis is on gathering information prior to defining the problem, rather than implementing a solution and then gathering information to find out why the solution did not work or was inadequate.

PRESEARCH was developed on the premise that an approach that simultaneously confronts several related problems is more cost effective than an approach that deals with problems as isolated entities. Cost effectiveness in this context considers such factors as dollars spent, time spent, emotional and physical energy spent (wear and tear on the manager), disruption of smooth operations, and deterioration of interpersonal relationships. A comparative cost-effective analysis of the multiple approach versus the single approach to quantify these variables was not conducted as PRESEARCH was evolving. Nevertheless, those who used the process in its developmental phase are in agreement that the outcomes

The PRESEARCH Process   5

have been well worth the expenditure of time and effort prior to defining the problems and taking subsequent actions.

Research Compared to Problem Solving

In Figure 1-1 a traditional problem-solving model is compared to the research model. In her book, *Guide for the Beginning Researcher*, Mabel Wandelt differentiates between the two in their statements of purpose: "The purpose of research is to reveal new knowledge; the purpose of

---

Figure 1-1 A Parallel Comparison of Scientific Research and the Art of Problem Solving

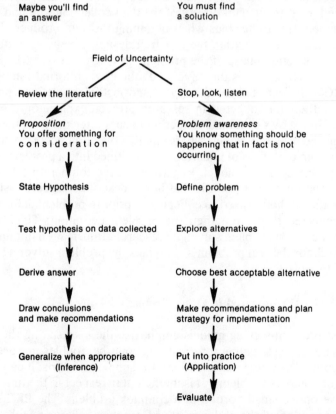

Source: Cecelia Golightly, *PRESEARCH: A New Approach to Creative Problem Solving for Hospitals and Other Health Care Agencies* (U.S.A.: Privately printed, 1978).

problem solving is to solve an immediate problem in a particular setting."[1] Research and problem solving differ in outcome as well as purpose and process. A good research model is designed so that it can be duplicated in another setting, whereas the "people" aspect of a problem-solving model recognizes the need to modify the solution to meet the needs of the people and the situation in each individual setting.

However, the data collection phase of the research can be applied to a problem-solving process, thereby enhancing the accuracy of the problem definition.

Research Compared to PRESEARCH

Figure 1-2 compares research to PRESEARCH by elaborating on the information gathering aspects of each model. In the research model, information is collected via a standardized, predetermined, and carefully designed instrument. Uniformity of the data collection tool and an effort to eliminate researcher bias when obtaining the data produce the purest information possible within the research design. Likewise, uniformity in the data collection phase of the problem-solving process, PRESEARCH, produces meaningful subjective and objective information. In PRESEARCH the data collected support and justify the defined problem(s) whereas the data collected in research are self-explanatory. A parallel comparison shows that data collection occurs after the hypothesis statement in the research model, whereas data collection occurs before information from the "field of uncertainty" is refined into a problem definition in the problem-solving model. Regardless of the comparative sequence of events, the significant point is that in the described process a structured systematic method is used to collect data prior to problem definition. The data collected then strengthen the problem definition. This, however, does not convert problem solving to research. Information obtained in the *pre*search for the real problem(s) provides the problem solver a base from which to work.

PRESEARCH Compared to Other Problem-Solving Methods

Most problem-solving models emphasize the user stating the problem before beginning to gather information about the troublesome area. While this approach is direct and necessary for simple problems, it can be inefficient for complex problems. It is inefficient in respect to the time required to solve only a small portion of a complex problem. The PRESEARCH developer adopted the philosophy of Dr. Jonas Salk who said "Answers preexist. It is the questions that need to be discovered."[2] Therefore the

Figure 1-2 A Comparison of Scientific Research and PRESEARCH

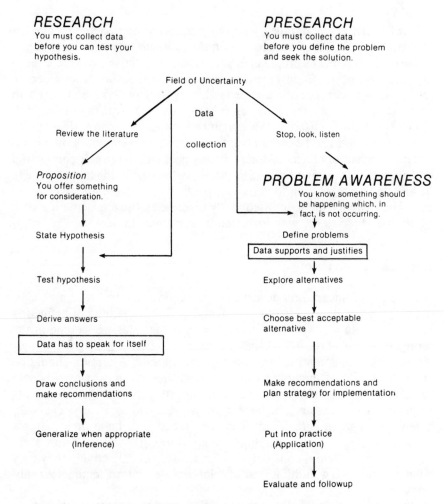

RESEARCH
You must collect data
before you can test your
hypothesis.

PRESEARCH
You must collect data
before you define the problem
and seek the solution.

Field of Uncertainty

Data

Review the literature

collection

Stop, look, listen

Proposition
You offer something
for consideration.

PROBLEM AWARENESS
You know something should
be happening which, in
fact, is not occurring.

State Hypothesis

Define problems

Data supports and justifies

Test hypothesis

Explore alternatives

Derive answers

Choose best acceptable
alternative

Data has to speak for itself

Draw conclusions and
make recommendations

Make recommendations and
plan strategy for implementation

Generalize when appropriate
(Inference)

Put into practice
(Application)

Evaluate and followup

Source: Cecelia Golightly, *PRESEARCH: A New Approach to Creative Problem Solving for Hospitals and Other Health Care Agencies* (U.S.A.: Privately printed, 1978).

*pre*search includes deliberative questioning prior to defining problems. It is this emphasis of data gathering that makes PRESEARCH unique.

In-depth discussions of problem-solving models and research techniques relating to the PRESEARCH method are presented in Part III of this book.

PRESEARCH—THE PEOPLE-CENTERED METHOD

PRESEARCH encourages a multidisciplinary approach to complex problems. The effect of the process on the problem solvers is fascinating. Since each step means progress toward a solution, those involved experience a sense of accomplishment as they progress. Although one person must function as a coordinator or facilitator, this method lends itself to group process. Since there are logical stopping points, many of the individual steps can be used as the structure for successive problem-solving committee meetings. Because an individual or group can work on a complicated project in blocks of time without backtracking, their energy and enthusiasm are sustained. PRESEARCH permits including those who will be affected by a solution in various aspects of the problem-solving process. Their involvement, consequently, increases their acceptance of a solution and paves the way for solution implementation.

The Field of Uncertainty

The field of uncertainty deserves exploration when received messages indicate that a situation is out of balance or that something ill-defined is interfering with an expected activity or outcome. Messages come in the form of "game playing," verbal and nonverbal feedback, gut feelings, written reports, committee minutes, or low morale. Attention should be given to a field of uncertainty from which multiple messages originate such as a nursing unit where the staff doesn't seem to get along, the employee turnover rate is higher than expected, and some physicians are happy with patient care while others are refusing to have their patients admitted to that unit. These symptoms are warning signals that may identify a single problem if considered individually, but collectively they may point to underlying multifaceted and interrelated interdisciplinary problems.

Once you have decided that the situation deserves attention, determine the purpose for exploring that field of uncertainty and state it in writing. The purpose can be simply to determine if the symptomatic feedback is significant. Write the reasons for investigating a situation. This will help you to set priorities and allocate time accordingly. Too often managers spend significantly more day-to-day problem-solving time in *urgent* "brushfire extinguishing" efforts that take priority over *important* long-range planning and crisis prevention efforts.

As you explore the field of uncertainty you will begin to examine more information. At this point you should decide how the data, once collected, will be used. Possible uses include assessing quality, determining appropriate community services, assessing learning, educating staff, evaluating performance, or analyzing a system. Correlate the anticipated use with the already identified reasons for obtaining more information. This will guide your decisions about how and in what depth you will collect factual information, and help you determine the kind of problem-solving efforts the situation deserves.

Identify the people or groups of people who are involved in this situation. Include those disciplines that might be affected by a solution (or change) to alleviate the symptoms of the suspected or ill-defined problem. For instance, if the symptoms are unrest among the nursing staff of a given unit, a high volume employee turnover, and disagreement among the physician users of the unit about the quality of patient care delivered, the appropriate target population would include the staff nurses in the unit, the head nurse, nurse supervisors, staff development personnel, and physician users of the unit.

Data Gathering

You should consider several methods of data collection and determine which one will be most appropriate for the situation. Some techniques to consider are personal interview, telephone survey, structured questionnaire, or methods analysis. Once a method is chosen, be certain that all data are collected on a standardized form and in a like manner. Pattern the data collection after the research model to assure consistency and to minimize the biasing influence of the person collecting the information. Thereafter formulate some questions whose answers should supply you with the needed information. You may develop a survey tool using either fixed alternative or open-ended questions (you may use both). Open-ended questions provide a frame of reference for participant responses, yet do not restrict the participant's manner of expression or content of answers. There is one distinct advantage of the open-ended question in this process. The respondents may give unexpected answers that identify aspects of the underlying problem not originally anticipated by those initiating or conducting the survey.

Settle on a time frame within which to collect the data and analyze the results. The complexity of the situation and the number of people included in your target population will greatly influence the amount of time required. It could be only a few hours or several weeks depending on the circumstances.

Collect the information in the chosen format. If you mail questionnaires, be sure to specify a deadline for returning the forms. Some of the pros and cons of useful data collection techniques are discussed at length in Chapter 3.

Data Analysis

PRESEARCH encourages the problem solver to collect subjective as well as objective data. This is based on the premise that interdisciplinary problems are potentially loaded with feelings. Therefore, the data analysis must acknowledge people's feelings as well as the facts. A content analysis approach is used to extract the issues imbedded in these responses. The objective data, on the other hand, can be tallied, graphed, compared, or associated as appropriate for the purposes of the problem solvers.

Issues Raise Questions about the Need for Change

After the subjective aspects of a situation have been addressed, the problem solver(s) must establish some goals or guides to restore equilibrium to the situation. The goal statements help the problem solver to stay on target while developing problem statements and exploring alternatives. Frequently, the goal can be a restatement of an already existing written or unwritten policy, philosophy, standard, or operating definition. It is important to realize that this is not merely a "goal writing exercise;" it is instead identifying an overall stabilizing course for problem-solving efforts.

Data Supports Problem Statements

Time has already been invested in collecting both objective and subjective information about the field of uncertainty. You have defined your desired state of equilibrium through goal statements. Now you must formulate the problem statements to incorporate numerous issues that have surfaced. The issues being addressed through problem statements are ones that need to be confronted, and the people involved in the problem solving need your help. For this reason, problem statements are developed by asking, "How can *we* (problem solvers) lend support to those affected by the imbalance?" This approach makes it possible to include those responsible for problem solving while acknowledging other relevant circumstances that will affect the strategy for implementation. Through this method the data collected support the problem statements because the statements are constructed from issues derived from that data as shown in Figure 1-2.

After developing problem statements it is imperative to identify the appropriate problem solver (the person who should be responsible) for each problem stated. Ask yourself, "Who owns this problem?" Don't try to solve a problem that does not belong to you. If you do, you will be conducting an exercise in futility. There will be times when you uncover an underlying problem that must be addressed and solved by someone else before you can proceed.

Group Process

PRESEARCH provides structure for group work. People come together for a well-defined common goal. They know what should be accomplished within the meeting time. Once a group cohesiveness is established, it is amazing how well members contribute to the meeting without the commonly encountered disruptive behavior that undermines unstructured meetings. Input from the people who will be affected by the solutions is considered extremely important in this process. Each group will need a facilitator. The facilitator has a key role because this person allows the participants to contribute any alternative, no matter how "far out," without questioning or being judgmental. If possible, the group facilitator should include the problem solver(s) when exploring alternative solutions to the problem. The larger number of alternative solutions posed, the greater the potential for a creative workable solution. The most creative approach combines several good elements from more than one alternative and generates a new alternative.

The person who is responsible for solving the problem should explore each alternative and concurrently consider factors affecting implementation. This can be done by examining the positive and negative forces that might facilitate, reinforce, or block its implementation. The *best* quality solution may not be the most acceptable solution. Look at the organization and scrutinize both its structure and its interrelated systems. Aim for the *best acceptable solution* because it *can* be implemented into the organization. If the best acceptable solution crosses departmental lines, state the desired solution in the form of a recommendation and make a formal presentation to the appropriate audience.

A Plan for Action

The action plan spells out how the solution will be implemented. It is not unusual to find that the best acceptable alternatives to the individual problems become steps or phases of the overall plan. Therefore, through the PRESEARCH process you build the plan. You will now need to add some time frames—what will be accomplished by whom, when. Several parts of the plan can take place simultaneously. You will also need to establish outcome criteria by which to measure the success of your problem-solving efforts. When you develop the outcome criteria, correlate those evaluative measures with your already established goals.

A strategy for implementing the plan must not be overlooked. The fact that you have already included many people in defining problems and exploring alternatives reduces the amount of time needed to explain "the problem" and the resulting need for change. If a formal proposal is indicated, be sure to include the rationale that was used to arrive at the best acceptable alternatives. This will strengthen and fortify both the proposal and you as the presenter. Graphs, charts, and conceptual models can also be used to enhance the proposal and to monitor implementation.

Measuring Results

Your plan will be implemented in phases; part of it may be an ongoing system maintenance effort. Therefore you measure results by evaluating individual segments of the plan as they are completed. This kind of evaluating gives the problem solvers opportunities to examine progress toward the goal at several points in time. Progress reports help to reinforce the importance of group effort and system maintenance in addition to providing a sense of accomplishment to those involved.

A followup mechanism should be built into the plan. After spending this much effort to restore balance to a situation, you will want to ensure that there is some way to institutionalize the action taken. Followup can be incorporated into some type of quality assurance program.

CONCLUSION

The philosophy of PRESEARCH is one of inquiry. The practicality of PRESEARCH is using available energy for the good of the organization. The PRESEARCH process is presented in depth in Chapters 2–9. It is summarized in a step-by-step procedure format at the conclusion of Part I in Chapter 9.

NOTES

1. Mabel A. Wandelt, *Guide for the Beginning Researcher* (New York: Appleton-Century-Crofts, 1970), p. xvii.
2. Jonas Salk, The National Foundation/March of Dimes Annual Report, 1973, p. 22.

Chapter 2

The Field of Uncertainty

THE FIELD OF UNCERTAINTY

The *field of uncertainty* represents a feeling of unsureness about some area of organizational behavior. You are aware that something should be happening which in fact is not occurring. You have reason to feel concerned, uneasy, perhaps even distressed. Somehow you are prompted to investigate the problem and discover that the closer you look, the more you uncover.

The concerned manager should approach the problem of unrest with a diagnostic orientation. An inquiring approach is essential because the field of uncertainty may stretch far beyond the presenting symptoms. Figure 2-1 presents a conceptual model of the field of uncertainty. The center of the model represents a person's area of freedom. In this context, *area of freedom* is defined as the parameters of one's job.[1] This framework represents the decision-making boundaries beyond which an individual cannot go without approval from the boss. The *field of uncertainty* encompasses all of the systems and subsystems that are interacting with or encroaching on the area of freedom. The field of uncertainty may stretch far beyond the unit in focus. This concept is equally applicable to work groups of all sizes, the institution, or the community as shown in Figure 2-2. The use of conceptual models in identifying and defining the field of uncertainty is presented in Part III, Chapter 18.

The manager recognizes the field of uncertainty as a disturbance that cannot be ignored. It can be a single event or a series of events. A crisis in one area often reveals a field of uncertainty in another area. The boss might say to you, "as long as you're looking into this, check out that other mess too." Or a procedure change that works well for one department can create havoc for another department. Systems that are established without a maintenance factor shift and change shape according to the users.

13

Figure 2-1 Area of Freedom within One's Job

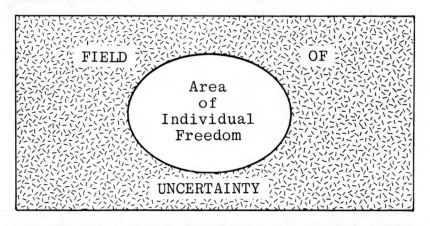

When a vital part of a functioning system gets neglected or remains unattended, the undesirable consequences command the manager's attention.

The way a manager responds to the warning signals depends on that person's own value system and life experiences. The manager's perception and tolerance level also influence how long the disturbance is allowed to continue. Long-term subtle disturbances can have a detrimental effect on the work group. These disturbances can become accepted by a work group as something they have to live with and work around. Disturbing situations encourage workers to build informal subsystems as coping

Figure 2-2 Area of Freedom of the Organization within the Community It Serves

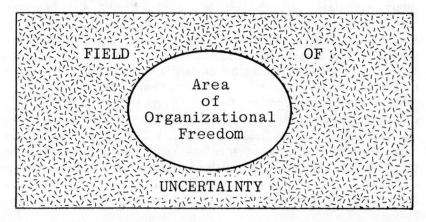

mechanisms. Sometimes these subsystems are functional. Other times they create a whole new set of problems. A close look may reveal the practice to be far removed from the original procedure.

A Warning System

The United States Weather Bureau has a highly sophisticated weather tracking system. Weather experts make up a 24-hour surveillance team. Their vigilance alerts them to changes in high and low pressure areas. A central control station warns the nation of impending turbulence. Local news media then inform the population of impending dangerous conditions.

Health care managers do not have a radarscope through which to view pressure changes as potential turbulence. Instead, through the years managers have learned to use the organizations' formal and informal communication network for warning signals.

According to Henry Mintzberg,[2] two behaviors of managers are monitoring and disturbance handling. In the "monitoring role," managers scan the environment for information constantly. They interrogate liaison contacts and subordinates. The unsolicited information they receive is a result of the network of personal contacts they have developed. Much of the information managers collect is in verbal form—often as gossip, hearsay, and speculation. The amount of information they receive depends on the extent of their communication network. The "disturbance handler role" depicts managers involuntarily responding to pressures and changes beyond their control. Managers must spend much of their time responding to high pressure disturbances. They must act because the situational pressures are too severe to be ignored. These pressures arise not only because poor managers ignore situations until they reach crisis proportions, but also because good managers cannot possibly anticipate all of the consequences of the actions they take. No health care agency can be so well run or so standardized that it has considered every contingency in the uncertain environment in advance.

Having a good communication network is not enough. Managers must use it. In her lectures to physicians and nurses, Pearl Rosenberg, a psychologist from the University of Minnesota, urges them "to listen to the music above the words." The manager must listen to the feelings that extend beyond verbalization. A musician might describe active listening as monitoring feeling tones, recognizing replays of the same tune, becoming aware of a new beat, and knowing when someone has written new words to an old melody. Similar descriptors identify happenings with, between, and among people. In a busy workday, the manager may hear only fleeting bars of the music. The ability to separate symphonic harmony from atonal discord is being sensitive to the warning signals.

Warning signals also come from nonverbal and written messages. It is wise to verify questionable nonverbal messages. Misinterpretation of signals can generate a series of disruptive events that could easily be avoided. Written communications such as interoffice memos, committee minutes, infection control reports, audits, budget reports, performance appraisals, meeting attendance records, and research findings should be used both as sources of information and as sources of verification. A trend noted by reading successive reports for a given time period may produce an unsuspected warning signal that the manager should be aware of.

It is possible to identify potential trouble areas. On a very simple Symptom Awareness Grid, as shown in Figure 2-3, you can list highly dependent work groups in specific departments. In the columns labeled "weeks," place a plus (+) or minus (−) indicating that you have received positive or negative information about specific interdependent groups within a department. This sheet will help you monitor negative messages and warn you that a specific segment of your work force deserves some of your attention. It will also alert you to give recognition to those who are performing well. This suggestion is based on Marguerite Schaefer's statements as a guest lecturer at a Patient Care Administration Seminar, Minneapolis, Minnesota, Spring of 1979.[3]

Conflicts occur between groups of people who have a high level of interdependency on each other. This is one reason for conflict in families. While we know that a certain amount of conflict is considered healthy, the

---

Figure 2-3 Symptom Awareness Grid

Interdependent Work Groups	Week date	1	2	3	4
Physician/Nurse ICU		+ + − − − − + −	− − + − − −		
Dietary/Nursing		− − + − + − − +	+ + − − − −		
Housekeeping/ Nursing		+ +	− + +		
Staffing coordinator/ Head nurses		− − + − −	+ + +		
Social service/ Discharge planning nurse		+ + +	+ +		

key is to recognize when conflict gets in the way of work group productivity.

Using the Symptom Awareness Grid in Figure 2-3, you should give attention and priority to the work relationships between the nurses and physicians in the intensive care unit (ICU). Obviously there is also some discord between the nursing and dietary departments. Further investigation of these two problem areas may narrow the focus to one nursing unit or even to a rift between one dietician and a nurse.

The relationship between housekeeping and nursing seems good, based on the information you are getting. It appears that there is less strife between the head nurses and the staffing coordinator in the second week than there was in the first week. Social service workers and the discharge planning nurse appear to be getting along well. With a few positive comments and recognition from you (their boss), they probably will continue to try to work in harmony. Monitoring interpersonal relationships in this manner, over a period of time, will provide you with a simple trend study of work group behavior among your employees.

Other authors, such as Virginia Satir, describe work groups as family-like units. Her workshops help large audiences recognize the similarities between family conflict and work group conflict. Likewise, transactional analysis (TA) deals with interactions among people behaving in parent, adult, and child roles. The TA model holds true every day, whether at home or at work. Being aware that the potential for conflict is ever with us, we must take time to examine why conflict occurs.

THE ANATOMY OF A CONFLICT

Margaret Roach, psychiatric nurse clinical specialist, lecturer, and colleague offers a unique interpretation of conflict to workshop audiences. Her explanation provides a basic understanding of "what is going on with people" involved in difficult situations. She describes simple conflict by using five progressive diagrams.

In Figure 2-4 the slanted line represents the desire that person A has for an object or goal. Desire in this context means the thought within A's mind. The thought may be "I want a new car." The mind is a field of energy that moves thought from the subconscious mind to conscious levels. The thought, once conscious, becomes reality. In other words, nothing man-made exists unless it was first a thought in someone's mind. For example, the automobile that person A desires was first conceptualized by someone else and later designed and manufactured. The goal of person A then is to obtain an automobile.

Figure 2-4 A's Goal Directed Behavior

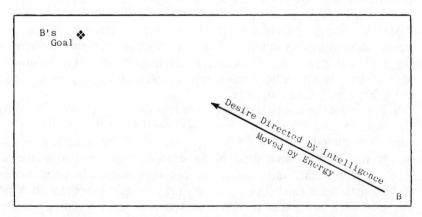

Source: Margaret Roach, St. Joseph's Hospital, St. Paul, Minnesota. Used with permission.

In Figure 2-5 person A and person B have a relationship of some sort. The goal of B, however, is to spend the same allocated amount of money on something else. He does not believe that the car is necessary or desirable. He wants to use that money for a different object. Here we have two people with desires raised to the conscious level through energy traveling on a collision course.

Figure 2-5 B's Goal Directed Behavior

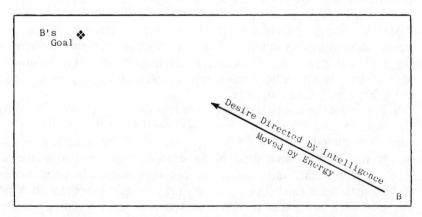

Source: Margaret Roach, St. Joseph's Hospital, St. Paul, Minnesota. Used with permission.

In Figure 2-6 the inevitable collision is due to each person's conflict of interest or goal directed behavior.

Figure 2-7 shows the collision occurring. This event causes an explosion of energy.

Figure 2-6 The Collision Course of A and B

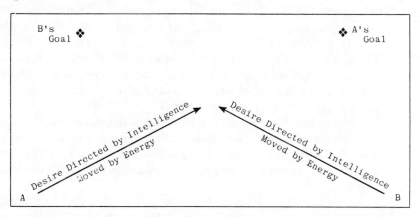

Source: Margaret Roach, St. Joseph's Hospital, St. Paul, Minnesota. Used with permission.

Figure 2-7 Explosion of Energy When Desires of A & B Collide

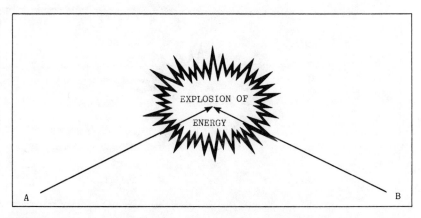

Source: Margaret Roach, St. Joseph's Hospital, St. Paul, Minnesota. Used with permission.

Figure 2-8 depicts the explosion of energy externally manifested through negative feelings. Once this has happened, people must cope with the negative feelings in one of the six following modes:[4]

I. Avoidance—This is an "I lose—you win" situation. It can be manifested when someone walks away from or turns his back on conflict.

II. Accommodation—This is an "I lose—you win" situation. It involves yielding or self-sacrifice on the part of one person who values his relationship with someone more than the desired object.

III. Competition—This is an "I win—you lose" situation. It occurs when you decide to pursue your own self-interests. More value is placed on the desired object than on the relationship with the person against whom you're competing.

IV. Compromise—This is an "I lose—you lose" situation. We both are able to give up something individual for our common good.

V. Collaboration—This is an "I win—you win" situation. Together we strive to arrive at a resolution that goes beyond our individual self-interests.

VI. Negotiation—This is an exchange situation. You and I exchange things we perceive to have equal value. Each of us clarifies our own self-interests and we bargain to protect them. This is done within the limits of maintaining our relationship.

Figure 2-8 Explosion of Energy Manifested through Negative Feelings

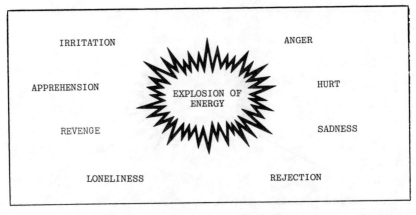

Source: Margaret Roach, St. Joseph's Hospital, St. Paul, Minnesota. Used with permission.

The manager who understands how conflicts originate and how people deal with them is prepared to confront disruptive situations. Staff members will seek the leadership of a manager who can help them confront conflict as a preliminary step toward problem solving.

Figures 2-4 through 2-8 depict simple conflict between two people. Based on years of crisis intervention, Margaret Roach has found that people who are involved in work group conflict often are experiencing severe conflict or crisis in their personal lives also. This observation is upheld by earlier industrial researchers. An extensive observant-listening study of workers' on-the-job behavior was conducted at the Western Electric Company in Hawthorne, Illinois, in the early 1920s. This research is frequently referred to as the Hawthorne Study. Elton Mayo, a Harvard University industrial researcher, reported:

> Many workers, I cannot say the majority for we have no statistics, seem to have something "on their minds," about which they wished to talk freely to a competent listener. And these topics were by no means confined to the matters affecting the company. . . .
>
> The researcher group began to talk about the need for "emotional release" and the great advantage that accrued to the individual when he had "talked off" his problem. The topics varied greatly. One worker two years before had been sharply reprimanded by his supervisor for not working as usual: in interview he wished to explain that on the night preceding the day of the incident, his wife and child had both died, apparently unexpectedly. At the time he was unable to explain; afterwards, he had no opportunity to do so. He told the story dramatically and in great detail; there was no doubt whatever that telling it thus benefited him greatly. But this story naturally was exceptional; more often a worker would speak of his family and domestic situation, of his church, of his relations with other members of the working group—quite usually the topic of which he spoke presented itself as a problem difficult for him to resolve. This led to the next successive illumination for the inquiry. It became manifest that, whatever problem, it was partly, and sometimes wholly, determined by the attitude of the individual worker. And this defect or distortion of attitude was consequent in his past experience or his present situation, or, more usually, and both at once.[5]

The study revealed the great benefit of employees being allowed emotional release and the extent to which every individual's problems are conditioned by personal history and situation. Mayo concluded that while an interview program retains importance, it must move beyond the individual's need for therapy.

Margaret Roach contends that workers who are having difficulty coping with stress in their personal lives are likely to replay this personal conflict or crisis in the work environment. This can surface in the form of a stressful work related situation or work group conflict similar to the conflict being experienced off the job. This is an unconscious attempt by the worker to solve a personal conflict or to show oneself that coping abilities exist. Consider the Roach premise with the findings of the observant listeners in the Hawthorne Study. This does not suggest that managers need to be minipsychologists. It does suggest that the manager who is astute will know what is going on with the workers. With such information the manager has a broader problem-solving knowledge, making it easier to prioritize the expenditures of managerial problem-solving energy.

The anatomy of *complex* conflict then can be described as one involving many people and many issues. It represents many people with desired goals. Some goals are work related, some are not. It is the manager's function to determine if these conflicts can be dealt with as simple matters or if they are so interrelated that the matter has become complex.

SIMPLE VERSUS COMPLEX SITUATIONS

Once a disturbance has gained the manager's attention, it is common to address a precipitating symptom as *the problem*. Often a symptom is stated as "the problem is . . . ," followed by the statement, "we had better do . . . to solve this." That approach works for simple, uncomplicated problems. The adage of the right solution to the wrong problem holds true when action is taken too quickly—in other words, before determining the matter to be complex.

Any one of the following examples has conflict potential:

- an inadequate or outdated policy is interpreted differently by individuals or groups
- job performance expectations are unclear
- territorial rights are misused
- individual selfish motives cause someone to obtain an increased amount of formal or informal power
- discrepancies exist between priorities of the boss and subordinate
- grapevine hearsay is interpreted as factual
- someone reports to more than one boss

- established channels of communication are bypassed
- an individual does not have the authority needed to carry out the job responsibilities
- people do not respect or trust their coworkers or superiors.

Each of these can result in an out-of-balance work situation. Furthermore, they could become either simple or complex situations. How does the manager separate the simple from the complex? One rule of thumb is to gather information and approximate the extent of the turbulence. This helps separate the simple from the complex and helps the manager make a decision about the type of problem-solving approach to take easier. To identify complex situations, you might ask:

1. How long has this been a problematic area? The best way to answer this question is to ask others at the grass roots level of the work group. Try to include those who are long-term employees and who have historical insight into the area involved. If there have been similar situations in the past involving the same categories of people, then it is likely to be a complex situation.
2. How many people or work groups are involved? The involvement of three or more work groups, either intra- or interdependent, indicates complexity.
3. To what degree has the situation interfered with work group activity? Ask the people affected by the turbulence to tell you how much time they are spending to cope with the situation. Then make a determination about the appropriateness of the time expenditure. An unreasonable amount of time means there is an underlying, complex situation.
4. How much of your management time is being focused on the symptoms? Also, how much time have you spent in this area? Are other areas getting shortchanged because of the amount of attention paid to this situation? If the presenting symptoms are repeatedly throwing your workday out of balance, then the situation is complex.
5. To what extent will the people involved have to change established behaviors to implement an acceptable solution? To what degree will the success of any solution depend upon the support of others? If the answer is "a great deal" to either of these questions, then you will need to involve other people in the solution-seeking process. When you have to build a support system to ensure a solution you have a complex situation.

CONFLICT AND THE ORGANIZATION'S ENERGY

An analogy can be drawn between a theory in physics and an organization stressed by conflict. The theory is that of entropy. It is usually expressed in mathematical terms. *Tabers Encyclopedic Medical Dictionary* defines entropy as "that portion of energy within a system which cannot be utilized for mechanical work but is available for internal use."[6] In *Chemical Principles,* Masterton states, "entropy is associated with the degree of disorder in substance."[7]

I am not a student of physics. At the risk of my interpretation being considered loose, I present my analogy. It is based on Masterton's definition. The amount of "trapped" nonusable energy is proportionate to the degree of disorder in the molecular makeup of a substance. Compare this to an organization experiencing stress. The greater the stressful situation, the higher degree of trapped nonproductive energy within the workers. When one reflects on relatively simple matters such as a dispute between management and staff over nurses wearing or not wearing their caps while on duty, you can quickly relate to this trapped energy theory. In this context, the trapped energy is being used tangentially to create discord. The discord consumes time and detracts from the usable available energy that should be focused on patient care.

The natural physical law discussed in sociological terms is not as farfetched as it may first appear. In 1977 a Belgian physical chemist, Illya Prigogine, was awarded a Nobel prize for his theory of entropy within living systems. He was intrigued by the tendency of organization within purely inanimate matter to decay eventually into disorder. A special issue of the *Brain Mind Bulletin* in May 1979 reported that he discovered entropy was nature's way of releasing new energy.[8] Consider an old deteriorating brick building. A physicist would tell us that there is energy within those bricks. As the building ages and the bricks start to crumble, trapped energy is being released. The analogous situation is a well-engineered system within an organization that begins to deteriorate over a period of time. Human service organizations are a combination of the inanimate and the animate. We usually need a building stocked with supplies and equipment from which to operate. The greatest resource, however, in human service organizations is the people who work there.

Prigogine mathematically proved that the law of entropy is even more noticeable in biology than in the study of lifeless systems. It is profoundly notable in the human brain, one of the highest known concentrations of energy that exists. Within any weakened system then, human energy is being released. Imagine the magnitude of energy being released minute by minute within health care agencies. Even in dying organizations untapped human energy exists. Recognizing the field of uncertainty is being aware of the place where a large concentration of "trapped" energy is being released.

The theory of entropy generated the PRESEARCH problem-solving philosophy. Problems in some form will always be with us. Managers will continue to spend a large part of every workday in problem-solving exercises. To recognize problems as a natural process puts a new focus on the art of problem solving. It then becomes a challenge. As responsible managers, we need to learn to recognize when to tap into the energy that is being released through the degenerating process and to channel that energy into change for the good of the organization. As Marguerite Schaefer says, a certain amount of conflict is healthy.[9] It sparks healthy competition. It contributes to a productive work environment. However, when conflict in a work situation becomes excessive, it then represents symptoms of a degenerating process.

CONCLUSION

In summary, the manager must tune in and listen to the music above the words. Managers need a structured framework to deal with complex situations. This is necessary because their workday does not permit lengthy periods of uninterrupted time to focus on the problem area. PRESEARCH provides this structure. It leads the problem solver through a step-by-step process. If the process is interrupted, it can be resumed hours, days, or weeks later. When this structured format is used, backtracking is minimized. The first step is to recognize that the field of uncertainty needs to be explored. Afterwards you must try to determine, through active listening, how many different disciplines are involved. If the matters of concern go beyond your area of freedom, you must get administrative backing to explore beyond your authority limits. Otherwise you will be spending countless hours trying to solve someone else's problems over which you have no control.

NOTES

1. Norman Maier, *Problem-solving Discussions and Conferences: Leadership Methods and Skills* (New York: McGraw-Hill, 1963), p. 70.
2. Henry Mintzberg, "The Manager's Job: Folklore or Fact," *Harvard Business Review,* July-August 1975, pp. 49–61.
3. Marguerite Schaefer, Ph.D., Patient Care Administration Seminar, Minneapolis, Minnesota, 1979.

4. "Conflict Coping Modes," in *Introduction to the Management of Conflict Workshop* (Minneapolis, Minn.: University of Minnesota, 1978), p. 15.

5. Elton Mayo, *The Social Problems of an Industrial Civilization* (Andover, Mass.: Andover Press, 1945), pp. 77–79.

6. *Tabers Encyclopedic Medical Dictionary*, 12th Edition (Philadelphia, Pa.: F. A. Davis, 1973), p. E–42.

7. William Masterton and Emil Slowinski, *Chemical Principles* (Philadelphia, Pa.: W. B. Saunders, 1969), pp. 330–335.

8. *Brain Mind Bulletin* (Los Angeles, Cal.: Interface Press, 1979), pp. 1–3.

9. Schaefer, Patient Care Seminar, 1979.

Chapter 3

Data Gathering

Systematic data gathering sets PRESEARCH apart from other problem-solving models. Figure 1-2 in Chapter 1 emphasizes the need to collect data before defining problems and seeking solutions. This chapter deals primarily with developing and using data gathering instruments. It also includes practical suggestions for the interviewer.

EXISTING FACTS, TRADITIONS, AND CONSTRAINTS

Within the context of problem solving it is helpful to subdivide the data gathering process into two distinct parts. The first part is the "givens" (existing facts, traditions or constraints) and the second part is the field of uncertainty. The "givens" encompass information from the literature, policies, rules, regulations, contracts, wage and hour laws, organizational structure, standards of practice, and actual practice.

One of the most underutilized resources available to a practicing manager is the hospital librarian. This person can assist you in a literature search. Reference materials will tell you what others have done and what has worked for them in similar situations. This frequently overlooked source of information can be of extreme value when identifying "givens." Other sources of information are masters' theses and doctoral dissertations. These often end up collecting dust on university library shelves. If you are dealing with very complex problems, it may be worth your while to glean information from such unpublished manuscripts. Some universities keep a card catalogue of these papers in the individual school offices. A telephone call to the school in which your topic of interest may be located can give you directions as to where unpublished manuscripts might be accessible.

The task of collecting "given" information can be delegated to someone other than the problem solver. An analysis of "what exists" helps the
manager determine the focus of problem-solving efforts. "Answers to
problems preexist. We must discover pertinent questions." This para-
phrase of an earlier quote from Dr. Jonas Salk emphasizes the *pre*search
aspect of the process.[1] The manager who examines the "givens" begins
to build a base for further questioning.

There will be times when the problem solver will gain enough information from examining "givens" to eliminate further data gathering. For
example, in one health care facility, position vacancies were of great
concern. Seven out of twenty-one part-time evening ward secretary positions were vacant. These vacancies created a severe handicap for the
evening nursing staff of the units concerned. The secretarial functions
were so vital to the units that staff registered nurses were being assigned
to replace the secretaries. Not only was this a very costly measure, it also
depleted the supply of available nurses. In this situation someone
suggested that the solution would be increasing the secretaries' salaries
and benefits. The person in charge decided not to settle on the suggested
solution before defining the problems. The following "givens" were
examined: the schedules of secretarial help on all nursing units, the staffing patterns of each position, the availability of trained secretarial personnel, and newspaper advertisements for ward secretary positions. Also,
demographic information about secretaries employed in part-time positions was compared to the demographic information of those employed in
full-time positions.

The data gathered revealed that position vacancies were a seasonal
problem. Further analysis indicated that each year students from a nearby
Licensed Practical Nurse (LPN) program had been employed in these
part-time positions. When the LPN classes graduated, positions were
vacated annually. Once this problem was recognized as seasonal, the
crisis intervention focus changed to a long-range planning focus. Temporary solutions were explored and accepted. In this case examining the
"givens" took approximately eight hours of one person's time. Although
the information gathered did not solve the problem, it supplied the problem solver with necessary information to do informed planning for future
hiring practices. It provided a knowledge base from which to work.

In summary, an examination of all known factors clustered together
provides:

1. enough information on which to make an informed decision, or
2. the base for further questioning.

When further questioning is needed, the information collected begins to give focus to the developer of a data-gathering instrument. At this point a decision must be made about how the data, once collected, will be used. Possible uses of the data include assessing quality, determining appropriate community services, assessing learning needs, educating staff, evaluating performance, and analyzing a system. The anticipated use of the collected data should be correlated with already identified reasons for obtaining more information. Deciding how you will use the information will help you determine the amount and in what depth to collect additional information. It will also help you establish problem-solving priorities and determine the amount of problem-solving effort the situation deserves.

EXPLORING THE FIELD OF UNCERTAINTY

The second part of data gathering should focus on the field of uncertainty. The problem solver may gather data from the field of uncertainty in several subsequent phases. It may be prudent to collect from a small population of key informants before expanding to a larger, more diverse population. For example, in a three-phase data collection process, phase one can provide valuable information that will help you proceed through phases two and three. You must have a survey instrument in order to do systematic data gathering. Developing and devising a questionnaire is an art. There are highly specialized firms that employ skilled personnel to develop survey instruments. Data gathering within the PRESEARCH framework can range from a simple opinion poll to a collection of quantitative or quantifiable data that are subsequently analyzed by statistical procedures.

The PRESEARCH emphasis is not on the sophistication of the data-gathering instrument but on a systematic, uniform approach to collecting data. In other words, it stresses collecting the same kind of information from a sampling of persons involved in the field of uncertainty. Without a systematic approach, the tendency is to ask the target population general questions that are somewhat related. With an unstructured approach, information is collected but participants are not asked to address the same subject or to give opinions in the same way. A systematic approach has the advantage of obtaining like kinds of information from your entire target population.

Developing a Survey Instrument

There are a few simple rules that must be followed when developing a survey instrument or questionnaire. Keep in mind that closed-ended questions are easy to tally, while open-ended questions may give you information that you had not anticipated. When preparing the survey instrument, one must avoid introducing bias, especially in closed-ended questions. Slanted questions will produce slanted results. When preparing your survey instrument you should observe the following rules:

1. Make the questions clear. Give the respondents all the information they will need to answer the question.
2. Avoid questions that have two central ideas or two themes.
3. Do not use jargon. Your target population must be competent to answer the questions you are asking. If they are not familiar with medical jargon, do not use it.
4. Keep questions relevant to the problem.
5. Keep questions short.
6. Avoid stating questions in the negative.
7. Design close-ended questions that are exhaustive, discreet, and nonoverlapping.
8. Provide enough response alternatives so that there is space for everyone to respond; for example, add a space for a write-in answer.

When preparing a survey instrument, avoid overkill. If a little is good, more is not always better. When you have a series of questions, start with broad, general questions and become sequentially more specific. When narrowing the focus of the questions, be cautious about becoming redundant. If questions sound redundant to the respondents, you may lose their cooperation. When people have responded to a question, they usually do not wish to respond to the same type of question again. The properly designed questionnaire makes information gathering easy for the researcher, the interviewer, and the respondent. Your goal should be to collect data in a comprehensive and efficient manner.

After you have prepared your survey instrument, be it one question or twenty, the next *must* is to pretest it. Ask your pretest audience to give you feedback on the clarity of your questions, the order of the questions, and the length of your survey instrument. Feedback from your pretest population will help you perfect the survey instrument. If there is an item in the questionnaire that poses a problem for several people in your pretest audience, you should examine the purpose for asking it. Thereafter, you may elect to reword or eliminate that question.

The Target Population

The size of the population depends on the complexity of the problem. One of the "givens" should be to determine the number of people who were directly or indirectly involved in the troublesome situation. The urgency of the matter and amount of time you can afford to spend collecting data will determine the number of people you can survey. If your target population is large, you may have to consider surveying only a sampling. When selecting your population sample, include at least one person from each discipline involved. Key informants should also be identified. While they are not necessarily involved in the problem immediately, they are people who have a broad overview of the situation at hand. For example, in a community survey an elderly gentleman may be asked, "Do you need help with the household chores?" If this question in any way threatens the gentleman's independence, dignity, or feelings of self-worth and stature within the community, his answer will more than likely be, "Oh, no." On the other hand, if a key informant (perhaps the head of the ministerial association) is asked about the needs of the community elderly in a corresponding questionnaire, he may respond, "The greatest needs of the elderly in this community are help with the yard work and household chores as well as transportation for grocery shopping." He further portrays the community as one in which people are proud, want to maintain their independence, desire to remain in their own homes, yet cannot handle the upkeep. The minister further clarifies that the thinking among the aging population is, "If you ask for help, you are looking for charity." In this example, had you interviewed only the geriatric population, your data would have been erroneous. This case illustrates how people will protect their own dignity and self-respect when answering questions. Getting more than one perspective about a given topic can prove extremely valuable in terms of problem solving.

SURVEY METHODS

There are three basic methods used to collect information from individuals who have undergone experiences which relate to the topic being investigated. They are (1) a face-to-face interview, (2) a telephone survey, and (3) a mailed-out or hand distributed questionnaire. Some advantages and disadvantages of each of the three methods are presented for consideration.

The Personal Interview

During a personal interview, the interviewer reads the same questions to all respondents, has the opportunity to interpret nonverbal messages, and establishes a rapport with the person during the data-collection phase. The interview climate allows the respondent to vent feelings or share additional information with the interviewer. In this type of survey, questions can be totally unstructured and completely nondirective. Unstructured questions allow the respondent more freedom in terms of reply.

On the other hand, the disadvantages are that personal interviews take a lot of time. Because of the time factor, they are costly. And, likewise, the time factor may force the interviewer to settle for a smaller sampling. There is also the risk of the interviewer introducing bias to the respondent through verbal and nonverbal messages. When bias is introduced, the information collected tends to be slanted. And finally, personal interviews do not allow the interviewer to collect anonymous information.

The Telephone Survey

Like the personal interview, in a telephone survey the interviewer reads the same written questions to all respondents. Telephone surveys have the advantage of being inexpensive, fast, and good for simple, short responses. On the other hand, two disadvantages of a telephone survey are that it is frequently used for sales, and it is an invasion of the person's privacy. Using this technique the interviewer has little chance to establish rapport with the respondent, nor can the interviewer observe nonverbal behavior or guarantee anonymity to the respondent.

The Questionnaire Sent by Mail

In this survey the lack of face-to-face contact with the person being interviewed can be an advantage or a disadvantage. However, anonymity can be guaranteed with this approach. Among the disadvantages one must consider is the amount of time needed to prepare a survey form that is clear enough for someone to complete independently. Usually this approach is used when the target population is extremely large. One must consider the high cost of mailing and the possibility of incorrect addresses when selecting this survey method. Researchers have raised questions about the type of persons who will respond to a questionnaire received in the mail. We do not know if there is a certain segment of the population representing some type of bias who do respond to questionnaires. Typically the rate of return mail is 50 percent or less.

Determining a Time Frame for Data Gathering

As stated earlier, the amount of time that you can afford to spend will help determine the size of your target population and your survey method. For example, if you decide on a personal interview, you should consider not only the number of respondents that you can interview within a given period of time but also the accessibility of the respondents. In other words, if you can schedule back-to-back interviews and are reasonably sure that people will be prompt for the interview appointment, you probably will schedule twenty-minute interviews at half-hour intervals. However, if you are scheduling twenty-minute interviews with physicians during hospital rounds and working hours, you probably should schedule one twenty-minute interview per hour. This type of scheduling allows for people who are not prompt and also eliminates the frustration of people having to sit and wait while someone else is being interviewed. Good planning is imperative to get a realistic estimate of the time needed to collect the data.

Summary

Identify the target population. Try to include those disciplines that might be affected by a solution (or change) to alleviate the symptoms of the suspected or ill-defined problem. For instance, if the symptoms are unrest among the nursing staff of a given unit, a high volume employee turnover, and a disagreement among the physician users of the unit about the quality of patient care delivered, the appropriate population would include the staff nurses on the unit, the head nurse, nurse supervisors, staff development personnel, and the physician users of the unit. It may also be advisable to obtain information from patients and families as well.

Examine several methods of data collection and determine which one will be most appropriate for the situation. Once a method (a personal interview, a telephone survey, or a mailed-out questionnaire) is chosen, be certain that all data are collected on a standardized form in a like manner. Pattern the data collection after the research model to assure consistency and to minimize the biasing influence of the person collecting the information.

Develop a survey tool using either fixed, alternative, or open-ended questions. You may decide to use either. Open-ended questions provide a frame of reference for participant responses, yet do not restrict the participant's manner of expression of content of answers. There is one distinct advantage of open-ended questions in this process: the respondents may give unexpected answers that identify aspects of the underlying problem not originally anticipated by the researcher.

Examine the appropriateness of each question in the survey instrument by asking:

1. Is the question related to the "field of uncertainty" and to the purpose of the study?

2. Is the type of question correct? (open-ended questions versus a clear-cut choice of two or more alternatives)
3. Is the question clear and unambiguous?
4. Does the question suggest a specific answer or a surveyor-preferred response?
5. Does the question suggest a socially desirable response?
6. Does the question demand knowledge or information that the respondent does not have?

If the answers to numbers one through three are "yes," keep the questions in the survey; if the answers to items four through six are "yes," reconstruct or discard those questions. Always pretest your survey tool before using it on your target population.

Decide on a time frame within which to collect the data. Try to consider the variables that might influence the time needed in the data-gathering phase. If your questions are well constructed and your target population includes all the disciplines involved in the complex process, the time invested in data gathering will be cost effective.

PRACTICAL HINTS FROM A FIELD RESEARCH ASSISTANT

The following down-to-earth comments were contributed by a close friend who preferred to remain anonymous. As a surveyor for both national and regional research firms, she gained unique insights into problems encountered while data gathering. Her interest in PRESEARCH and its audiences prompted her to share this practical information.

Icebreaker

Whenever any type of survey information is collected, an icebreaker is essential. Inside or outside an organization an introductory explanatory letter should precede the interviewer. This is also true if you are doing a mailing, telephone survey, or personal interview. If you are meeting the interviewee face-to-face, you should present some type of printed material that summarizes the survey and tells why you are there. If at that time, the person hesitates to participate, the interviewer should explain how the person was chosen to be part of the survey population. If an opinion survey is being conducted, stress that this is an opportunity for the participants to express their feelings about the topic at hand.

Interview Climate

The person needing the information from the systematic data gathering should select a neutral person to collect internal information on sensitive issues. It is ideal to hire an outside research assistant. When this is not possible, an alternative is to find someone within the organization who is considered neutral. Perhaps a chaplain or social service worker might have time to collect information for you through a survey instrument. The neutrality of the interviewer is extremely important. If the respondents are threatened by the survey, the results will definitely be slanted. Respondents who are insecure within the organization will probably read something into the survey process itself. When people are protecting their work positions, they are likely to answer the questions in a way that they believe will please the boss. During the interview thoughts like, "How does answering this question affect me and my job?", or "How am I perceived by the interviewer?" may influence their responses.

An astute manager will consider what is happening organizationally before launching into a large scale, formal, data-gathering process. If the department has recently been restructured, it is not a time to ask people if they like their jobs. At this time the common response will be, "Me, oh yes, I love my job." Other responses that you can expect to get in a situation like this are, "I'm really excited about the changes," or "I'm sure things will be better."

Positive reinforcement helps when people are becoming accustomed to responding to systematic data gathering. If a simple survey is foreign to members of your organization, it is advisable to start by investigating a nagging problem to which a solution would mean a reward for everyone involved. After one good experience with organized information collection, the workers will be more willing to cooperate in an elaborate survey. It definitely helps to get people within the organization accustomed to data collection. They also will need to be conditioned to the fact that data collection is done not for punitive measures, but for the common good of those involved in a complex situation.

Filling out a Form versus Interviewing

Always provide privacy for the respondent when asking for information. During the interview, the surveyor is able to reinforce the need for the participant to be part of the survey. If, for example, the respondent says to you, "Well, what's this all about anyway?" you might answer, "The best way I can explain it is to get started with the interview." It is up to the interviewer to sell the respondent on the idea of proceeding through the survey instrument together. The participant usually cooperates with just a small amount of reassurance. Generally, you will obtain a much greater degree of participation by interviewing the respondent from a questionnaire than by asking the person to sit down and fill out a form. With the structured interview approach, the interviewer becomes the pencil that writes on the paper.

Facilitating the Interview

As an interviewer, you may encounter people who appear unwilling to participate. Hesitation to be interviewed can result from many unexpressed feelings. The person from whom you need cooperation may be thinking any one of the following:

"I don't want to appear foolish."

"I don't want to appear dumb."

"I may not be as educated as someone else, and I don't want to give you the wrong answer."

"Hey, answering these interview questions could jeopardize my position in the community so I had better not get involved."

Therefore, the first thing that the interviewer must stress to the person being interviewed is that there are no right or wrong answers in an opinion survey. An additional comment that might be used is: "We are interested in what you think and what your feelings are." Several times during the interview, if the person answers "I don't know," rather than giving an opinion, you may have to stress again that there are no right or wrong answers but that you need input from everyone.

If the respondent gives you an answer that is indirect or one that needs interpretation, the interviewer's only resort is to restate the question. Often you will find that when you ask a question, the person being interviewed will think out loud rather than answer the question directly. The appropriate way to deal with an indirect or nonspecific response is to restate the question. The interviewer may say "Let me reread the question and let's see exactly what the questionnaire is asking." A few steadfast rules for the surveyor are:

- Do not rephrase questions.
- Do not redefine things.
- Do not give opinions.
- Do not interpret.

A neutral stance for the interviewer is learned behavior. You will find that the better educated people are, the better they will tend to track with you during the interview. Those who are less educated or lonely will tend to drift. It is your responsibility, as the interviewer, to get the interviewee back on target without using putdowns. Once this is done, you generally have and can keep the respondent's attention. If in the process of the interview the informant introduces some information that is relative to the questionnaire but not included in it, make a note of that information for the researcher. Sometimes, during a survey with a large population, there may be a topic related to the questionnaire that keeps coming up as a pattern. It is very important to make a note of such information for those analyzing the data.

Introducing Bias

The greatest risk of interviewing is introducing bias. Body language, a nod of the head, a smile, or any type of positive or negative reinforcement the interviewee offers as an answer tends to bias the information collected in the interview. If a biased response is solicited early in the interview, a question further into the interview may cause the respondent to think, "I remember how she nodded when I answered the other question; I probably should answer this one the same way." It is very difficult to interview all people in a like manner and not introduce bias.

Rights of the Participants

Every survey participant should have access to a summary of the analyzed data that was collected. The data collection process should leave the interviewees in no worse condition than existed prior to the interview. In other words, interviews should not introduce variables into their lives that would not otherwise have existed. They have a right to be informed about the purpose of the survey and also to know how that information will be used once it is collected. They should know before they participate if there is a possibility of the results being published and how that information will be presented. Some people will say, "Yes, I'll participate in the survey, but I want to know the results." Many times in large surveys the results are sent only to those people who request it.

CONCLUSION

Most health care managers will not have the opportunity to have the experiences of a field researcher. It is hoped that the insight shared in this chapter will highlight the sophistication of a truly unbiased approach. This is not meant to discourage the novice surveyor; rather it is intended to encourage you through an understanding that each person responds to a questionnaire from his or her own perspective.

NOTE

1. Jonas Salk, The National Foundation/March of Dimes Annual Report, 1973. p. 22.

Chapter 4

Examining Survey Responses

Data analysis in research means examing pieces of information and drawing conclusions about how the pieces fit together. The data from research is frequently subjected to statistical analysis in order to demonstrate significant relationships or associations among identified variables. In the PRESEARCH method data analysis is the close examination of survey responses to identify key facts and issues directly and indirectly related to the complex problem situation. Structured data gathering produces information from which problem statements are constructed. Chapter 5 demonstrates the process of transforming facts, opinions, and "givens" into problem statements.

Two methods that are useful for examining survey responses are numerical tabulations and content analysis. Numerical tabulations include simple tallies, ratios, and percentages of responses to closed-ended questions. Content analysis is extracting key words and phrases embedded in responses to open-ended questions. The design of the questionnaire determines the process of choice. Closed-ended questions lend themselves to numerical analysis. Adding the number of "yes" and "no" responses to this type of question can be done quickly and easily. Thereafter, tallied information can be arranged and displayed in tables and graphs for comparative and reporting purposes. Nevertheless, the majority of questionnaires designed by problem solvers will include open-ended questions. This design allows the respondents to express their feelings and perceptions about the matter at hand subjectively. Processing subjective responses is time consuming. However, analysis of subjective responses reveals unanticipated information. The questionnaire in Figure 4-1 exemplifies the use of closed- and open-ended questions. Actual survey responses are compared later using simple mathematical interpretations. Content analysis is demonstrated by extracting key words and phrases from the open-ended questions.

Figure 4-1 Flexible Scheduling Questionnaire

Name: **Unit:**
Check the appropriate box for each of the following questions.

Position Title:
Registered Nurse ( )   Licensed Practical Nurse ( )
Nursing Assistant ( )   Operating Room Technician ( )
Ward Secretary ( )   Other ( )

Age:

Under 21 ( )	31–35 ( )	46–50 ( )
21–25 ( )	36–40 ( )	51–55 ( )
26–30 ( )	41–45 ( )	over 55 ( )

Length of Time Employed at This Hospital:
Less than one year ( )   37 months to 10 years ( )
13 months to three years ( )   More than 10 years ( )

Employment Status:
Full-time ( )   Regular Part-time ( )   Casual Part-time ( )

Present Schedule:
Straight shift   days ( )   evenings ( )   nights ( )
Rotating shift   day/evening ( )   day/night ( )   evening/night ( )

Factors Influencing Availability to Work:
Are there factors that influence how and when you are available to work?
Yes ( )   No ( )
If yes, please indicate:
School ( )   Car Pool ( )   Available child care ( )
Other ( )_____

Flexible Schedule:
A flexible schedule does ( ) does not ( ) appeal to you.
If yes, which type of schedule:
10 hour shift/4 days a week ( )
12 hour shift/3 days a week ( )
Other schedule ( )
If other, indicate schedule

Why does it appeal to you?

Source: Eitel Hospital, Minneapolis, Minnesota. Used with permission.

This questionnaire was designed in response to staff nurses asking for schedules other than the traditional 8-hour shifts. Their request came at a time when the hospital had numerous unfilled budgeted positions and the nurse shortage was a national concern. The director of nursing recognized that rigid staffing patterns were affecting the turnover rate among nursing staff members. She did not know if the request from a few was representative of the desires of the full staff. Therefore, the questionnaire was designed to determine the amount of interest in alternative scheduling and to identify those factors that influence the nurse's availability to work.

The questionnaire was short, straightforward, and did not require much explanation. It took, at most, three minutes to complete. The interest of the nursing staff in this subject was reflected by an 87 percent return rate. Of the 172 questionnaires distributed throughout the department, 149 were completed and returned. This questionnaire is used as an example to show how closed-ended questions lend themselves to a variety of data display possibilities. The use of tables is helpful for those who interpret the significance of the responses. The following tables helped the manager to differentiate between those who were and were not interested in flexible scheduling. Responses for the entire department are displayed by job title, age, length of service, employment status, and unit.

Table 4-1 displays the responses by job title for the total department.

The response rate to the questionnaire was 149. Of those participating in the survey, 98 indicated that they were interested in flexible scheduling, 41 indicated that they were not, and 10 were undecided. Converted to percentages, 66 percent indicated an interest in flexible scheduling, 27 percent indicated that they were not and 7 percent were undecided.

Tables 4-2 through 4-5 show the responses by age of the respondents, length of service, employment status, and present work schedule. Displaying the data several different ways revealed that the interest in flexible scheduling was not limited to any one group whether based on age, longevity, employment status, or schedule.

It is interesting to note that in all age categories the positive response is equal to or outweighs the negative. Had the data not been sorted this way,

Table 4-1 Questionnaire Response Rate by Title—Entire Department*

Position	Yes	No	Uncertain	Total
RN	61	21	5	87
LPN	25	8	2	35
NA	3	7	2	12
WS	5	2	1	8
OR Tech	2	2		4
Other	2	1		3
Total	98	41	10	149

* *Note:* Tables 4-1 through 4-17 are from the same source—Eitel Hospital, Minneapolis, Minnesota. All are used here with permission.

Table 4-2 Questionnaire Response Rate by Age—Entire Department

Age	Yes	No	Uncertain	Total
over 55	5	4	1	10
51–55	6	4	1	11
46–50	6	4	2	12
41–45	2	2	1	5
36–40	11	3		14
31–35	11	3	1	15
26–30	27	10		37
21–25	28	10	4	42
under 21	2	1		3
Total	98	41	10	149

Table 4-3 Questionnaire Response Rate by Service Longevity—
Entire Department

Length of Service	Yes	No	Uncertain	Total
More than 10 years	15	9	4	28
37 months to 10 years	14	14	1	29
13 months to 3 years	30	7	1	38
Less than 1 year	39	11	4	54
Total	98	41	10	149

Table 4-4 Questionnaire Response Rate by Employment Status—
Entire Department

Employment Status	Yes	No	Uncertain	Total
Full-time	69	28	5	102
Regular Part-time	25	10	4	39
Casual Part-time	4	3	1	8
Total	98	41	10	149

it might have been assumed that a flexible schedule would appeal to some age groups more than others.

Table 4-3 again shows the positive responses equal to or greater than the negative responses in each of the length of service clusters. It is interesting to note that the positive responses are proportionately greater in the "Less than 1 year" and the "13 months to 3 years" categories. In these clusters their response was 72 percent and 79 percent respectively. It is also interesting to note that the positive responses were 53 percent in

Table 4-5 Questionnaire Response Rate by Work Schedule—Entire Department

Present Work Schedule	Yes	No	Uncertain	Total
Straight Days	31	17	1	49
Straight Evenings	15	5	3	23
Straight Nights	8	5	2	15
Rotating Day/Evening	23	8	3	34
Rotating Day/Night	17	4		21
Rotating Evening/Night	4	2	1	7
Total	98	41	10	149

the "More than 10 year" category which is slightly higher than the responses in the "37 month to 10 year" cluster which was 48 percent.

Table 4-4 shows that when the data was sorted by employment status, 50 percent or more in each classification were supportive of exploring flexible scheduling. It is interesting to note that 67 percent of the full-time employees, 64 percent of the part-time employees, and 50 percent of the casual part-time employees found flexible schedules appealing.

When the responses were sorted by work schedules, Table 4-5 shows that again the interest crossed all work schedules.

Because the interest in exploring scheduling alternatives was not confined to any one group (at least as we had classified the information), data was further analyzed by unit to determine where the interest level was the highest. This information was needed to identify appropriate pilot units. It stands to reason that where the interest level was the greatest, the probability of successful implementation would also be high. The tables are constructed for the nursing units in a similar manner. The positions along the left hand column include Registered Nurse (RN), Licensed Practical Nurse (LPN), Nursing Assistant (NA), Ward Secretary (WS), and Operating Room Technician (ORT). The information was not only displayed according to position, but was also converted to percentage of total interest or lack of it within each nursing unit. The percentage figures were most useful in identifying the pilot units.

On the Third South Unit there were 14 respondents of a possible 15. (See Table 4-6.) Of those responding 1 RN, 5 LPNs, 1 NA and 1 WS indicated that flexible scheduling appealed to them. Four RNs, 1 LPN and 1 NA indicated that it did not appeal. Converted to percentages, 57 percent responded "yes" and 43 percent responded "no."

In Nursing Unit Four South there were 19 respondents out of a possible 19. (See Table 4-7.) Of those responding, 9 RNs, 5 LPNs and 1 NA indicated that a flexible schedule appealed to them. One RN and 1 NA

Table 4-6 Questionnaire Response Rate by Employee Category—
Third South Unit

Position	Yes	No	Uncertain	Total
RN	1	4		5
LPN	5	1		6
NA	1	1		2
WS	1			1
Total	8	6		14

Table 4-7 Questionnaire Response Rate by Employee Category—
Fourth South Unit

Position	Yes	No	Uncertain	Total
RN	9	1		10
LPN	5			5
NA	1	1	2	4
Total	15	2	2	19

indicated that it did not appeal. Two NAs indicated that they were uncertain. Converted to percentages, 78 percent responded "yes," 11 percent responded "no," and 11 percent responded "uncertain."

In Nursing Unit Five South there were 16 respondents out of a possible 21. Table 4-8 shows that of those responding, 6 RNs and 4 LPNs indicated that a flexible schedule appealed to them. Two RNs, 1 LPN, and 1 NA indicated that it did not appeal. One RN and 1 WS indicated that they were uncertain. Converted to percentages, 63 percent responded "yes," 25 percent responded "no," and 12 percent were "uncertain."

In Nursing Unit Six South there were 14 respondents out of a possible 16. Table 4-9 shows that of those responding, 3 RNs, 3 LPNs, and 1 NA

Table 4-8 Questionnaire Response Rate by Employee Category—
Fifth South Unit

Position	Yes	No	Uncertain	Total
RN	6	2	1	9
LPN	4	1		5
NA		1		1
WS			1	1
Total	10	4	2	16

Table 4-9 Questionnaire Response Rate by Employee Category—
Sixth South Unit

Position	Yes	No	Uncertain	Total
RN	3	1	2	6
LPN	3	1	1	5
NA	1	1		2
WS		1		1
Total	7	4	3	14

indicated that a flexible schedule appealed to them. One RN, 1 LPN, 1 NA, and 1 WS indicated that it did not appeal. Two RNs and 1 LPN indicated that they were uncertain. Converted to percentages, 50 percent responded "yes," 29 percent responded "no," and 21 percent were "uncertain."

In the Intensive Care Unit there were 10 respondents out of a possible 13. Table 4-10 shows that of those responding, 3 RNs, and 1 LPN indicated that a flexible schedule appealed to them. Four RNs, 1 LPN, and 1 WS indicated that it did not appeal. Converted to percentages, 40 percent responded "yes," 60 percent responded "no," and none responded "uncertain."

In the Coronary Care Unit (CCU) there were 10 respondents out of a possible 12. Table 4-11 shows that of those responding 6 RNs, 1 LPN, and 1 WS indicated that flexible scheduling appealed to them. One RN and 1 LPN indicated that it did not appeal. Converted to percentages, 80 percent responded "yes," 20 percent responded "no," and no responses were "uncertain."

In the Obstetrics Unit there were 14 respondents out of a possible 20. Table 4-12 shows that of those responding, 11 RNs and 2 LPNs indicated that a flexible schedule appealed to them. One RN indicated that it did not

Table 4-10 Questionnaire Response Rate by Employee Category—
ICU

Position	Yes	No	Uncertain	Total
RN	3	4		7
LPN	1	1		2
WS		1		1
Total	4	6		10

Table 4-11 Questionnaire Response Rate by Employee Category—
CCU

Position	Yes	No	Uncertain	Total
RN	6	1		7
LPN	1	1		2
WS	1			1
Total	8	2		10

Table 4-12 Questionnaire Response Rate by Employee Category—
Obstetrics Unit

Position	Yes	No	Uncertain	Total
RN	11	1		12
LPN	2			2
Total	13	1		14

appeal. Converting to percentages, 92 percent responded "yes" and 8 percent responded "no."

In the Pediatric Unit there were four respondents out of a possible four. Of those responding, as shown in Table 4-13, 2 RNs and 1 LPN indicated that a flexible schedule appealed to them. One RN indicated that she was uncertain. Converted to percentages, 75 percent responded "yes" and 25 percent responded "uncertain."

In the Emergency Room there were ten respondents out of a possible ten. Of those responding, Table 4-14 shows that three RNs and one WS indicated that a flexible schedule appealed to them. Two RNs and three LPNs indicated that it did not appeal. One RN indicated that she was uncertain. Converted to percentages, 40 percent responded "yes," 50 percent responded "no," and 10 percent responded "uncertain."

Table 4-13 Questionnaire Response Rate by Employee Category—
Pediatrics Unit

Position	Yes	No	Uncertain	Total
RN	2		1	3
LPN	1			1
Total	3		1	4

Table 4-14 Questionnaire Response Rate by Employee Category—
Emergency Room

Position	Yes	No	Uncertain	Total
RN	3	2	1	6
LPN		3		3
WS	1			1
Total	4	5	1	10

Table 4-15 shows that in the Operating Room there were 18 respondents out of a possible 19. Of those responding 5 RNs, 2 LPNs, 1 WS, and 2 ORTs indicated that a flexible schedule appealed to them. Three RNs, 3 NAs, and 2 ORTs indicated that it did not appeal. Converted to percentages 55 percent responded "yes" and 45 percent responded "no."

In the hospital Float Pool there were five respondents out of a possible seven. Of those responding, one RN, one LPN, and one WS indicated that a flexible schedule appealed to them as shown in Table 4-16. One RN indicated that it did not appeal. One LPN indicated uncertainty. Converted to percentages, 60 percent responded "yes," 20 percent responded "no," and 20 percent responded "uncertain."

Table 4-15 Questionnaire Response Rate by Employee Category—
Operating Room

Position	Yes	No	Uncertain	Total
RN	5	3		8
LPN	2			2
NA		3		3
WS	1			1
ORT	2	2		4
Total	10	8		18

Table 4-16 Questionnaire Response Rate by Employee Category—
Float Pool

Position	Yes	No	Uncertain	Total
RN	1	1		2
LPN	1		1	2
WS	1			1
Total	3	1	1	5

Table 4-17 shows that in Nursing Administration there were 15 respondents out of a possible 15. Of those responding, 11 RNs and 2 other employees indicated that a flexible schedule appealed to them. One RN and one other employee indicated that it did not appeal. Converted to percentages, 87 percent responded "yes'" and 13 percent responded "no."

In summary, a manager can display data in tables for reporting purposes. When converted to percentages, the results help to pinpoint those units with greatest interest at the time of the survey. Rationale for sorting data, rather than considering it information of the whole, can be demonstrated with the following example.

The three ICU RNs who responded to the questionnaire and indicated an interest in flexible scheduling were the ones who made the original suggestion at a staff meeting. Prior to the investigation, an erroneous assumption was made that the Intensive Care Unit would be a good place to introduce flexible schedules. The survey, however, corrected the assumption.

Closed-Ended Question, A Second Example

Another example in the use of a closed-ended question follows:

In response to the question (See last question in Flexible Scheduling Questionnaire) about factors influencing individuals' availability to work, 73 people responded "yes" that there were factors that influenced when they were able to work, and 73 people responded that they did not have factors influencing their availability to work. Of those people responding "yes," the following factors were identified:

school	19
car pool	2
available child care	24
other (not specified)	8

Table 4-17 Questionnaire Response Rate by Employee Category— Administration

Position	Yes	No	Uncertain	Total
RN	11	1		12
Other	2	1		3
Total	13	2		15

other (specified)

family obligations	6
bus	2
weather	1
health	1
prenatal classes	1
Alcoholics Anonymous Meetings	1
life style	8
straight days only	2
spouse's work schedule	3
Total	76

Three of the respondents had more than one factor that influenced their availability to work. In this example it is important to note the use of the category "other." A total of 35 responses fell into this category. Closed-ended questions that do not provide an opportunity for individual input limit the respondent's ability to specify information that might be important to the surveyor. In problem solving it is vitally important to get as much information as possible about the field of uncertainty. Therefore, always give the respondents an opportunity to supply you with information that you may not have.

CONTENT ANALYSIS

Content analysis is examining responses to open-ended questions to identify issues. It acknowledges people's feelings as well as facts. Through this technique the manager selectively extracts attitudes, ideas, actions, philosophies, constraints, and events that were expressed by the respondents.

For problem-solving purposes, the raw data is processed by compiling issues (a list of key words and phrases) from the data-gathering instrument. After each questionnaire has been processed, the next step is to combine like or related responses under broad topic headings. You'll find that there will be response patterns. People convey like or related messages using different terminology. The data that has been collected supports and justifies the problem definition. This conversion does not change problem solving to research. However, the information obtained in the *pre*search provides the problem solver with a knowledge base from which to work. Chapter 5 deals with converting these responses into problem statements.

Content analysis is demonstrated using actual responses to the quest on "Why does it (flexible scheduling) appeal to you?" The issues that were extracted from that open-ended question were grouped under broad topic headings. The topics and issues were as follows:

General:
   would like more information (2)*;
   flexibility prevents monotony;
   need example schedules for staff to see;
   like to try something new (2)*;
   hope it's on a trial basis.
Nurse Shortage:
   need to increase our present staff;
   willing to try if it will help nursing shortage, maybe flexible schedul-
      ing will make staffing easier and increase morale;
   would like to try if we have adequate staffing;
   concerned about the number of "pool" nurses we are using now;
   concerned about present shortage of help.
Weekends:
   am considering leaving hospital nursing because of every other
      weekend schedules, would consider staying if scheduled to work
      every third weekend;
   possibility of fewer weekends (2)*;
   possibility of a three-day weekend (4)*.
Start Time:
   would like a later start time for A.M. shifts;
   would like an earlier start time (2)*.
Shift Length:
   would consider working full-time with a four-day week (2)*;
   twelve-hour shifts are desirable on weekends;
   shorter partial shifts (2)*;
   willing to try twelve-hour shifts (5)*.
Formal Education:
   flexibility will make it possible to work and attend school (5)*;
   with short shifts (four or six hours) I can go to school full-time (2)*.
Patient Care:
   more complete patient care possible (2)*.
More Free Time:
   extra free days (44)*;
   don't have to come to work so often, yet get in my hours (28)*;
   a longer work day would maximize the use of work time (14)*;
   easier to arrange personal and social life with long shifts;
   could get more things done at home;
   more time off is physically and psychologically refreshing.

Babysitting:
  easier to get a babysitter for long shifts (2)*;
  harder to get a babysitter for long shifts (3)*.
Concern about Long Shifts:
  at my age I can barely manage eight hours;
  hard to work long shifts with a family;
  don't believe anyone could work twelve-hour day, but almost all of
    us work ten hours at least once a week;
  eight hours is all I can handle (3)*.
General Concerns:
  question the impact of long schedule on employee illness rate,
  question the compatibility of flexible scheduling with the union con-
    tracts;
  may interfere with management responsibilities (2)*;
  prefer to work eight hours a day five days a week for continuity (2)*.

SUMMARY

Answers to closed-ended questions can be tabulated and sorted in several ways. Issues can be extracted from open-ended questions through
content analysis. Responses from an actual survey demonstrated how
problem solvers can expand their knowledge base through systematic
data gathering and thereafter examining survey responses.

Note: * indicates the number of people who addressed the same issue in almost identical
terms.

Chapter 5

Issues Raise Questions about the Need for Change

Data gathering may uncover unanticipated information. When new or unforeseen variables are discovered it is possible to lose sight of the original intent of the problem-solving effort. The manager may even discover that the intent was identified inadequately in the beginning.

In people-centered problem solving, the manager must consider the persons who will be affected by an outcome or change that results from a solution. The people about to be involved in a change have their own personal biases about the out-of-balance situation. It is therefore essential for the manager to establish an overall outcome goal for the problem-solving efforts. This goal statement should be consistent with the organization's philosophy, policies, goals, and objectives. Once written, the goal statement should be posted in a prominent place as a reminder whenever a person or group of people are working toward the solution. If a committee is involved, the common goal statement helps the chairperson to keep the group on target. A common goal promotes group unity and team building. It also helps to diffuse emotionalism and promote objectivity.

Consider, for a moment a hypothetical situation. You are the manager who has called together a small task force to examine the results of the flexible scheduling questionnaire used in Chapter 4 and to develop the problem statements from it. One committee member has difficulty obtaining adequate child care while at work. This person focuses on the 24 respondents who indicated that provision for child care influenced their availability to work. This particular person is quite assertive and manages to dominate the entire committee meeting with the trials and tribulations of the working parent. If the committee chairperson had been provided with the following outcome goal statements:

Flexible scheduling will

- provide employees the option of alternatives to traditional eight-hour work schedules, as evidenced by staffing patterns which include four, six, ten, or twelve hour shifts;
- provide employees the option of more scheduled time off duty, as evidenced by three-day weekends replacing two-day weekends; and
- decrease the number of staff members who leave the hospital to join outside nursing personnel agencies, as evidenced by a decreasing number giving this reason for termination;

the group leader could have acknowledged this person's concern, but could have averted a disproportionate amount of time and attention being paid to one aspect or element of the data. These outcome goal statements become very useful tools in helping the chairperson stay on target and move the meeting along at an appropriate pace. With well-stated outcome goals, several groups of people can be developing problem statements for different aspects of the solution simultaneously. Hence, a large group can be subdivided into several small groups and within a very short period of time all of the problem statements can be defined. In *Goal Analysis*, Mager presents a procedure that is useful in helping describe the meanings of the goals you hope to achieve, whether these goals deal with attitudes, appreciations, or understandings. The purpose of his book "is to help you understand your own intents better so that you will be able to make better decisions toward their achievement and be able to recognize progress and success."[1]

In the preface, Mager tells this fable:

Once upon a time in the land of Fuzz, King Aling called in his cousin Ding and commanded, "Go ye out into all of Fuzzland and find me the goodest of men, whom I shall reward for his goodness."

"But how will I know when I see one?" asked the Fuzzy.

"Why, he will be *sincere*," scoffed the king, and whacked off a leg for his impertinence.

So, Fuzzy limped out to find a good man. But soon he returned, confused and empty-handed.

"But how will I know one when I see one?" he asked again.

"Why, he will be *dedicated*," grumbled the king, and whacked off another leg for his impertinence.

So the Fuzzy hobbled away once more to look for the goodest of men. But again he returned, confused and empty-handed.

"But how will I know one when I see one?" he pleaded.

"Why, he will have *internalized his growing awareness,*" fumed the king, and whacked off another leg for his impertinence.

So the Fuzzy, now on his last leg, hopped out to continue his search. In time, he returned with the wisest, most sincere and dedicated Fuzzy in all of Fuzzland, and stood him before the King.

"Why, this man won't do at all," roared the king. "He is much too thin to suit me." Whereupon he whacked off the last leg of the Fuzzy, who fell to the floor with a squishy thump.

The moral of this fable is that . . . *If you can't tell one when you see one, you may wind up without a leg to stand on.*

If your goals are important to achieve, it is essential that you do more than talk about them in "fuzzy" terminology. Broad statements of intent can be achieved only to the degree that their meaning is understood, *to the degree that you will know one when you see one.*[2]

As David Campbell, a well-known psychologist and author says, "If you don't know where you're going, you'll probably wind up somewhere else."[3] It is extremely important to know what you are trying to accomplish at this point in the problem-solving process. Likewise, in PRE-SEARCH I recommend that you develop your outcome goal statements before you write the problem statements. By doing so you can determine how those facts, givens, and issues you extracted through content analysis present difficulties in relationship to the desired outcome. Then the goal statements represent the situation as viewed *in balance.* You have recognized that things that should be occurring to maintain balance in fact are not occurring. You have explored the field of uncertainty and have confirmed that many parts of a given situation or system are unbalanced. Those parts have been identified as issues, givens, and facts. Once you are aware of the factors influencing the out-of-balance situation, you become more keenly aware of how you wish to define the *in balance* state of affairs.

Source: From *Goal Analysis* by Robert F. Mager © 1972 by Fearon Publishers, Inc. Reprinted by permission.

SUMMARY

Outcome goal statements provide you and your problem-solving colleagues with achievable, measureable outcome criteria. You will find the goal statement extremely valuable when you are conducting evaluative followup. At that point you will not have to go back and establish measurement criteria because you will already have it. Probably the most you will have to do is to develop a tool to measure the criteria you have already developed.

Chapter 6 deals with constructing problem statements from the data you have collected. The purpose for constructing multiple problem statements is to ask comprehensive questions, the solutions to which will produce the desired outcome results.

NOTES

1. Robert F. Mager, *Goal Analysis* (Belmont, California: Lear Siegler, Inc./Fearon Publishers, 1972), pp. v–vi.
2. Ibid.
3. David Campbell, *If You Don't Know Where You're Going, You'll Probably End up Somewhere Else* (Niles, Ill.: Argus Communications, 1974).

Data Supports Problem Statements

Problem definition is recognizing and confronting the field of uncertainty. It is blending or synthesizing the information that has been collected about the out-of-balance situation. It might be described as the culmination of efforts that have been put forth. In a very real sense, it is having enough information to prompt comprehensive questioning. Therefore, as we look at the complexities that face us, we combine the issues that have been extracted from the questionnaire with the givens or known facts we have at our disposal. By putting these pieces of information together, we build a series of interrogatory problem statements. A complex situation deserves this kind of approach because it helps identify the many variables that interface and that must be addressed before a solution can be formulated.

FORMULA FOR DEFINING PROBLEMS

A formula for building problem statements can be stated as

Issues + Facts + Givens = Problem Statements

People-centeredness is again emphasized as the problem statements are constructed. Therefore, the author recommends that problem statements be constructed in a noncritical manner such as "How can *we* help establish equilibrium?"

Management's willingness to help conveys a very important support message to the work group. Many situations that confront you are a product of interactions of people, systems, and behavioral patterns that have developed over a period of time. In these situations, it is extremely difficult to identify the source of the disequilibrium and determine why the process is self-perpetuating. The question "How can *we* help close the gap between *current practice* (as it exists) and *desired practice* (as it should be)?" has proven to be a very effective approach.

Applying the Formula

As you read through the list of extracted issues in Chapter 4, you probably had a sense that there was a logical clustering of content. Some of the responses dealt with delivering patient care, others focused on free time, and some dealt with such issues as combining school and work. Information from the flexible scheduling questionnaire is used here to illustrate how issues, facts, and givens are translated into problem statements. Content analysis of responses to the open-ended question, "Why does it (flexible scheduling) appeal to you?" revealed that seven people indicated combining school and work was an issue for them. These responses were clustered under the broad heading of Formal Education. Immediately preceding that portion of the questionnaire, in the section where people were asked to elaborate and explain why alternative scheduling appealed to them, 19 people identified school as a factor that influenced their availability to work. This indicates that 7 of these 19 people felt strongly enough about combining school and work to comment on that subject in the open-ended response space. In this instance, problem solvers constructed the following problem statement:

"How can we provide scheduling patterns that will provide adequate patient care coverage (*given*) yet allow the kind of flexibility that is needed by employees who choose to, or must work (*fact*) while they attend school either on a part-time or full-time basis (*issue*)?"

This problem statement addresses one portion of the complex situation. In this statement you will note that three main factors are combined. The first portion of the statement is the outcome we were trying to achieve—alternative scheduling patterns. The second portion of the statement is a given. In this case the given is a predetermined ratio of the nursing care hours needed per patient day on a shift basis. The third and final portion of the statement recognizes the fact that there are employees who desire or who must work while they attend school part-time or full-time which may or may not be an issue. This problem statement is in keeping with the goal statements from Chapter 5. For easy reference they are restated below. Flexible scheduling will:

- provide employees the option of alternatives to traditional eight-hour work schedules, shown in staffing patterns that include four, six, ten, or twelve hour shifts;
- provide employees the option of more scheduled time off duty, as shown by three-day weekends replacing two-day weekends; and
- decrease the number of staff members who leave the hospital to join outside nursing personnel agencies, as shown by a decreasing number giving this reason for termination.

Figure 6-1 illustrates expansion and condensation of information as the problem solvers proceed toward establishing problem solutions.

This model is composed of three funnels to indicate how the information from the field of uncertainty was collected, in a broad sense, through systematic data gathering. This same information was processed to produce issues, facts, and givens and expanded into problem statements. This process is illustrated by an inverted funnel to show that there are many problem statements, not just one. In a complex situation, there are so many variables known and unknown that the problem statements may overlap. This overlapping becomes apparent when exploring alternative solutions for each problem statement. Often one comprehensive solution will solve more than one aspect of the broad problem so that the solutions condense the information into a manageable action plan including outcome criteria, strategies for implementation, a plan for followup, and a way to measure results. Chapter 7 explains how it is possible to arrive at one solution that will solve one or more of the individual component problem statements. As a problem solver, you will find that issues become more manageable when they are distributed under broad topic headings. The number of issues that are clustered under one broad heading will help the problem solver determine the number of problem statements that should be constructed for each.

INVOLVING THE PEOPLE WHO WILL BE AFFECTED BY PROBLEM SOLUTION

In an earlier chapter the author discussed the necessity of collecting information from the various disciplines or work groups involved in the field of uncertainty. Just as it was necessary to identify the scope and complexity of the situation, it is equally important to involve a representative group as you begin to define the situation at hand. While managers can single handedly design the questionnaire, collect the data, process it, and get it to a reportable stage, they must also decide at what point to

Figure 6-1 The Funnel Analogy

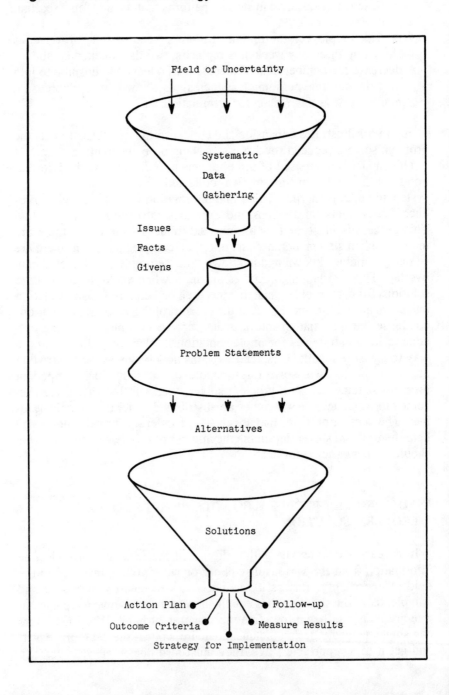

involve members of the work group to facilitate a change process. Repeatedly we have noted that paying attention to the work group begins to improve the out-of-balance state. The fact that the manager has taken time to collect information from the work group seems to establish a climate in which change is anticipated.

Once the data has been processed, the issues extracted and divided under broad topic headings, constructing problem statements can be a very meaningful way for a task force to become involved in a problem-solving project.

Defining a problem lends itself to small group work. Because the issues have been clustered under broad topic headings, the subject matter can be quickly divided among committee members. It works well to divide the committee into subgroups of two members each. The pairs should be allowed to select the topic headings of most interest to them. The overall goal statement of the problem-solving effort should be available for each subgroup as a quick reference as they proceed. This is a very effective way to get a task force involved immediately in a project—converting the raw data into problem statements. It gives them an immediate sense of involvement and ownership. You will be amazed at the amount of work they will accomplish within a short period of time using this process. Their involvement assures them that working on this task force will be a meaningful and rewarding experience. The members will leave the meetings with a sense of closure and feeling that they have produced and developed something concrete. They have developed material that will be addressed at sequential meetings when the task force begins to explore alternative solutions to each of the problem statements.

If you appoint a committee or task force to convert the issues, facts, and givens into problem statements, the chairperson must understand the PRESEARCH process. The group leader must be given more than a general overview in order to understand how one phase of this people-centered process leads to another. Be sure to allow the person whom you select enough time to become familiar with the process before chairing the committee.

It will be the chairperson's responsibility to create a climate within which a committee can work as a team toward mutual goals. Numerous useful references on effective small group process are available. A selected reference list follows at the end of this chapter for those who are interested in expanding their knowledge about small group behavior.

People-centered problem solving provides the manager with a systematic method to implement planned change. Theorists emphasize involving the work group early in the change process. When you allow a committee to formulate problem statements from the results of the survey, you not only foster their involvement but also provide for their ownership of the solution. Involvement of the work group at this point enhances the change agents' effectiveness. It also accelerates group acceptance of subsequent changes that may result from the solutions. Planned change theory in PRESEARCH is discussed in greater depth in Part III.

SUMMARY

The problem solver uses the information collected as a base for problem definition. A people-centered approach allows the manager to involve individuals systematically in the problem-solving process. Hence, the benefits of involving people from the work group begin to appear. The data-gathering phase gave them an opportunity to have input and express feelings. Constructing problem statements expanded their understanding of what you, the manager, were up against. It fostered a team effort in solution seeking. And, as you will discover in future chapters, involvement fosters their desire to participate in restoring balance to the unwieldy situation at hand. People-centeredness facilitates the planned change process from the manager's point of view and it recognizes the individual worth of the worker. People in a work group need to be recognized and they like being involved. If they perceive their involvement as worthwhile, they become supporters of the change process and develop a vested interest in the success of the problem-solving efforts.

Small Group Behavior Suggested References

Argyris, Chris. *An Introduction to Interaction Theory and Field Theory*. New Haven, Conn.: Labor and Management Center, Yale University, 1952.
Berne, Eric. *The Structure and Dynamics of Organizations and Groups*. New York: Grove Press, 1963.
Friedman, William. *How to do Groups*. New York: Jason Aronsen Publishers, 1979.
Hare, A., Borgatta, E., and Boles, R., eds., *Small Group Studies in Social Interactions*. New York: Alfred A. Knopf, 1961.
Lewin, Kurt. *Field Theory in Social Science*. New York: Harper and Row, 1951.
Shaw, M. *Group Dynamics: The Psychology of Small Group Behavior* 2nd ed. New York: McGraw Hill, 1976.

Chapter 7

Exploring Alternatives and Arriving at Solutions

The complex problem has been defined through a series of interrogatory statements. Each of the problem statements is closely linked to the next. If you recall in Chapter 1 the problem statements were likened to a chain of paper dolls cut from the newspaper. Each doll represents a different part of the complex situation, yet it is difficult, sometimes impossible, to discern where one problem stops and the next begins. One distinct advantage of dividing the complex problem into numerous component parts is that the manager is then able to distinguish where the problem-solving responsibilities and efforts should lie.

The person in charge of the problem-solving efforts has the responsibility of identifying who the appropriate problem solver is for each problem statement. In other words, this person must identify who *owns the problem*. It is useless to try to solve or rectify a problem over which you have no authority or control. If, for example, a problem is within the realm of the medical staff bylaws and hospital administrative policy, and you are the chief laboratory technologist, it is imperative to bring that portion of the problem to the hospital administrator's attention. In an earlier part of the book, we discussed the necessity of having administrative backing prior to attempting to tackle complex interdepartmental problems. When solutions require a cooperative effort from several individuals, it is imperative that each of the departments participate in formulating the overall goal and solution. Consequently, it truly becomes a synergetic interdisciplinary effort. If, on the other hand, you are unable to gain cooperation, you will be able to present your case to your boss from a position of strength. As a manager, you will be able to carry out your responsibility for the solution of certain aspects of the complex problem. Other aspects may be beyond the scope of your authority. The data-gathering process that you have undertaken provides you with the concrete evidence that you will need to explain why your problem-solving efforts will have limited effectiveness.

An example of a situation where a director of nursing was limited in his problem-solving capabilities is shown in the following situation. In a relatively small hospital, the evening supervisors were complaining bitterly about having to spend time in the pharmacy looking up and obtaining medications for patients. They were upset about not being able to concentrate on the patient care responsibilities they saw as top priority for their job. The chief pharmacist did not agree that the workload warranted scheduling someone to cover the pharmacy during off-shift hours. It is not uncommon to find a situation that presents a problem for one department is not viewed as a problem of the same magnitude by another department. The key to arriving at a mutually acceptable solution is a willingness for departments to cooperate or compromise. Unless the pharmacist in this situation is willing to participate in finding a way to lessen the amount of time the supervisors are spending in the pharmacy, the nursing efforts will be of no avail. There may be times when two departments reach a deadlock. Should this occur it may be necessary for someone in a higher position of authority to provide direction.

GENERATING ALTERNATIVES

Generating alternatives to the problem statements can be an extremely good use of committee time. If the person responsible for the problem-solving project has set the right climate, one where people feel free to speak without fear of being criticized, brainstorming for solutions can be energizing, fun, and productive. In his book *Excellence in Leadership*, Frank Goble discussed the use of brainstorming.

> Myron Allen, Director of Creative Growth Center in Los Gatos, California, believes that brainstorming works best when all members of the group are of approximately equal rank in the organization and the problem is not too controversial. Otherwise, fear of embarrassment, lack of self-esteem, and fear of reprisal greatly limit the willingness of group members to contribute.[1]

Usually after a group has experienced what it feels like to toss around ideas that might solve the problem, they become looser and feel freer to participate. The manager's explanation to the group that every idea, no matter how remote or ridiculous, has some bit of merit helps to reassure the group. The person in charge should also explain that a solution may evolve by combining elements from several of the suggested alternatives. If the group is reserved, a good place to start is for the leader to suggest an absolutely ridiculous alternative to the question at hand. This will let the group know that it is all right to expand their thinking and to suggest approaches other than those that have been tried and true methods of the past.

Goble describes the brainstorming process as one of the best-known approaches to creativity. He explains:

> In brainstorming, the leader gives the group some specific problem—the more specific the better. Everyone is encouraged to contribute as many ideas as possible and a secretary records it all. No value judgments or criticisms are permitted and participants are encouraged to hitchhike on other people's ideas. Wild ideas are encouraged because they stimulate the imagination. (Alex) Osborne who developed the use of brainstorming in business, recommended a time limit. After the session is over, the secretary types the ideas into a list. Then, and only then, are the ideas criticized and evaluated by those responsible for solving the problem under discussion. Charles Clark, one of the country's leading exponents of brainstorming, says that experience shows at least six per cent of the ideas are usable. Sometimes the percentage is much higher.[2]

David Campbell in *Take the Road to Creativity and Get Off Your Deadend* describes what he calls the phases of creativity.

> Creative people frequently report that in coming up with a new idea or product, they went through several phases, usually in the following order:
>
> PREPARATION—laying the ground work. Learning the background of the situation.
> CONCENTRATION—being totally absorbed in the specific problem.
> INCUBATION—taking time out, a rest period. Seeking distractions.
> ILLUMINATION (AHA!)—getting the answer, the idea! The lightbulb goes on.
> VERIFICATION/PRODUCTION—confronting and solving the practical problems. Other people are persuaded and enlisted. The work gets done.[3]

It is especially important for the committee chairperson to understand how to recognize and avoid "killer phrases." These are putdowns or judgmental biases or comments that committee members might express when someone else comes up with an alternative. In his book, *Brainstorming,* Charles Clark encourages the use of a bell at brainstorming sessions.[4] He suggests that whenever someone uses a "killer phrase," whoever is nearest the bell rings it. The following are some examples of "killer phrases":

- We don't have enough help to do that.
- We don't have enough time to do that.
- The doctors won't like it.
- That's a dumb thought.
- That will never work.
- We tried that years ago.
- We're too busy for that.
- We're too small an institution for that.
- The contract won't allow it.
- Get down out of your ivory tower—come into the real world.
- We didn't budget for that.
- We're not ready for another change.

The bell ringing technique, where committee members are monitoring each other's rule-breaking behavior, helps to establish an "everybody participate" atmosphere.

Although brainstorming for alternatives can be an extremely energizing and enjoyable experience, the energy level of the people involved begins to wane after one hour of time. As Alex Osborne suggests, it is advisable to plan the committee's brainstorming session with time limits.[5] The larger the number of alternative solutions generated, the greater potential there is for arriving at a creative, workable solution. For efficiency's sake a committee or task force can be subdivided into pairs. Groups of two can produce lengthy lists of alternatives and later share them with the group as a whole. The large group can be afforded the opportunity to expand the list of alternatives if that is deemed desirable. David Campbell identified the need for incubation time as a phase of creativity.[6] Experience has proven that it is advisable to allow a time lapse between the original brainstorming sessions, when the committee is generating alternatives, and the time set aside for them to recommend solutions.

DETERMINING SOLUTIONS

How do you know which alternative will produce the best acceptable solution? Earlier in this chapter, the author stated that no single alternative produces a solution that is all right or all wrong. Problem solvers should aim for the best fit. In other words, aim for the solution that most nearly will achieve the set objectives. The solution should be compatible with and implementable within the organization. All problem solving requires decision making. Within each organization there are decision-making constraints. Some of the things to consider when determining the best acceptable alternatives are:

- Timing—What else is going on within the institution or within work groups; what will be happening to work groups at the time the solution will be implemented?
- Budget—What cost factors are directly or indirectly related to implementation of the solution; will the solution require adding employees or purchasing new equipment and/or supplies?
- History—How have changes comparable to this one been accepted in the past; are circumstances different now that would make accepting a change easier or more difficult?
- External Factors—What is happening outside of the organization that might influence the implementation of the solution?
- Mission Statement, Philosophy, Policies—How compatible is the solution with basic beliefs, current practices, long- and short-range goals of the institution?
- Interdepartmental Impact—Which departments will be affected by a solution; would the solution be compatible with the capabilities and limitations of other work groups?
- Health Care Trends—Does the solution represent a step backwards or is it progressive; which direction is most in keeping with the posture of the institution?

These are just a few items you should consider as you enter a decision-making process and subsequently choose one solution over another.

After reviewing this list, it is plain to see that the person with the ultimate decision-making responsibility for choosing the best acceptable alternative must have an in-depth knowledge of the organization. If it is an interdisciplinary problem, it is not only advisable, but essential to include the disciplines affected by the solution when the decision is made. Some people find it helpful to use a solution analysis grid such as Figure 7-1.

This solution analysis grid can be a worksheet, although I prefer to think of it as a permanent record. At the top of the grid is a place to state the problem-solving objective. A problem-solving objective should be developed for each broad topic heading as discussed in Chapter 5. When

Figure 7-1 Solution Analysis Grid

Problem Solving Objective: _____

Problem Statement: _____

LIST OF ALTERNATIVE SOLUTIONS	CONTRIBUTION TO OBJECTIVE	COST IN DOLLARS	TIME FRAME	FEASIBILITY
1.				
2.				
3.				
4.				
5.				
6.				
7.				
8.				
9.				
10.				

Best Acceptable Solution: _____

that objective is determined, it can be entered on this sheet and retained as a permanent on-going, hand-written or typed record.

After the objective has been stated, the next step in the process is to develop problem statements for each broad topic heading as discussed in Chapter 6. There is space on the Solution Analysis Grid for the individual problem statements to be entered. If you decide to use this sheet during committee meetings it can be distributed at the beginning of the meeting and collected at the conclusion. I have found this to be a very effective and efficient record-keeping method. It replaces writing minutes of problem-solving meetings. All you will need in addition is a meeting attendance record.

During the brainstorming sessions the alternatives generated by the group can be listed on this same grid sheet. Thereby, when the person or persons who have decision-making responsibility reach the point of determining the best acceptable solution, they have all of the necessary data before them. The procedure for completing the four columns to the right of the alternatives is listed below:

Procedure for Use of the Solution Analysis Grid

1. **Contribution to Objective**   In this column rank the alternative's contribution to the problem-solving objective using the qualifiers high—medium—low.
2. **Cost in Dollars**   In this column estimate the cost for preparation and implementation of the alternative. Use the symbols of three dollar marks ($$$), two dollar marks ($$), or one dollar mark ($) to indicate relative estimated dollar amounts.
3. **Time Frame**   In this column estimate the amount of time it will take to prepare and implement a program that might result from the alternative. Use the qualifiers *Long-Range—Short-Range—Immediate* in this section.
4. **Feasibility**   In this column enter *yes* or *no*. Your affirmative or negative answer should be based on the decision-making constraints of the organization.
5. Use a process of elimination to delete all alternatives that are deemed *not feasible*. Delete those alternatives that have a low contribution to the objective. Retain those alternatives that have a high or moderate contribution to the objective.

SELECTING THE BEST ACCEPTABLE SOLUTION

Often it is desirable to combine several elements of different alternatives to come up with the best acceptable solution. Figure 7-2 graphically shows how parts of an idea can be combined to move an alternative along a continuum from the unacceptable to the acceptable. I was first exposed to this concept at the Center for Creative Leadership in Greensboro, North Carolina. The instructors at the center teach men and women to take a creative approach to management responsibilities and life in general. They stress that no solution is either all right or all wrong. The staff there urge problem solvers to expand their thinking when looking for the best fit. In Figure 7-2 the "•s" represent ideas that build on each other to create an alternative that has more merit because it combines the best qualities of several alternatives.

After narrowing the list of alternatives on the Solution Analysis Grid, it is advisable to examine the remaining alternatives that fall into the realm of the feasible. Ask yourself, "What parts of each of these alternatives are meritorious and could be combined to generate a solution?" The result should be one that capitalizes on the strong points of each of the remaining alternatives. You will notice in Figure 7-2 that all solutions can be placed somewhere along the continuum from unacceptable to outstand-

Figure 7-2 Piecing Together an Alternative

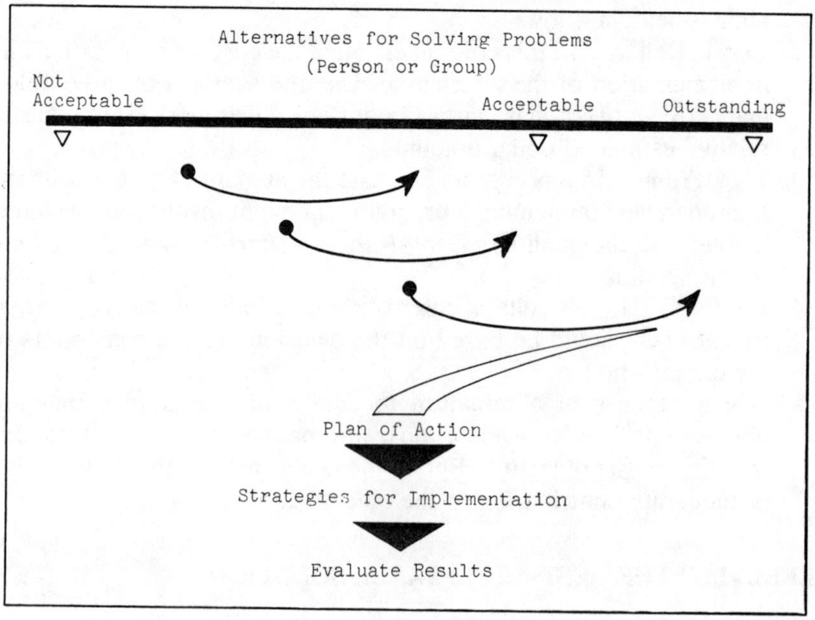

Source: From materials presented at the Center for Creative Leadership, Greensboro, North Carolina. Used with permission.

ing. By combining elements from a brainstorming session you can expand a totally unacceptable alternative by adding other ideas that move it into the realm of the acceptable. When you feel satisfied that you have arrived at the best acceptable solution, enter it in the space at the bottom of the Solution Analysis Grid. This completed sheet then becomes a very valuable record for your file. In the future when someone asks why certain choices were made, you can quickly refer to these sheets and provide very accurate information about why and how you arrived at certain solutions.

The next phase of the PRESEARCH process is to develop the action plan. When developing your plan, you can spread these individual Solution Analysis Grids before you. The solutions to each one of the individual problems must be compatible. This is essential for they will be incorporated into the overall action plan. In fact, in reality they become a series of events or component parts that must take place within the total plan of action.

SUMMARY

Brainstorming is an excellent technique for generating creative alternatives to problems. Frank Goble states that brainstorming works best when the problems are specific.[7] Certainly with the PRESEARCH process you will have specific problems on which to work. David Campbell describes getting "totally absorbed in the specific problem" as one of the phases of creativity.[8] Indeed, it is the aim of people-centered problem solving to involve people in the process. People involvement is accomplished by allowing those who will be affected by the solution to participate in the solution-seeking process. They should also be included in development of the action plan.

Figure 7-3 shows a set of Rules for Solution Seekers. This checklist includes crucial points to be considered before exploring solution alternatives.

Once you have accomplished each of the items in the checklist, you proceed with your planning. After you have explored alternatives and arrived at the best acceptable solution for each component part of the problem, you will have your essential plan developed.

Figure 7-3 Solution Checklist

RULES FOR SOLUTION SEEKERS

_____ Get approval to proceed.
_____ Get agreement from the boss that the goals as stated are appropriate.
_____ Determine who owns each of the problems.
_____ Determine that your interdisciplinary counterparts are willing to participate
         in an overall problem-solving effort.
_____ Be certain that the appointed group leader understands group process and
         the use of brainstorming techniques.
_____ Gather the decision-making constraints which exist in written and un-
         written form within your organization.

NOTES

1. Frank Goble, *Excellence in Leadership* (New York, N.Y.: American Management Association, 1972), p. 24.
2. See *supra* note 1, p. 23.
3. David Campbell, *Take the Road to Creativity and Get Off Your Dead End* (Niles, Ill.: Argus Communications, 1977), p. 30.
4. Charles Clark, *Brainstorming* (Garden City, N.Y.: Doubleday, 1958), p. 55.
5. Goble, *Excellence in Leadership*, p. 24.
6. Campbell, *Road to Creativity*, p. 30.
7. Goble, *Excellence in Leadership*, p. 24.
8. Campbell, *Road to Creativity*, p. 30.

Chapter 8

The Action Plan

A blending of the best acceptable solutions from each component part of the problem produces the action plan. The plan is knowing what needs to be done and planning how and when actions and events must take place to accomplish the desired outcome. Relationships between the events that must occur need to be considered carefully. Two techniques which can be used to plot out an action plan are Management By Objectives (MBO) and Performance Evaluation Review Technique (PERT) charting.

MANAGEMENT BY OBJECTIVES

An example of a Programmed Planning and Implementation Calendar is shown in Figure 8-1. This particular MBO planning sheet is set up for a four month time period. On it there is space to type the overall outcome objective. The program steps are the solutions that you have identified. This kind of calendar requires that each step of the program be given a target scheduled completion date. That date is entered in an appropriate box on the four month calendar. Beside the date place a capital "S" indicating that the date entered is the date that this segment of the plan is scheduled to be accomplished. Each of the program steps is entered and given its own scheduled date of accomplishment. As the program steps are completed, whether ahead of schedule, on target, or overdue, an "A" is entered in an appropriate calendar box. This indicates when the program step is actually completed. An MBO calendar of this nature works quite well for programs that can be accomplished in a relatively short period of time. There is space at the bottom of the page to enter comments about the progress, or lack of it, within the specified time frame.

73

Figure 8-1 Program Planning and Implementation Calendar

Topic _____

OBJECTIVE: _____

Period from_____ to_____

PROGRAM STEPS	TIME PERIOD			
	JAN.	FEB.	MAR.	APR.

COMMENTS: _____

S = Scheduled date of accomplishment
A = Date accomplished

PERFORMANCE EVALUATION REVIEW TECHNIQUE CHARTING

A simple PERT network is another tool that is quite useful in mapping a problem-solving project. It is especially beneficial when there are many people or departments whose actions must be synchronized. More explicitly, PERT charting is advantageous when the total efforts of many must mesh at the completion of the project. A PERT chart is essentially a system flow chart. It presents a visible network of events and activities necessary to complete a project, from its inception to its completion. Events and activities are linked together in a chain-like manner. Unlike the MBO program planning and implementation calendar, where you will probably list the first step at the top of the page and work downward, backward chaining is necessary to develop a PERT flow chart. This process requires you to describe the last step in the anticipated process and work backwards, event by event, to the first step. In a PERT network the program steps are called events. These are signified on the PERT network as circles. Each event is brought about by an activity. An activity is indicated by a straight line that connects one circle to another in the chart. A PERT chart forces you to consider the time required between the occurrence of each event. It thereby helps you to determine a reasonable time frame within which to accomplish the project.

An excellent example of PERT charting is provided by Dirk J. Wassenaar in *Principles and Applications of PERT/CPM*.[1] In the title of this little book PERT stands for Program Evaluation Review Technique and CPM means Critical Path Method. In a PERT chart all major events must be identified. The relationships between the events must be clearly identified or indicated. In the literature some authors discuss the Critical Path Method as an intricate aspect of PERT charting. Others describe the Critical Path Method as a separate tool for diagramming a complex project. For the purpose of discussing how PERT charting can be used in mapping out a PRESEARCH problem-solving project, a simple PERT network as described by Wassenaar is presented below.

A Simple PERT Network

Figure 8-2 shows a simple PERT chart for the construction of a storage shed.

Major events are indicated, including the start of the project. The diagram shows, for instance, that it is expected to take five weeks to get the plans approved. After approval of the plans it will take five weeks to finish the foundations, and two weeks to

Figure 8-2 PERT Network

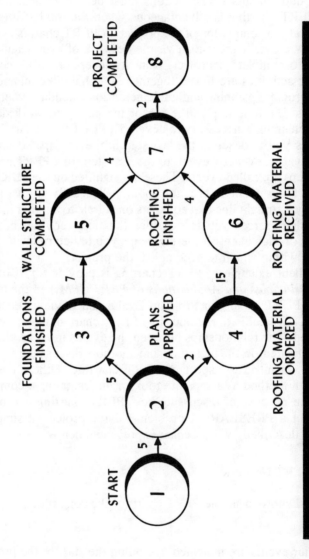

A SIMPLE PERT NETWORK

HOW MUCH TIME IS NEEDED TO COMPLETE THE PROJECT?

Source: Principles and Applications of PERT/CPM, Dirk J. Wassenaar, Ph.D. Used with permission.

order the roofing material. (Note that the last two activities can take place simultaneously.) The wall structure is expected to be completed seven weeks after the foundations are finished, and the expected delivery time for the roofing material is fifteen weeks. Roofing can be finished four weeks after the completion of the walls, and the receipt of the roofing materials.

How long will it take to complete this project? The answer is found as follows: it takes 21 weeks to move from event two to event seven (note that the lower branch of the network dominates the upper branch; in other words, the lower branch represents the critical path). Add to this the five weeks for activity 1–2, and the two weeks for activity 7–8 and the total project time is found to be 28 weeks. The critical path in this case is 1–2–4–6–7–8. If one would like to speed up this project, it would do no good to speed up work on the foundations or wall construction. Instead, the ordering and delivery of roofing materials should be expedited.

The question might come up why this PERT chart indicated ordering and delivery of roofing material but that nothing is shown about ordering and delivery of foundation and wall structure materials. The answer is simple: in this case the latter materials were on hand (or readily available) and therefore the availability of these materials was not considered critical.

PERT charting helps one visualize which events can occur simultaneously and which ones must occur in rapid sequence. It serves as a double check on the proper sequencing of the action plan. Backward chaining often identifies a previously overlooked step in the action plan. Those who have used the PRESEARCH process agree that PERT charting augments the process at the action plan phase. Literature about the use of the Performance Evaluation Review Technique is extensive. A selected bibliography is included at the end of this chapter for those who wish to read more about its use and application.

Problem Analysis and Strategy

Power: Use It or Lose It by the National League for Nursing includes a problem analysis and strategy planning model and questionnaire.[2] (See Figure 8-3.) These thought provoking questions, shown in Exhibit 8-1, are included here because the strategy information they generate aid the problem solver in action planning.

Figure 8-3 Problem Analysis and Strategy Planning

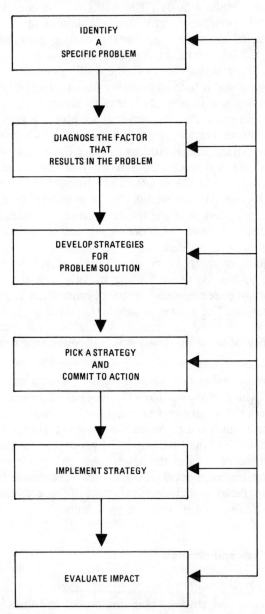

Source: "Problem Analysis and Strategy Planning Questionnaire," in *Power: Use It or Lose It* (New York: National League for Nursing, 1977), pp. 24–26. Reprinted with permission of the publisher.

Exhibit 8-1 Problem Analysis and Strategy Planning Questionnaire

1. What is the difficulty, the concern, the problem?
   - Who sees it as a problem?
   - Who is affected by it?
   - How are they affected?
   - What significant events or typical incidents illustrate the problem?
   - To what extent are there differences in goals toward which individuals or groups are working in this situation?
2. Identify the various values (assumptions, beliefs, or feelings that serve as goal determining criteria of the total organization, any groups, and the individual persons involved.
3. Identify the various norms (i.e., behavior patterns highly valued or discouraged) of the total organization and any of its groups.
4. Identify the various individuals and groups that influence (i.e., have power and/or status) the decisions and behavior of the total organization, its groups, and individuals.
5. Identify the various sanctions (i.e., punishments and rewards) by which norms are maintained in groups or the total organization.
6. Identify your roles (i.e., positions and functions) in the situation. What other roles seem important in the situation? As you refer to other people, explain the relationships between you and them.
7. Identify the various patterns of communication (i.e., who talks to whom, formally and informally). You may wish to diagram this.
8. Identify the various steps (i.e., defining, clarifying, developing alternatives, etc.) and categories by which the group makes decisions.
9. Identify the various actions that relevant groups take to help the organization maintain its identity and separateness.
10. Identify the means by which groups maintain linkage (communication) with other groups.
11. In reviewing your diagnosis, now what seems to be the underlying problems?
12. Which elements or processes seem to be most critical to the problem?

Exhibit 8-1 continued

13. List what you have tried to do about the problem within the past six months. (Include as specifically as possible the goals and strategy that informed your actions, as well as the effects of the actions.)
14. What do you think you might try to do about the problem within the next six months? List as many specific actions as you can, and your anticipation of their effect on relevant organization elements and processes.

Source: National League for Nursing, *Power: Use It or Lose It,* 1977.

While preparing your tactics you will need to ask the following questions from the same questions that have been paraphrased and expanded:

- Are there any self-interest groups involved in the problem?
- Who informally sanctions activities that might involve change in the problem area?
- Whose ideas are normally accepted and implemented in situations such as this?
- Who can everyone count on to get things done?
- How can you tap into the grapevine and gain support of the informal leaders?
- What tactics will communicate your concerns and mobilize support for them?
- How will you identify and organize your problem-solving resources?
- What further strategies seem relevant and need to be developed?

When problems are addressed, in all cases except when the best acceptable solution is determined to be "do nothing," *change* is indicated. In their book *Nursing Management,*[3] Joan and Warren Ganong discuss managing organizational change. They describe the effect of change within an organization in the following manner:

Despite careful planning, a change of any magnitude produces some degree of trauma. People don't resist change as much as they resist being changed by others. The manager can help staff members respond to the requirements and risks of change by treating such requirements and risks as new opportunities for personnel growth and progress.

Hirschowitz says that the failure of organizations to appreciate the complexity of human beings and their multiplicity of needs is a contributing factor in lack of adaptation to change. He cites three predictable sequential phases experienced by people going through change: (1) impact, (2) recoil-turmoil, and (3) adjustment and reconstruction. From experience with systems in transition, he suggests what does and does not help ease the difficulty of adjusting to change.[4] Briefly, and with a few additions, these are:

What Helps

- Involvement in planning and problem solving
- Support and reassurance
- Guidance
- Presence and proximity of superiors
- Talking about feelings
- Clarification of roles
- Respect for values and dignity
- Hope, through communicative leadership
- Planning
- Timing
- Trust

What Does Not Help

- Denial (by those who must face up to change)
- Simplifying complexities
- Overspecializing, by trying to overdevelop functions and domains
- Holding onto cherished habits, routines, and rituals
- Hidden agendas

What Friedman says about changing behavior in therapy groups applies to people in any group:

> The facilitation of change involves an assessment of discrepancies. There may be discrepancies in the way the group member has organized his understanding of what happened in the past; discrepancies between his experience of himself and the way others perceive his actions in the present; discrepancies between where he is now, in relations to his needs, wants, and expectations, and where he would like to be. These discrepancies may be

more visible or obvious to others than to the individual who experiences and maintains them.[5]

The list of "what helps" presented by the Ganongs addresses the needs of the group that will be affected by the change. Lang, Dittrich, and White propose a problem-solving process that emphasizes the abilities of the chief problem solver. They contend that

> two kinds of ability are necessary for problem-solving performance. Ability One is cognitive problem-solving ability—the ability of the problem solver to develop and select a potentially successful solution. Ability One includes both personal problem-solving talent and supporting information and computational resources. It also includes validity of environmental perceptions and use of information. Ability Two is actual possession of skills (or a command of resources) that can, in fact, implement the chosen solution to the problem.[6]

They further elaborate that while Ability One and Ability Two are necessary for problem-solving performance, motivation to attempt to resolve the problem is also necessary. The PRESEARCH process is designed to address and consider the needs of the group as well as provide the person in charge with support tools to supplement his or her problem-solving ability and skills. Motivation in an organizational problem-solving sense is directly related to the manager's desire to perform his job. In other words, problem-solving motivation is related to the manager's perceptions of the contributions he should make to the whole organization or a specific work group.

SUMMARY

The action plan is composed of the best acceptable solutions to each segment of the complex problem. The manager is responsible for developing the comprehensive action plan and establishing reasonable target dates within which to accomplish the desired outcome. Besides mapping the plan, a problem solver must determine implementation strategies for achieving the change. In order to be an effective change agent, the manager must develop tactics, have the trust of the work group, and be able to offer guidance, support, and reassurance to them as a group and as individuals. In complex problem-solving projects, such as the ones PRE-SEARCH is designed to address, charting the action plan does not simplify complexities. It divides the complex situation into manageable parts of the whole.

NOTES

1. Dirk W. Wassenaar, *Principles and Applications of PERT/CPM* (San Jose, Calif.: Lansford Publishing Co., 1975), pp. 4–5.
2. National League for Nursing, *Power: Use It or Lose It* (New York, N.Y.: National League for Nursing Publication No. 52-1675, 1977).
3. Joan Ganong and Warren Ganong, *Nursing Management*, 2d ed. (Rockville, Md.: Aspen Systems Corp., 1980), pp. 277–278.
4. R. J. Hirschowitz, "The Human Aspects of Managing Transition," *Personnel* (Hartford, Conn.: Connecticut General Hospital *Notes and Quotes*, July 1974), pp. 8–17.
5. William Friedman, *How To Do Groups* (New York: Jason Aronson, 1979), p. 28.
6. James R. Lang, John E. Dittrich, and Sam E. White, "Managerial Problem Solving Models: A Review and a Proposal," in *The Academy of Management Review* (Mississippi State, Miss.: Academy of Management, October 1978), p. 860.

Suggested Reading List—PERT/CPM

Dusenbury, Warren, "CPM for New Product Introductions," *Harvard Business Review*, July-August 1977, pp. 124–139.
Levy, F. K., Thompson, G. L., and West, J. D., "The ABCs of the Critical Path Method," *Harvard Business Review*, September-October 1963, pp. 98–108.
Miller, Robert W., "How to Plan and Control with PERT," *Harvard Business Review*, March-April 1962, pp. 93–104.
Paige, Hillard W., "How PERT-Cost Helps the General Manager," *Harvard Business Review*, November-December 1963, pp. 87–95.
Wassenaar, Dirk J., *Principles and Applications of PERT/CPM* (San Jose, Calif.: Lansford Publishing Co., Inc., 1975).
West, Jerome D., and Levy, Ferdinand K., *A Management Guide to PERT/CPM: With GERT/PDM/DCPM and Other Networks* (Englewood Cliffs, N.J.: Prentice-Hall, Inc., 1977).

Chapter 9

Evaluation and Followup

Evaluation and followup are the stepchildren of management. Too often these elements have been viewed as extra work. They get pushed low on the priority list and may eventually be neglected totally. When this happens you will hear managers say, "Now, why did that happen? That was such a good plan and everything was going so well!" The tendency in such cases is to blame the work force for not following directions or for being uncooperative, while often the opposite is true. The fault may lie with the change agent for not supporting or monitoring the impact of the change and its acceptance by the work group.

The PRESEARCH process stresses negating the concept that evaluation and followup have to be "trumped up procedures" that satisfy educators and theorists. Chapter 5 emphasized developing measureable outcome goals. At this point in the process, an evaluative tool must be developed to measure those goals. It is up to you, the manager, to determine the intervals at which followup should occur. An attitude, "If I check on them, they'll think I don't trust them," must be eradicated. The work force views appropriate followup as the manager being interested in what they are doing. It also gives the staff an opportunity to explain snags or pitfalls in the implementation process. Hereby, the manager can deal with difficulties in a timely fashion. The astute manager will be able to determine when the followup should be shared by the work force. Involvement increases the awareness of the need to correctly implement the change.

How much followup? I recommend at least twice during the project. One followup should be held soon after the plan is implemented. The second one should be determined by the results of the first evaluation. If all is well and there is a smooth transition, you can probably wait six months or a year before the second evaluation. If, on the other hand, the work group is having difficulty, it will be up to the manager to determine what else is needed. Does the work group need more instruction or simply need additional support through the change process? If the latter is true, both informal and formal evaluations at rather short intervals are essential. The amount of evaluation and followup depends on the circumstances in each situation. You as a manager must make decisions about "how much." I strongly advise against your deciding not to do any evaluations or followup because you "trust" the work group. You can however, delegate this aspect of the project to those you trust and allow them to report the findings back to you.

In some problem-solving models, several authors discuss evaluation as the first step in problem solving. Evaluation, as discussed in this chapter, is not the same. In this context followup means evaluative monitoring. Expressly, it means that you assess progress, or the lack of it, against predetermined criteria. The results of this kind of evaluation may uncover other problems. It has been written that in problem solving, every solution creates another problem. However, the PRESEARCH process encourages the problem solver to develop an awareness of other problems that may be generated by a potential solution. Hence, the problems uncovered in the evaluative phase most likely will be minor and fairly predictable ones.

A good example of an evaluative tool is presented in Chapter 15, Interdepartmental Problem Solving. Another example is presented in Figure 9-1 which is a conversion of an excerpt from the job performance standard into an evaluative tool found in Chapter 11.

This evaluative criterion was derived directly from the job performance standards. Staff nurses were involved in the development of these standards. The document was widely circulated and discussed. At the time the standards were being developed, two questions had been asked: "Does this standard tell the staff nurses what is expected of them?" and "Do you believe that this is a fair tool by which to evaluate a nurse's performance?" The staff nurses' answers to both of those questions were a unanimous yes. The nurses who worked on these general duty performance standards were instrumental in initiating individual chart audits using Figure 9-1 as the evaluative tool. Initially they conducted a retrospective audit. The results of that audit indicated the need to educate the other nurses about the department's expectations of their individual use of the nursing process. Thereafter, the staff nurses from the original task force engaged in a concurrent peer review (of charting). They went from unit to unit and taught their peers to use the evaluative criteria. They also demonstrated the process of giving each other constructive feedback. It is anticipated that a retrospective audit six months in the future will show a significant documentation improvement. This assumption is based on the

Figure 9-1 General Duty Registered Nurse Performance Evaluative Tool

Medical record # _____ Primary Nurse _____ Reviewer _____ Date _____

PERFORMANCE STANDARDS	ASSESSMENT CRITERIA	COMPLIANCE (circle one)			REVIEWER COMMENTS
A. Demonstrates an understanding of and ability to use the nursing process.	Was the patient's condition assessed by a registered nurse at the time of admission?	yes	no	n/a	
	Was the admission data sheet completed within 24 hours of admission?	yes	no	n/a	
	Has an individualized care plan been initiated?	yes	no	n/a	
	Has the care plan been reviewed and updated on a daily basis?	yes	no	n/a	
	Has the care plan been revised according to the changes in the patient's condition?	yes	no	n/a	
	Is there an indication that the RN approved patient care written by an LPN?	yes	no	n/a	
	Is there evidence that the patient and/or family were given an opportunity to participate in the care plan?	yes	no	n/a	
	Were recognized standards used to develop this patient care plan?	yes	no	n/a	
	Have appropriate nursing directives been initiated?	yes	no	n/a	

Figure 9-1 continued

PERFORMANCE STANDARDS	ASSESSMENT CRITERIA	COMPLIANCE (circle one)	REVIEWER COMMENTS
	Is there documented evidence that discharge planning has been initiated?	yes no n/a	
	Have appropriate interdisciplinary personnel been contacted for discharge planning purposes?	yes no n/a	
	Have the patient's learning needs been identified?	yes no n/a	
	Has the patient's learning readiness been assessed?	yes no n/a	
	Has an individualized patient teaching plan been designed?	yes no n/a	

Source: Format for this evaluative tool is an adaptation of the department's self-assessment tool devised by the Joint Commission on Accreditation of Hospitals. Eitel Hospital *Performance Standards* General Duty Registered Nurse. Used with permission.

fact that each staff nurse will be increasingly aware of the documentation expectations of their use of the nursing process. This kind of followup assures the departmental director that expected standards are recognized and practiced.

SUMMARY

Evaluation and followup are essential parts of a problem-solving project. Any manager who has invested the amount of time required in the initial phases of PRESEARCH will agree that followup is imperative. Although periodic evaluation is required throughout the problem-solving process, the project essentially is not finalized until the manager is satisfied with the results of evaluation based on predetermined outcome criteria.

CONCLUSION

A common complaint among health care managers is that there is an inadequate amount of time allocated for planning purposes. People-centered problem solving requires an investment of time and energy at the beginning. Many elements of planned change theory are incorporated as people are involved in the process. Elements of research are incorporated from which the problem-solving data base is built. This systematic approach forces people to spend time planning before implementing.

The PRESEARCH emphasis is on time spent in an intelligent planning process rather than extinguishing brushfires. It also forces people to come to grips with the situation at hand before tackling an isolated aspect of the problem and using the Bandaid approach. Because of the people involvement in the process, interdisciplinary staff share ownership in the outcome. The process fosters a team working together for a common goal from which the individuals and organization mutually benefit.

For your quick reference and future use, the entire people-centered PRESEARCH process is presented in Exhibit 9-1 as a step by step procedure.

DELEGATING PROBLEM-SOLVING RESPONSIBILITIES

Often the problem solver must delegate responsibility to others or subdivide responsibilities for accomplishing the goals. Delegation makes good management sense. In a very complex situation the challenge for the person in charge becomes, "How can I possibly keep apprised of the

Exhibit 9-1 The PRESEARCH Process

METHOD:

Step I. Recognize a field of uncertainty. This can surface in various symptomatic ways, for example, through a nursing unit when the staff doesn't work well together, the employee turnover rate is higher than expected, and some physicians are happy with patient care while others refuse to have their patients admitted to that unit. These symptoms are warning signals, that, if considered individually, may identify a single problem, but collectively they may point to underlying multifaceted and interrelated interdisciplinary problems.

Step II. Determine and state the purpose for exploring the field of uncertainty. The purpose may simply be to decide if the symptomatic feedback is significant. It could be, however, to pursue more complex problems systematically.

Step III. Decide how the data, once collected, will be used. Correlate the anticipated use with the stated purpose in Step II—education, evaluation, or problem solving.

Step IV. Identify the target population. Try to include those disciplines that might be affected by a solution (or change) to alleviate the symptoms of the suspected or ill-defined problem. For instance, if the symptoms are unrest among the nursing staff of a given unit, a high volume employee turnover, and disagreement among the physician users of the unit about the quality of patient care delivered, the appropriate target population would include the staff nurses on the unit, the head nurse, nurse supervisors, staff development personnel, patients, and physician users of the unit.

Step V. Examine several methods of data collection and determine which one will be most appropriate for the situation. Once a method—personal interview, telephone survey, or structured questionnaire—is chosen, be certain that all data are collected on a standardized form and in a like manner. Pattern the data collection after the research model to assure consistency and to minimize the biasing influence of the person collecting the information.

Step VI. Develop a survey tool using either fixed alternative or open-ended questions, or both. Open-ended questions provide a frame of reference for participant responses, yet do not restrict the

Exhibit 9-1 continued

participant's manner of expression or the content of answers. There is one distinct advantage of the open-ended question in this process; the respondents may give unexpected answers that identify aspects of the underlying problem not originally anticipated by those initiating or those conducting the survey.

Step VII. Examine the appropriateness of each question in the survey instrument by asking:

1. Is the question related to the "field of uncertainty" and to the purpose of the study?
2. Is the type of question right? (open-ended question versus a clear-cut choice of two or more alternatives)
3. Is the question clear and unambiguous?
4. Does the question suggest an answer or a surveyor-preferred response?
5. Does the question suggest a socially desirable response?
6. Does the question demand knowledge or information that the respondent does not have?

If the answers to items 1–3 are "yes," keep the questions in the survey; if the answers to items 4–6 are "yes," then reconstruct or discard those questions.

Step VIII. Decide on a time frame within which to collect the data and analyze the results.

Step IX. Collect the data.

Step X. Combine the subjective feedback from all respondents. Sort the responses and group or classify them under several broad topic headings. These headings can be interpreted as problem areas, and the data can be defined as constructive criticism. One general heading can have more than one problem area.

Step XI. Extract the issues from the constructive criticism by listing words or phrases within the content of the data.

Step XII. Group the issues by clustering like or related content.

Step XIII. Specify measureable outcome goals or changes that should be accomplished for each problem area.

Step XIV. Construct one or more problem statements by incorporating associated issues, facts, and givens into a sentence beginning "How can we . . . , while . . . ?"

Exhibit 9-1 continued

Step XV. Identify the problem solvers by asking, "Who really owns this problem?" The owner, person or group, should be the one responsible for solving the problem.

Step XVI. If possible include those who will be affected by a change when brainstorming for possible solutions to the problem. The larger number of alternative solutions posed, the greater the potential for a creative workable solution.

Step XVII. Explore each alternative. Consider all the factors necessary to implement the alternative. Examine the positive and negative forces that might facilitate, reinforce, or block its implementation. The most creative approach is to combine several good elements from more than one alternative and generate a new alternative. With the most unique creative solution, do not neglect to consider the pros and cons of its implementation. The *best* quality solution may not be the most *acceptable* solution. Look at the organization, scrutinize its structure and its interrelated systems. Aim for the *best acceptable solution* because it *can* be implemented into the organization. If the best acceptable solution crosses departmental lines, state the desired solution in the form of a recommendation and make a formal presentation to the appropriate audience.

Step XVIII. Establish evaluative tools by which to measure the implementation. Evaluative criteria must be compatible with the goal statements in Step XIII.

Step XIX. Develop the action plan or strategy for implementation. Include planned change theory when developing tactics.

Step XX. Implement the best acceptable solution.

Step XXI. Measure the results of the problem-solving effort through evaluative monitoring and followup.

Prior to initiating a large problem-solving study, it is advisable to obtain administrative approval. As mentioned in Step VI, a survey may produce some unexpected results, that may need administrative support when you make recommendations or implement the best acceptable solutions.

Source: Cecelia Golightly, *PRESEARCH—A New Approach to Creative Problem Solving for Hospitals and Other Health Care Agencies* (USA: Privately printed, 1978).

project's progress, individually and collectively?'' Figure 9-2 is an example of a work flow chart which was developed for an extremely complex project.

This graphic display provides space to enter the major aspects of the entire process. Note that you can enter the:

- people who will be affected by the changes,
- field of uncertainty,
- broad topic headings,
- problem segments under each heading,
- plans for action,
- person responsible for carrying out each part of the plan,
- person from whom approval will be needed,
- target date for implementation,
- actual date implemented,
- outcome or results of the action taken,
- followup methods,
- date evaluative followup is planned, and
- person responsible for the followup.

This kind of chart centralizes project information. It could be considered an MBO chart. It is a working model and, like the chart described in Chapter 8, it too can be a prominent wall hanging. The advantage of this flow chart is the inclusion of "Outcome" or results and "Followup." It also includes identifying those responsible for the action plans, those from whom approval must be obtained, and those responsible for followup. If the chart is kept current, anyone can go to the chart and see the overall progress on a daily basis. It is another useful management tool. This one is especially handy when delegating portions of the project is necessary.

Figure 9-2 Flow Chart for Complex Projects

Which involves:	Broad Topic Headings	Problem Segment	Plan of Action	Person Responsible	Approval from	Target date	Actual date	Outcome	Follow-up	Date	Person Responsible
A.		1.									
B.		2.									
C.	______	3.									
D.		4.									
E.		5.									
F.											
		1.									
		2.									
	______	3.									
		4.									
		5.									
		1.									
		2.									
	______	3.									
		4.									
		5.									
Field of		1.									
<u>Uncertainty</u>		2.									
	______	3.									
		4.									
		5.									
		1.									
		2.									
	______	3.									
		4.									
		5.									
		1.									
		2.									
	______	3.									
		4.									
		5.									
		1.									
		2.									
	______	3.									
		4.									
		5.									

Part II

The Application

INTRODUCTION

This section provides a variety of case examples that demonstrate the wide application potential of this process. These situations will stimulate your thinking and facilitate your implementing the process in your individual institutions.

Chapter 10 focuses on a small group of people who staffed the continuing education department in a 425 bed hospital. Although this example occurred in an acute care setting, similarities exist in all health care agencies. This case was chosen because it vividly portrays all aspects of PRESEARCH. It traces actual events over an eighteen month period. It exemplifies the interrelatedness of the confronted problems. The case demonstrates the far reaching effects of one problem-solving effort—one that started out simply to clarify roles and resulted in the reorganization of the department.

Chapter 11 presents a review of the literature, definitions of quality assessment, quality assurance, outcome criteria, process criteria, structure criteria, and peer review. In this chapter a case study is presented that describes how the department of nursing at Eitel Hospital, Minneapolis, Minnesota, rebuilt their committee structure around quality assurance. The use of the PRESEARCH method is discussed as a necessary and vital part of a total quality assurance program. This chapter also provides a protocol for documenting quality assurance problem-solving projects.

Chapter 12 describes the use of PRESEARCH concepts in a problem prevention mode rather than a problem-solving mode. Examples from Eitel Hospital, Minneapolis, Minnesota, are used to illustrate an oral and written interview process for key positions. The selection process as well as an Applicant Rating Grid is included in the text.

Chapter 13 describes a situation where a system that works well for two departments is causing problems for another department. Systematic data gathering proves helpful in defining the area of decision-making freedom for the director of nursing in this case. An interdepartmental compromise is then described and the director is able to make a few minor adjustments that reduce the adverse effects caused by the system on her department.

Chapter 14 is the reprint of a student's project paper. Martyann Penberth, an instructor at a nontraditional second step baccalaureate program at St. Joseph's College in North Windham, Maine, offered her students the option of using the PRESEARCH process for conducting their required projects. Adriane Weaver was one of the students who selected to do so. She not only used the process in problem solving, she also organized her paper using the sequential steps of the process.

The final chapter in this section is a system example for the care of patient valuables at St. Joseph's Hospital, St. Paul, Minnesota. This example includes a problem that affects patients, the admitting office staff, the cashier, the nurses, and the nursing administrative staff. This case demonstrates how methods analysis can be used as the data-gathering tool for problem definition. In this case an elaborate, involved system was simplified as a result of actively listening to those involved in the process. An example of PERT charting is included to show how the action plan was charted and time frames established.

Chapter 10

Case Study—An Education Department Reorganized

How discouraging it is to see well qualified, competent people functioning at a mediocre level. Such was the case of four registered professional
nurses who staffed the continuing education department of a large metropolitan hospital. There was no great upheaval that signalled the problem; no crisis, just subtle intradepartmental changes which resulted in
feelings of unrest.

The educators' job encompassed new employee orientation, in-service
education, continuing education, and staff development; also included
was a clinical resource component. Clinical responsibilities were divided
among three staff members; the fourth person was mainly responsible for
new employee orientation. Their professional backgrounds were quite
diverse. Each one emphasized the area of greatest expertise on her assigned units. Discussion among the four went something like this:

"I want to do a good job, but I don't really understand what my
job encompasses. When I took this position, I thought I understood my responsibilities. Head nurses don't expect the same
thing from my time that my supervisor does. I know that I'm not
carrying out my responsibilities in the same way that the other
two staff development nurses are. Yet, our job descriptions are
the same."

"We are pulled in too many different ways. I don't even have
time to go to the library for reference material that I need for
program development."

"I never get any feedback from the head nurses about the
people I have had in orientation. Sometimes the new nurses get
'lost in the system.' I never see them again until something goes

wrong and then I'm called to the rescue. I am also annoyed that some head nurses manage to keep their new personnel on 'orientation' status much longer than others. We need some standardization around here."

"I know what you mean. There's no time to prepare for classes. I am constantly interrupted by calls from the nursing units. Some of the head nurses are using me as a sounding board for management problems instead of a staff developer."

IDENTIFYING THE FIELD OF UNCERTAINTY

Their supervisor listened to the music above these words. She also was aware that the staff's confusion over job responsibilities made evaluating their performance a difficult task. This was a classic example of a situation where job performance expectations were unclear. Also there were discrepancies between the priorities of the boss and the subordinates. Furthermore, the supervisor wanted to upgrade the educational efforts of the department. She exerted pressure on those reporting to her to do long-range program planning and to develop house-wide educational programs. The pressure exerted meant a shift in job emphasis. This was viewed by the educators as changing their job focus and incorporating additional duties into an already busy schedule. Numerous tasks were already pulling them in many different directions. As their discomfort increased, they began to question their own abilities. This was more than the educators could cope with alone.

Within a relatively short period of time the head nurses asked the educators to come to one of the head nurse meetings to talk about in-service education. Discussion at the meeting indicated that there was polarization among the head nurse group about the duties and responsibilities of the educators in the nursing units. This head nurse meeting caused the associate directors of nursing to realize that they had expectations of the educators that had not been shared between highly interdependent work groups. Simple and complex conflicts were abounding. The head nurses needed the educators to prepare and develop their staffs, while the educators needed appropriate input and feedback from the head nurses.

The field of uncertainty therefore was emerging through the head nurses, the educational staff and their immediate supervisor, as well as the associate directors of nursing. The supervisor was aware that her perception of the staff developer's role was not in concert with those reporting to her. Furthermore, her expectations did not necessarily agree with those of the head nurse group or the associate directors.

The field of uncertainty stretched beyond the supervisor's area of freedom, because it involved her educators functioning as clinical resource persons. For this aspect of their job they reported to the associate directors of nursing. The educators were experiencing internal conflict between their educational commitments and their clinical responsibility. They believed education should be their primary function but their own time allocations did not permit education to outrank their clinical responsibilities. Fortunately, the supervisor was sensitive to the frustrations of her subordinates. She recognized that "trapped" energy was being spent dealing with job-related frustrations. Conflict had gone beyond the healthy state. It was interfering with the work group's productivity. The continuing education staff were working hard but they felt they were going around in circles. They had little sense of accomplishment and no job satisfaction.

About the time that annual departmental goals were due, two of the educators announced plans for retirement. The timing was perfect to analyze the situation and set new priorities. The educators, under the direction of their supervisor, took this opportunity to examine the past, deal with the present, and prepare for the future.

COLLECTING DATA SYSTEMATICALLY

The educators' supervisor decided on a two-phase data collection approach. Since role conflict seemed to be the predominant message from the staff education coordinators, the initial phase focused on internal group conflict. The coordinators' supervisor, wishing to remain impartial, sought the assistance of the project director for the department of nursing. This person was viewed as neutral (in terms of the existing conflicts) and functioned as a facilitator to the data gathering and subsequent phases of the project. A copy of the first survey instrument is shown in Figure 10-1.

It should be noted that this specific job description questionnaire has two distinct foci. One was designed to instill hope. It allowed the staff development coordinators to express their personal concept of what the position should include. Part of the questionnaire was designed to explore the "givens." Givens in this instance focused on time allocation and existing practices.

The supervisor explained the format of the data-gathering instrument and the anticipated sessions through which the group would redefine the staff development coordinator role. In spite of this, there was a certain uneasiness among the coordinators about the process which lay ahead of them. Nevertheless, they were extremely cooperative from the very beginning. They filled out the first survey instrument independently prior to

Figure 10-1 Continuing Education Survey Questionnaire, Survey I

NAME _____

DATE _____

CONTINUING EDUCATION SURVEY I

1. Describe (in your opinion) what the job responsibilities and tasks of a Staff Development Coordinator would ideally include.

2. How does the above description correspond to your job description? What would need to be changed (added or deleted) to accomplish your description of "the ideal?" (Be specific)

3. In your opinion, what portion of your time *should* be allocated to:
   a. conducting orientation _____
   b. being a clinical resource _____
   c. assisting the unit in-service nurses to develop programs _____
   d. developing and presenting house-wide education programs _____
   e. participating in other activities _____
4. In actuality what portion of your time is spent:
   a. conducting orientation _____
   b. being a clinical resource _____
   c. assisting the unit in-service nurses to develop programs _____
   d. developing and presenting house-wide education programs _____
   e. participating in other activities _____
5. Estimate the number of hours you spend per month conducting orientation classes _____ or doing one:one followup on the unit with orientees _____ .
6. Estimate the number of hours you spend per month as a clinical resource:
   a. evaluating a patient for someone by request _____
   b. being involved in one:one staff development (teaching at bedside) _____
   c. being involved in one:one staff development (teaching at nurses' station) ___
   d. consulting with head nurse/charge nurse as a management resource _____
   e. consulting with associate director about management problems encountered on the units _____
   f. providing direct patient care (crisis intervention or relieving nurses giving care)
   g. providing other services (specify) _____
   _____
7. Estimate the number of hours per month you spend assisting the unit in-service nurses develop programs _____
   helping to present unit programs _____
8. Estimate the number of hours per month you spend developing house-wide education programs _____
   presenting house-wide programs _____

Figure 10-1 continued

9. Estimate the number of hours you spend per month on other activities (add to the list under appropriate categories):

    Committees _____

    Meetings with Supervisor _____

    Educational meetings _____

    Other (be specific) _____

10. Does the amount of time you spend on your assigned units vary from week to week? Do you consistently spend a larger portion of your time on a/some unit(s) than others? If so, why?

    _____

    _____

    _____

11. Estimate the number of on-the-job hours you allow for your own professional growth _____

12. You may use the back of the sheet for any additional comments you wish to make.

Source: St. Joseph's Hospital, St. Paul, Minnesota. Used with permission.

---

coming together face-to-face. They each used their survey forms as a reference during the discussion. While together, they compared their actual practice to their existing job description. They also discussed the division of their work week. The dissimilarities in their practices were dramatic. The unlikenesses revealed that they were emphasizing their own areas of expertise heavily, and each had a personal perception of the expectations of those for whom they provided service. The coordinators' need for role clarification precipitated a discussion of what the position ideally should include. Within a short period of time they agreed that the role of the staff development coordinator must be redefined completely and that the redefined job must allow coordinators to have feelings of accomplishment from their work. Furthermore, the new position description should include responsibility for:

- developing educational programs and housewide classes
- one-to-one teaching on the nursing units
- following up on new procedures and practices (Formerly, as new procedures were written there was marginal followup, little assurance of consistency, no long-term standardization of practice, and no competency testing.)
- attending workshops and provision for reading time in the library (They felt a strong need to be knowledgeable of current nursing trends and changing practices.)

- identifying staff learning needs (They needed to be able to spend time on the nursing units with the staff nurses, and they also needed enough clinical exposure to be competent with the procedures and to maintain credibility with the staff.)
- assisting unit in-service nurses as they planned unit classes
- participating in committee work (They wanted to be able to coordinate or follow through on the educational aspects of committee recommendations.)
- following up on individual orientation, and
- testing of new employees for competency and skill level prior to their assignment to the nursing unit.

The coordinators each had their own concept of how the staff members and head nurses perceived them. To avoid role clarity getting mixed with personal performance, the phase two survey instrument was designed to assess the *system* of staff development rather than the individual coordinator's performance. The people who had the most information about how the total *system* was functioning were the head nurses, the unit in-service nurses, the associate directors of nursing, the staff development coordinators and their supervisor. The concept of key informant is essential to emphasize at this point. The staff development coordinators, their supervisor, and the associate directors of nursing were key informants. These people had the most information about the expected outcomes of their efforts and about what the position should and could be in terms of allocation of time, people, and budgetary resources.

Copies of the letter and survey form which were distributed to all participants in this phase are shown in Figures 10-2 and 10-3. The questionnaires were distributed to each participant. One calendar week was allowed for the data collection. Those questionnaires which were not returned to the nursing office in that time period, were individually collected from the nurses involved. After gathering this information, it was time to move into the data analysis process.

ANALYZING THE DATA

The educators tabulated the key informants' closed-ended responses separately from those of the head nurses and unit in-service nurses. Table 10-1 shows the distribution of responses from the two groups.

From the above comparisons, the educators were able to determine quickly that the key informants were more in agreement than the rest of the respondents. The exception was in the area of patient education where there was almost a fifty-fifty split in both groups.

Figure 10-2 Letter to Survey Participants

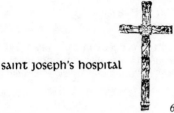

saint joseph's hospital

69 *West Exchange Street   Saint Paul, Minnesota*   55102

November 1, 1978

Dear Survey Participant,

This is a short survey to gain information about our continuing education system within the Department of Nursing. Information will be collected from staff development coordinators, head nurses, inservice education nurses, and from nursing administration.

You must return the completed questionnaire sheet to the nursing office on or before November 8, in order to be included in the survey.

Thanking you in advance for your cooperation.

Sincerely,

Cecelia Golightly   Martha Lehmann
Project Director   Assistant Director
                     of Continuing
                     Education

Source: St. Joseph's Hospital, St. Paul, Minnesota. Used with permission.

The education coordinators also participated in content analysis of the open-ended questions. They clustered the extracted issues under the following broad headings:

- orientation
- basic skills
- clinical resources
- unit in-service education
- continuing education
- patient education

Figure 10-3 Continuing Education Survey Questionnaire, Survey II

CONTINUING EDUCATION SURVEY II
November, 1978

Instructions: In each section of the question, place a check in the "yes" □ if the continuing education system meets your unit needs; if the system does not meet your needs, place a check in the "no" □. For each "no" or "uncertain" answer explain why or what else is needed in the space provided.

Does the present system meet unit needs in:

1. New employee orientation
   Yes □   No □   Uncertain □

2. Unit in-service education
   Yes □   No □   Uncertain □

3. Continuing education
   Yes □   No □   Uncertain □

4. Clinical resource/teaching
   Yes □   No □   Uncertain □

5. Patient education
   Yes □   No □   Uncertain □

Source: St. Joseph's Hospital, St. Paul, Minnesota. Used with permission.

These were essentially the same ones addressed in the questionnaire. However, since there were so many comments about the orientation process, the educators decided to differentiate orientation from basic skills. As a group, they defined each term prior to writing a goal for their problem-solving project.

Establishing a Project Goal Based on Identified Issues

As a result of the information they had collected, the educators had a sense of direction. From it, they developed the following overall goal to serve as their problem-solving guide.

Overall Goal. An evaluation and reorganization of the nursing department education activities will result in a revitalized education department which will be evidenced by:

1. Staff Development Coordinator role clarification,
2. revised curriculum content, and
3. clearly defined purposes for the department.

Table 10-1 Summary of Closed-ended Questions

KEY INFORMANTS (8)

1. new employee orientation
    yes *8*   no *0*   uncertain *0*
2. unit in-service education
    yes *7*   no *1*   uncertain *0*
3. continuing education
    yes *8*   no *0*   uncertain *0*
4. clinical resource/teaching
    yes *6*   no *2*   uncertain *0*
5. patient education
    yes *4*   no *4*   uncertain *0*   not applicable *0*

HEAD NURSE AND UNIT IN-SERVICE NURSES (35)

1. new employee orientation
    yes *16*   no *18*   uncertain *1*
2. unit in-service education
    yes *23*   no *12*   uncertain *0*
3. continuing education
    yes *18*   no *16*   uncertain *1*
4. clinical resource/teaching
    yes *20*   no *14*   uncertain *1*
5. patient education
    yes *16*   no *16*   uncertain *1*   not applicable *2*

Source: St. Joseph's Hospital, St. Paul, Minnesota. Used with permission.

STATING THE PROBLEMS

The educators individually and collectively participated in the development of the goal and problem statements for each broad topic heading. The first topic was orientation. Their goal and problem statements follow:

Goal. The revised orientation program will provide new employees with information they need to become incorporated into the nursing department as evidenced by each experienced nurse and each new graduate completing an evaluative tool within a specified time period.

Problem No. 1. How can we provide the new employees with the information that they need to begin the integration process?

Problem No. 2. How can we follow up to evaluate whether employees have completed orientation tasks?

Problem No. 3. How can we separate orientation from skill development and assure a basic level of competency?

The second broad topic heading they addressed was basic skills. The goal as they defined it and the related problems follow:

Goal. A new basic skills program will be designed and it will provide the new employee with an opportunity to develop basic nursing skills as evidenced by new graduates being able to function at a defined safe level of practice.

Problem No. 1. How can we provide sufficient resources to develop and provide such a program?

Problem No. 2. How can we develop a competency testing tool which will determine the individual's learning needs?

Problem No. 3. How can we establish an acceptable time frame for completion of basic skills?

Problem No. 4. How can we evaluate employee's progress and skill development and provide feedback to the head nurses?

Problem No. 5. How can we help the employee gain entry into the assigned work group while still providing needed learning opportunities?

Problem No. 6. How can we determine the basic content needed by employees working in all areas?

Problem No. 7. How can we effectively provide standardized content when new staff come to us with diverse skills and varied learning experiences?

Problem No. 8. How can we determine the best time to schedule an employee into a basic skills program while considering staffing needs as well?

Problem No. 9. How can we assure that the hospital receives a reasonable return on its investment in employee development?

The third broad topic heading was clinical resource. The goal and subsequent problems as they defined them for clinical resource follow:

Goal. The clinical resource role of the staff development coordinator will be understood by staff nurses as evidenced by the educators being called to assist with clinical problem solving on the nursing units.

Problem No. 1. How can we assess the needs of the education system and clarify the role responsibilities of the staff development coordinator?

Problem No. 2. How can we determine whether a central clinical resource person is appropriate for a decentralized department where head nurses are determining which hospital resources are appropriate for an individual situation?

Problem No. 3. How should the staff development coordinator function as a clinical resource when others are available and are providing this assistance throughout the hospital?

Problem No. 4. How can we determine the nonnegotiable trade-offs for the staff development coordinator?

Problem No. 5. How can we identify the appropriate amount of assistance to be provided by the staff development coordinators?

The fourth broad topic heading was unit in-service education. The goal and subsequent problems as they defined them for unit in-service education follow:

Goal. The unit in-service nurses will provide timely instructional programs in the work setting as evidenced by their doing a learning needs assessment and using the staff development coordinators as program planning resources.

Problem No. 1. How can we expect unit in-service nurses to identify needs and conduct instructional programs on the unit, while their patient care assignments remain the same as other staff nurses?

Problem No. 2. How can we provide the float nurses with an opportunity to participate in in-service programs while they are usually assigned to remain on the unit while the unit personnel attend educational programs?

Problem No. 3. How can we provide a central mechanism for coordinating in-service programs throughout the hospital while allowing for individual unit in-service needs?

Problem No. 4. How can we separate mandated, hospitalwide education needs from individual unit needs?

Problem No. 5. How can we assure well-developed programs, taught by qualified people, that will provide content appropriate for individual level of competency and that will keep people updated in their area of practice?

Problem No. 6. How can we identify needs in subsequent programs which will promote: enthusiasm of the in-service nurses, support by the head nurse, and participation of the staff nurses?

Problem No. 7. How can we determine if in-service programs should be offered more than once?

The fifth broad topic heading was patient education. The staff development coordinators did not perceive themselves responsible for patient education programs. Therefore, the goal statement and problem statement which follow reflect that.

Goal. Planning and coordinating patient education programs will not be the responsibility of the staff development coordinators as evidenced by the development of a patient education coordinator position with that specific job responsibility.

Problem No. 1. How can we present our position of wanting to eliminate the responsibility for developing and coordinating the patient education program in a positive constructive manner?

The final broad topic heading was continuing education. The staff development coordinators defined continuing education programs as those conducted outside of the hospital. Therefore their definition is reflected in the goal and problem statements.

Goal. The extent to which the staff development coordinators will be involved in continuing education will be clarified as evidenced by new policies and procedures being defined, written, and followed.

Problem No. 1. How can we clarify and foster an understanding of the hospital's responsibility and the individual's responsibility for continuing education?

After developing the problem statements the educators' reaction was, "How can we possibly do all of this?" They knew it needed to be done, yet they were almost overwhelmed by the magnitude of the project that lay ahead of them in the months to come. The most frustrating aspect was that they truly needed the end products (such as developed course content, competency test, evaluative tools, job descriptions, and policies and procedures) at that time. The process shown in Figure 6-1 helped them to understand that one solution could solve more than one problem. They remained skeptical for they knew that not only must they do an extensive amount of planning and revising, but they must also be able to keep up with their present day-to-day workload.

Before proceeding any further with this problem-solving venture, the staff development coordinators made certain that their supervisor agreed with and approved the goals for the challenge that lay before them. They also obtained agreement that this extensive project took a top priority position in the months ahead. They freed blocks of time to work together in exploring alternatives and the subsequent action that was needed. They agreed that all other program planning would remain in a holding position. They also determined which programs could be postponed or omitted for a period of time until they could get the action plan ready for implementation. Once these arrangements were made they moved quickly into exploring alternatives.

EXPLORING ALTERNATIVES

The staff development coordinators scheduled specific times during their work week when they could generate alternative solutions for each of the problem statements. To facilitate the process, each person had solution analysis grids on which goals, problems, and alternatives were sequentially entered.

Figure 10-4 shows a Solution Analysis Grid for one of the identified orientation problems that illustrates combining several aspects of suggested alternatives into a solution.

In this example the best acceptable solution was developed by combining aspects of the alternatives after eliminating item 10. The resulting solution was both implementable and compatible with the decision-making constraints of the organization.

The staff development coordinators used this process to address each problem statement. When completed, they were able to recommend a comprehensive action plan that completely reassessed and revised the orientation program as well as developed the basic skills program.

CHARTING THE ACTION PLAN

The staff development coordinators decided on a target date by which to complete the total action plan. They charted their orientation and basic skills program on a PERT network as shown in Figure 10-5.

Although this PERT network helped them to determine target dates for completion, they felt they needed some type of chart on which to display each of the topics included in those programs. This was necessary because decisions had to be made about the content, the method of presentation, and the presenter of each of those classes. Consequently, they developed the wall chart shown in Figure 10-6 which displayed the information they needed to work from on a daily basis during the developmental phase.

Figure 10-4 Solution Analysis Grid

Problem Solving Objective: Orientation: to provide the new employees with information they need to become incorporated into the nursing department as evidenced by completion of an orientation evaluative tool.

Problem Statement: How can we follow-up whether an employee has completed orientation tasks?

LIST OF ALTERNATIVE SOLUTIONS	CONTRIBUTION TO OBJECTIVE	COST IN DOLLARS	TIME FRAME	FEASIBILITY
1. Written statement of completion	High	$	Moderate	Yes
2. An individual interview	High	$	Immediate	Yes
3. Group testing	Medium	$	Moderate	Yes
4. Head nurse verified completion	Medium	$	Immediate	Yes
5. Critical incidence	High	$	Immediate	Yes
6. Ask doctors and other staff	Low	$	Immediate	Yes
7. Develop a case study	Medium	$	Moderate	Yes
8. Hold the employee responsible	High	$	Immediate	Yes
9. Measure completion against outcome criteria	High	$	Moderate	Yes
10. Assume all is well unless negative feedback	Low	$	Immediate	No

Best Acceptable Solution: Develop a written checklist (including outcome criteria) which must be completed by the staff development coordinator and the orientee within three weeks of starting date.

Source: St. Joseph's Hospital, St. Paul, Minnesota. Used with permission.

They constructed the chart by pasting together six sheets of graph paper. It was a working model and they retained it in the freehand form.

This chart contained ten columns consecutively spaced across the joined pages. Each column had a distinct purpose and contained valuable action plan information. Their blueprint for action is described below:

- *Present Content* was the first column on the chart. Under this heading they listed each of the 22 classes in the existing orientation program.
- *Nursing Orientation/General Orientation* headed the second column. As a group the staff development coordinators decided which of the 22 classes belonged in general orientation and which did not. In the same process they determined which ones should be specifically in nursing orientation.
- *Orientation/Basic Skills,* column 3, offered an opportunity for more fine-tuning. Again as a group, the educators determined which of those classes categorized as "nursing orientation" were properly labeled. They asked themselves, "Did the course content address a basic nursing skill or orientation?" They defined orientation—the information one needs to become integrated into the department. Basic skills were defined—those elementary procedural skills that a nurse must master to be considered a safe entry level practitioner.
- *Presenter* was the column where those who were currently conducting the classes were listed.
- *Presentation Method* was the column in which to list the current methods used. Content was offered in the following teaching/learning techniques: lecture, discussion, role play, demonstration/return demonstration, film, and tour. Likewise, one or more methods was indicated for each class listed.
- *Retain/Change* column was used for recording their decisions about keeping the class "as is" or revising it in some way—content, presenter, method of presentation, and so forth.
- *Proposed Change* was a wide space in which they briefly recorded "what" and "how much" revision was needed if revision or change had been indicated.
- *Responsible for Change* was the column in which they entered the name of the person who was designated to accomplish the tasks indicated in the preceding columns. Each staff development coordinator chose a personal color and they color-coded the wall chart. This way each coordinator could quickly identify who was responsible for which aspect of the whole project.

Figure 10-5 PERT Chart for Orientation and Basic Skills Program

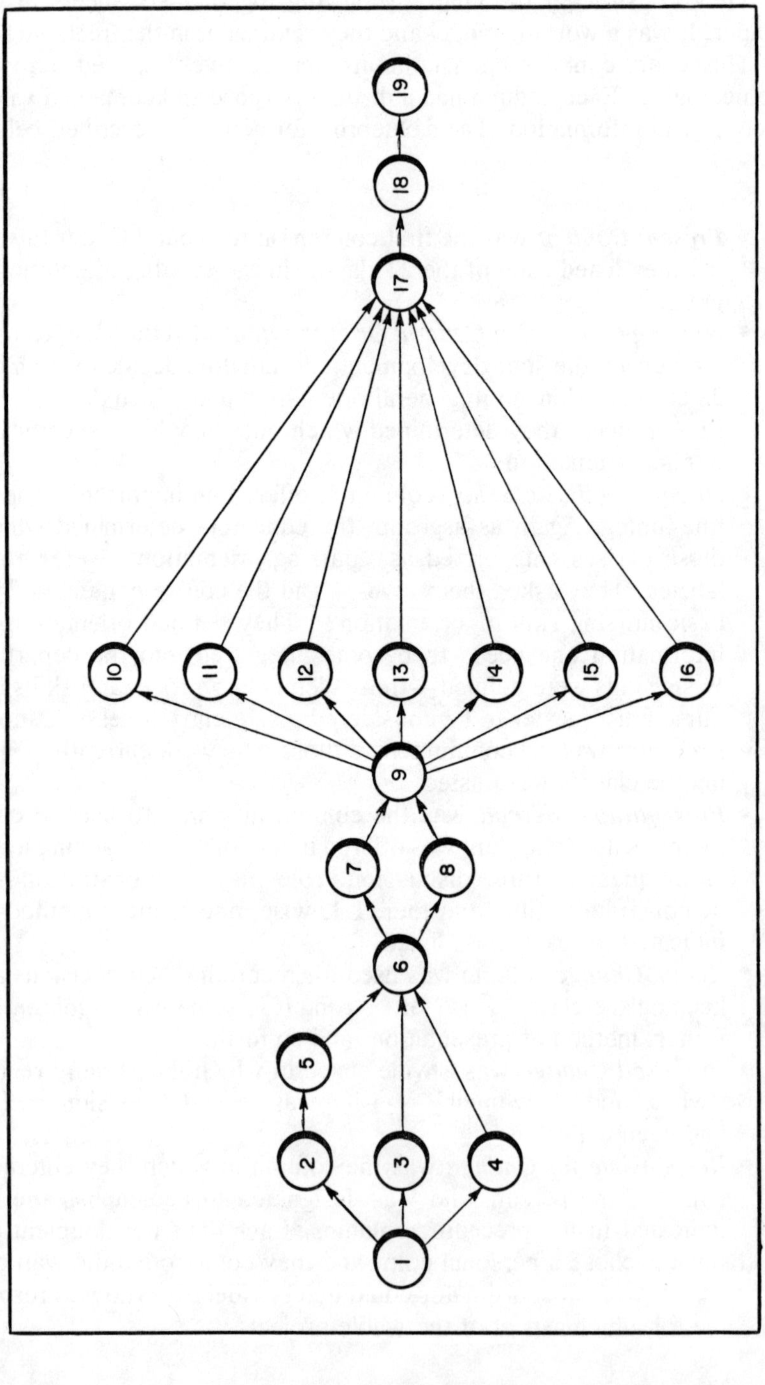

Source: St. Joseph's Hospital, St. Paul, Minnesota. Used with permission.

Key for Orientation and Basic Skills PERT Chart in Figure 10-5

1. Start—develop a program proposal that incorporates feedback from surveys.
2. Conduct a literature search.
3. Visit three other hospital education departments.
4. Hold a meeting for head nurse input into proposal.
5. Review current literature on nursing department orientation and basic entry-level skills.
6. Finalize program proposal that separates orientation from basic skills.
7. Define content and criteria for revised orientation program.
8. Define content and criteria for basic skills course.
9. Determine the budgetary needs of the proposed programs.
10. Define acceptable methods of competency testing that can be used in the proposed classes.
11. Evaluate each existing program or class.
12. Devise methods for evaluating the effectiveness of new program content.
13. Develop feedback systems and procedures for information flow between head nurses and staff development coordinators.
14. Develop a followup and record-keeping system for those who attend the programs.
15. Develop testing methods that will include present as well as new staff members.
16. Determine which classes will lend themselves to self-learning packages and/or independent study modules.
17. Present the overall action plan to nursing administration for approval.
18. Present the approved plan of action to the head nurse council.
19. Implement the revised orientation and basic skills programs.

Figure 10-6 A Blueprint for Action: Nursing Orientation Program

1 Present Content	2 Nursing Orientation/ General Orientation	3 Orientation/ Basic Skill	4 Presenter	5 Presentation Method
1.				
2.				
3.				
4.				
5.				

6 Retain/ Change	7 Proposed Change	8 Responsible for Change	9 Target Date	10 Comments
1.				
2.				
3.				
4.				
5.				

Source: St. Joseph's Hospital, St. Paul, Minnesota. Used with permission.

- *Target Date* was the space where they recorded their scheduled dates of accomplishment. By listing dates in this way, they were able to set priorities.
- *Comments* labeled the last column. This provided a place where anyone could enter notes, suggestions, ideas, references, and encountered problems as the project progressed.

This improvised blueprint permitted the educators to map their strategies and their tactics. They displayed their chart on their office wall for the entire 6-month program development period. As each part of the action plan was completed it was implemented without confusion. This was possible because each individual element meshed to accomplish the total desired outcome.

EVALUATING THE PROJECT

The staff development coordinators no longer complained about a lack of role clarity. Quite the opposite; they now exemplify the epitome of goal directed behavior. They are busier than ever and love it! There is no doubt about their contributions to the department of nursing.

Eighteen months after the inception of their major problem-solving project, the author interviewed Mary Riley, the staff development supervisor. She reported positive outcomes even greater than originally had been expected.

For evaluative purposes of comparing actual to projected outcomes, their goals are restated. Following each goal statement is an assessment of the outcome quoted from the interview with Mary Riley.

Goal No. 1. The revised orientation program will provide new employees with information they need to become incorporated into the nursing department as evidenced by each experienced nurse and each new graduate completing an evaluative tool within a specified time period.

> Okay, we come up with two options for orientation. Option One is a three-week total orientation and basic skills program. It is for nurses who have some experience and who can complete all competency testing and return demonstrations in three weeks. In fact, some experienced nurses complete their orientation in two weeks. All classes are required: they're mandatory. No one is exempt unless there is some special reason. But we do have flexibility built into this option. An experienced nurse doesn't need to spend as much learning time as an inexperienced nurse. Option Two is a five-week plan. It's designed particularly for new graduates. It includes a class on transcription of physicians' orders and another class on reality shock.
>
> Our evaluative tool is a checklist. Indicators that learning has occurred are specified for each class. Surprisingly enough new nurses are completing them. On the reverse side, there is space for head nurse comments. They have a conference and set performance objectives. The employee has space for comments and the staff development coordinator can comment also. The completed checklist is kept in their personnel file. Attached to the checklist is a preaddressed memo. It goes to the evening and night supervisors. One of our problems was: "How do we get word to nursing supervisors that there's someone new starting on a unit?" They could not keep track of all these new people. When the checklist is completed, the head nurse fills in that little preaddressed slip of paper and sends it down to the supervisor's office. They consistently do it, which just amazes us! The supervisors love it. This magic little sheet of paper has improved communication immensely.

Goal No. 2. A new basic skills program will be designed and it will provide the new employee with an opportunity to develop basic nursing skills as evidenced by new graduates being able to function at a defined safe level of practice.

> The basic skills program has really turned our department around. It is now a visible and a viable department. We get positive verbal feedback from head nurses. We hear that things are so much better now with regard to orientation. Part of it is due to the checklist that must be completed. We also require return demonstrations and competency testing for certain basic skills.
>
> The basic skills program became a recruiting tool. We advertised this program in local newspapers. We had approximately 15 nurses returned to practice after about 10 years away. They were really skeptical of being able to assume their role as care givers because they had been away so long. It was just fun to watch them as they went through the skills classes. After they had brushed up on their skills, they found that the patients had not changed and everything fell right into place. It was just neat. Many of those returning nurses who have been away from practice said that they had also been through a refresher program. They felt this was far superior, far superior.
>
> Another nice thing has happened. Some head nurses are sending old staff members to attend some of the classes. A head nurse was down the other day and he said that he was going to come through himself. He had not been through an orientation class for 12 years. He really wanted an update on policies and procedures. He is coming and he is going to send his entire staff through the skills class. We're even thinking of giving some contact hours for some of the classes.

Goal No. 3. The clinical resource role of the staff development coordinator will be understood by staff nurses as evidenced by the educators being called to assist with clinical problem solving on the nursing units.

> There's actually very little time for the staff development people to do those management kind of things that used to happen a lot. Occasionally the staff development people go around and gather reports, which is now a management job. Other than that they are being used as clinical resources. Clarifying our roles not only helped us internally; it helped the staff nurses too.

Goal No. 4. The unit in-service nurses will provide timely instructional programs in the work setting as evidenced by their doing a learning needs assessment and using the staff development coordinators as program planning resources.

> We did not spend much time with the unit in-service nurses this year. When I filed my annual report, I discovered that just as many classes were held on the units this year as last. The earlier training we had for them really paid off. These nurses are using the staff development coordinators more appropriately as program planning resources. Individual nurses are beginning to identify their own education needs. That is a real good sign!

Goal No. 5. Planning and coordinating patient education programs will not be the responsibility of the staff development coordinators as evidenced by the development of a patient education coordinator position with that specific job responsibility.

> The hospital did hire a patient education coordinator. That was a big relief.

Goal No. 6. The extent to which the staff development coordinators will be involved in continuing education will be clarified as evidenced by new policies and procedures being defined, written, and followed.

> We wrote procedures that spelled out the hospital's responsibility and the nurse's personal responsibility for continuing education. This has not been a headache.

CONCLUSION

In summary and as our conversation ended, I asked Mary if the time expenditure in planning had been worthwhile. Mary replied,

> Indeed it was. We have about a year's worth of experience with this project. The biggest thing in my mind is: Since we have implemented our action plan, we have had just very minimal changes; there have been no additional problems identified; and there has been no need for crisis intervention.

Chapter 11

PRESEARCH: An Integral Part of Quality Assurance

Quality assurance is a topic foremost in the minds of health care providers. Physicians talk about it in terms of Professional Standards Review Organization (PSRO) and Utilization Review, hospitals echo the physicians and add joint audit, while nurses discuss the American Nurses Association's (ANA) Standards of Nursing Practice, peer review, and nursing audit. In an effort to bring institutional quality assurance under one umbrella, the 1980 Joint Commission on Accreditation of Hospitals (JCAH) standards require each facility to have a written plan that describes an overall program. The scope of the effort is broadening while the phenomenon of quality assurance is still in its infancy, quite elusive and difficult to manage. At best we can try to organize existing high level achievement activities and add elements of control.

WHAT IS QUALITY ASSURANCE?

If you were to conduct a "define quality" survey of the next ten people you meet, the odds of your getting ten different answers are great. You might hear: first rate, excellent, superior, grade A, or high level. These are qualifiers or descriptors. Each one denotes a degree of merit or achievement. They all leave room for individual interpretation. Assurance, on the other hand, means guarantee. Brucker and Reedy define quality assurance as "a guarantee of improvement of care through continual evaluation."[1] An expanded version of their definition follows:

> Quality assurance is a guarantee that on-going evaluations of direct and/or indirect patient care occur. Evaluation in this context means a comparison of existing practice against:

1. the client's perceptions and expectations of the total experience within an acute, intermediate or long-term care facility. This includes what the client and/or significant others would or should expect if adequately informed.
2. predetermined criteria that qualify and quantify expected levels of practice,
3. the health care provider's philosophy or policies, and/or
4. the department's policies and procedures.

The purpose of evaluative monitoring is to improve or maintain a defined level of practice for the benefit of the client.

In order to guarantee a consistent level of practice, you must first define the desired level. After that you assess a particular practice at a given period of time. Following the assessment, analyze the resulting data and determine if a quality improvement or a quality maintenance program is needed. You may find that what you are doing is quite acceptable and decide to keep it that way. Finally, you develop some type of monitoring system to assure that the specified level of practice is achieved consistently. In my experience, developing an effective evaluating system is often minimized. This is one reason that good programs fall apart after implementation. To assure quality you need to know that work groups are adhering to certain specified standards. To do this, you must provide for feedback. Feedback alerts you to reassessment needs.

What Are Its Characteristics?

O'Regan reported the findings of an Institute of Medicine (IOM) study that specified the characteristics of an ideal quality assurance program. These were:

1. existence of an organization structure for assessing quality,
2. establishment of standards or criteria against which quality is assessed,
3. a routine system for gathering information,
4. information from a representative sampling of the population (of patients),
5. a process of providing results of review to patients, providers, sponsoring organizations, and the public, and
6. methods of instituting corrective actions and programs.[2]

A more general description was offered by Hover and Zimmer when they described all quality assurance programs as including two main factors: "#1. the evaluation of care, and #2. the improvement of care for groups of patients." They further described the quality assurance approach as "one that replaces individualization with standardization, professional assessment with scientific measurement procedures, and self accountability with institutional responsibility for quality of care."[3]

Brooke and Avery suggested that during the next five to ten years, researchers will develop methods for:

1. a valid measure of the art of care,
2. disease specific process criteria that use principles of decision analysis,
3. disease specific short term outcome measures,
4. disease taxonomies that group patients into prognostically homogeneous strata, and
5. a set of instruments that permits a valid assessment of the process of care.[4]

These quotations represent differing opinions about the makeup of quality assurance programs. All of these opinions have merit. However, I am in agreement with Egdahl and Gertman who wrote "any attempt to develop an 'ideal standardized' quality assurance system in the next few years is folly."[5] Although the "ideal" may be folly, we are still confronted with the reality that quality assurance is mandated by two federal laws, the Professional Standards Review Organization and Utilization Review Programs and one professional body, JCAH.

What Does It Cost?

In their book *Quality Assurance and Health Care,* Egdahl and Gertman stated that "if quality assurance efforts become fully operational in the 1980's, they are likely to consume two to five percent of the dollars spent on personal medical services—or about two to five billion dollars per year."[6] Their book deals entirely with the physician/hospital aspects of quality assurance programs. Estimate the amount of money spent on quality assurance efforts in all service areas of the hospital, and I feel certain that their figures would rise considerably. If, for example, we were able to count just the hours spent each week by the dietary, anesthesia, inhalation therapy, and nursing departments in efforts to assess, establish, and assure quality, we would be astonished. Because of cost, the JCAH is promoting results-oriented quality assurance programs.[7] In other words, the Commission is now saying, "if you're going to spend the money, get results."

How Does It Benefit the Consumer?

The most obvious benefit of quality assurance to the consumer is rais-
ing substandard practices to an acceptable level. Consumers do think of
health care providers in terms of quality services. For instance, a preg-
nant woman and her husband may choose the hospital where she will
deliver their baby because it offers prenatal classes, family centered
maternity nursing care which includes allowing the father in the delivery
room, provision for the care of high-risk infants (in case their baby may
need special attention), in-patient baby care classes, and out-patient par-
enting classes. They recognize this as a quality maternity program, perceive themselves needing it, and feel reasonably certain that by choosing
a certain hospital they will be assured the quality that this concept represents.

Someone jokingly defined quality care as "the consumer leaving the
institution in no worse condition than he was when he entered." Ponder
that a moment. Consider the elderly gentleman who falls out of bed and
breaks his hip while hospitalized, or the woman who goes to surgery and
has the wrong ovary removed, or the post-operative patient who develops
serum hepatitis. One goal of a quality assurance program should be to
provide the consumer with a safe environment in which to receive treatment. To provide quality services to the consumer consistently, there
must be quality control.

How Does It Benefit the Hospital?

An effective quality assurance program can help build and sustain a
hospital's reputation in the community. A good reputation attracts a high
caliber of people to seek employment within the institution. Qualified,
competent, and caring practitioners enhance the services available to the
consumer. A well designed quality assurance program within a hospital
provides direct and indirect internal control. It can be described as an
evaluative monitoring of the systems and subsystems within the organization. Furthermore, a quality assurance program that meets the federal
requirements and JCAH criteria is in the best interest of the hospital's
survival.

How Can It Become a Detriment to the Hospital?

Care must be taken to establish achievable standards. This does not
mean being satisfied with mediocrity. It does mean exercising prudence.
If unattainable practice standards are set exclusively by an administrative

team for implementation by a team of bedside care givers, the result may be frustrated, angry care givers. Overly idealistic standards can work against the institution. I agree with Hover and Zimmer who wrote "improvement of care is most likely to occur when the care providers participate in the decisions about assessment and improvement."[8] They must also be given time to reach the desired standards.

Overly idealistic standards not attainable within a reasonable period of time can also work against an organization in a court of law. In a malpractice suit, one of the first things the hospital's defense attorney will ask hospital personnel before the deposition is, "What was the existing standard of practice at the time this incident occurred?" If the care provided to the patient in question did not measure up to those existing standards, and if the prosecuting attorney discovers it, he can have a courtroom field day. A good quality assurance program can and should be established without jeopardizing the integrity of competent practitioners.

PRESEARCH'S RELEVANCE TO THE JCAH STANDARD OF QUALITY ASSURANCE IN THE DEPARTMENT OF NURSING

An excerpt from the 1980 JCAH Standards, is included here for quick reference. The case study presented later in this chapter exemplifies the compatibility of the JCAH requirements and PRESEARCH.

Excerpt From JCAH Nursing Standards
1980 Edition[9]

STANDARD VII The nursing department/service shall provide mechanisms for the regular review and evaluation of the quality and appropriateness of nursing department/service practice and functions. Such mechanisms shall be designed to attain optimal achievable standards of nursing care.

INTERPRETATION The nurse administrator shall be responsible for assuring that a review and evaluation of the quality and appropriateness of nursing care is accomplished in a timely manner. The review and evaluation may be performed by the nursing department/service as a whole or by a designated representative committee, or by the professional nursing staff assigned to clinical departments, services, or units. When possible, nursing quality assurance efforts should be integrated with similar activities in the hospital. The review and evaluation shall be based upon written criteria, shall be performed at least quarterly, and should examine the provision of nursing care and its effect on patients.

Methods of review and evaluation may include, but are not necessarily limited to, patient observation or interview, specific monitoring functions, or use of the patient medical record. Nursing staff personnel who provide patient care shall participate in the review. When possible, the medical record department should help the nursing department/service perform medical record functions related to the nursing department's/service's review of nursing care. The quality and appropriateness of nursing care provided by personnel who are not hospital employees, that is, those obtained through agencies, registries, or other outside sources, shall be included in the regular review of nursing care.

A mechanism shall be designed to assure that pertinent findings from the evaluation of nursing care are disseminated within the nursing department/service, and that appropriate action is taken.

The 1980 Standards emphasize that audit is only one component of a quality assurance program. Why are audits being de-emphasized as the method of identifying patient care practice deficiencies? It is because audits can be and have been manipulated. Criteria were established that identified minimal deficiencies. Depending on the way the criteria were defined, the resulting problem definitions were often biased and narrowly focused. In many instances, "corrective" action was taken in the form of a one shot educational program or a reaudit six months later. According to the 1980 criteria, audits can be conducted, but they should be only one way of gathering information. This represents a definite emphasis shift *from* developing criteria and conducting an audit for problem identification *to* recognizing problems and taking subsequent action to correct them. Because it uses time and human resources to identify problems and to assure that standards of practice are maintained, the problem-solving approach has been recognized as more cost effective than an audit procedure. The protocol shown in Figure 11-1 for documenting problem-solving projects within a quality assurance program includes the elements set forth in the JCAH Standards and combines them with the PRESEARCH concept.

This outline can be used as a guide for documenting individual or group problem-solving efforts. When problem-solving projects are approached in this manner, you have documented evidence of assessing and assuring a defined level of quality. As presented in earlier chapters, the PRESEARCH process can be applied to review and evaluate numerous situations that directly or indirectly affect patient care. It permits input from

Figure 11-1 Protocol for Documenting Quality Assurance Problem-solving Projects (Combining JCAH Requirements and PRESEARCH Concepts)

I. Describe the quality assessment topic or problem.
II. Identify the type of criteria to be used: Process, outcome, structure or prospective.
III. State *how* the need for quality assessment was recognized.
IV. State *why* this is a timely effort.
V. State *what* approach will be used to assess the level of quality. (Audit, PRESEARCH, or other analytical methods)
VI. State *who* will be involved in the quality assessment efforts. Identify how and to whom results will be reported.
VII. Estimate *when* the assessment project will begin and end.
VIII. Supply appropriate support documentation which reflects the ongoing progress and status of the project. (Meeting minutes, etc.)
IX. Discuss the direct and/or indirect impact of the problem-solving efforts on patient care.
X. Define a quality assurance mechanism for maintaining a specified level of practice, standard of care, or functional system. Include person(s) responsible for on-going monitoring and frequency of same. Identify how and to whom results will be reported.
XI. If the problem-solving efforts did not resolve the problems, state a plan for further action(s) to be taken.

Source: Eitel Hospital, Minneapolis, Minnesota. Used with permission.

personnel at all departmental levels. They subsequently become committed implementers of appropriate action.

Summary

PRESEARCH is a mechanism that has been designed to recognize and resolve multifaceted problems within an organization. It allows a person or a group of people to identify the potential problem components in a field of uncertainty. It provides an interdisciplinary framework for identifying problems, developing creative solutions, selecting the best acceptable solution, implementing action plans, and evaluating the results of the problem-solving efforts. Quality assessment is accomplished through the data-gathering process. Quality assurance is the on-going or periodic monitoring mechanism that results from the overall problem-solving efforts. The PRESEARCH philosophy and method have a vital place in every quality assurance program.

DEVELOPMENT OF A QUALITY ASSURANCE PROGRAM IN A NURSING DEPARTMENT

The following example explains how a department in one hospital included PRESEARCH in a quality assurance program. The protocol for documenting problem-solving projects offers the option of using a variety of approaches to assess quality. When the problems are complex, you may choose PRESEARCH because it provides a framework within which to work. When you use the protocol as a record-keeping guide, you have documented evidence of assessing a situation, defining it, determining an action plan, and evaluating the outcome. In addition, you have an ongoing account to explain the rationale for decisions made along the way.

Eitel Hospital: A Case Example

Eitel Hospital is a 144-bed, nonprofit, acute-care facility in downtown Minneapolis, Minnesota. The hospital's mission statement clearly defines it as a community oriented institution that emphasizes personalized patient care. In response to the changing community service demands, the nursing department was completely reorganized. This was an ideal opportunity to incorporate a quality assurance program into every aspect of the department. Following an extensive search of the literature, the nursing administrative team developed a master plan. This plan described the components necessary for a solid quality assurance program. The following elements were included in the master plan:

1. Development of definitions for such terms as quality of care, quality assessment, quality assurance, criteria, structure, process, outcome, prospective, and peer review (see Figure 11-5 at the end of this chapter).
2. Delineation of responsibility for direct and indirect patient care evaluation.
3. Standardization of a method of documenting quality assessment efforts using a problem-solving approach.
4. Development of a mechanism for periodic review of the overall quality assurance efforts.
5. Delineation of nursing's role in the total hospital quality assurance program.
6. Clarification of open communication channels to allow information to flow from the care givers to nursing administration and vice-versa.

7. Provision for interdisciplinary participation in quality assessment and assurance where appropriate.

The Joint Commission's quality assurance standards state "Nursing staff personnel who provide patient care shall participate in the review."[10] Eitel's nursing management team wanted to provide an opportunity for the staff to participate in standard setting as well as in review. Therefore, when the department was reorganized the committee structure was expanded to include three councils. There is one policy making body, the Nursing Administrative Council, and two operational groups—the Nursing Practice Council and the Nursing Management Council. In Figure 11-2 a triangle represents the committee structure of the department of nursing with quality assurance as the central focus.

The arrows on the sides and base of the triangle indicate that there is provision for information to flow between each of the councils. Each council has a defined purpose and membership.

Figure 11-2 Nursing Department Committee Structure

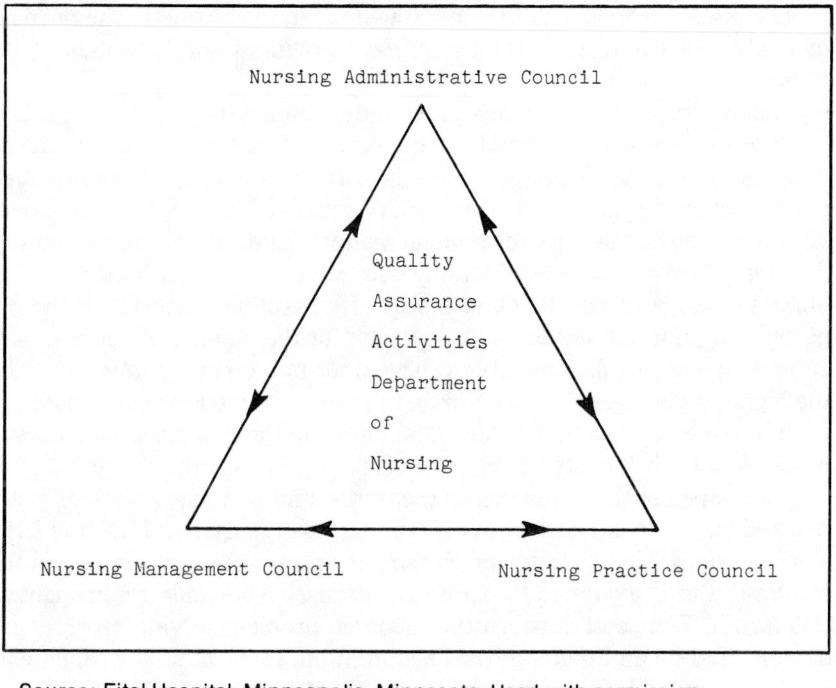

Source: Eitel Hospital, Minneapolis, Minnesota. Used with permission.

The Nursing Administrative Council is composed of the director of nursing and all nurse managers with direct line accountability to the director. The purpose of this council is:

- to develop long- and short-range goals for the department of nursing consistent with those of the hospital,
- to make policy decisions for the department, and
- to act on recommendations made by the Nursing Practice and Nursing Management Councils.

The Nursing Management Council is composed of head nurses, educators, clinical coordinators, and supervisors. The purpose of this council is to examine management activities and practices which indirectly affect the delivery of direct patient care and patient care systems. The management issues often focus on interdepartmental as well as intradepartmental relationships.

The Nursing Practice Council is composed of the nurse designated to be responsible for monitoring quality assurance activities, a clinical coordinator, a supervisor, a nurse educator, a head nurse, and a staff nurse representative from each of the nursing units in the hospital. The purpose of this council is to examine the clinical practices and activities of the nursing department.

Each of the councils has the option of developing subgroups for specific tasks or purposes. For example, the Nursing Management Council designated subgroups to develop, review, and revise the patient classification system, chart forms, and nursing care plans. The Nursing Practice Council designated subgroups to conduct patient care audits, and others to develop, review, and revise nursing care standards and procedures. The nurse in charge of coordinating the quality assurance efforts for the department of nursing serves as chairperson for the Nursing Practice Council and also serves as a member of the other two councils. Minutes from the Nursing Management and Nursing Practice Councils are distributed to each nursing unit at regular intervals following the meetings. One person on each unit is designated to be responsible for incorporating the information contained in the minutes into the unit's staff meetings. Nursing practice and management issues are also discussed at the general RN and LPN staff meetings. The Director of Nursing is an ex-officio participant in the meetings and is available to clarify or discuss issues that are brought to this forum. Topics of concern that become problem-solving projects are documented on an on-going basis according to the protocol outlined earlier in Figure 11-2. In other words, traditional minutes are replaced by an on-going account of the project's status. Hence, at the completion of a problem-solving effort the entire process is fully documented.

There is a significant relationship between the department's committee structure and the hospital's quality assurance program. Figure 11-3 shows the Department of Nursing committee structure in relation to the hospital quality assurance program. In this diagram the nursing committee structure is symbolized by a small triangle that overlaps a larger triangle representing the hospital's quality assurance program. The greater portion of overlapping is in the area of nursing practice. The chairperson of the Nursing Practice Council and the director of nursing served as active members on the hospital's Quality Assurance Committee. The chairperson for the Nursing Practice Council also represents the department of nursing on the hospital's Patient Care Committee (represented by a smaller triangle) which is also concerned with quality.

Figure 11-3 Department of Nursing Committee Structure in Relation to Hospital Quality Assurance Program

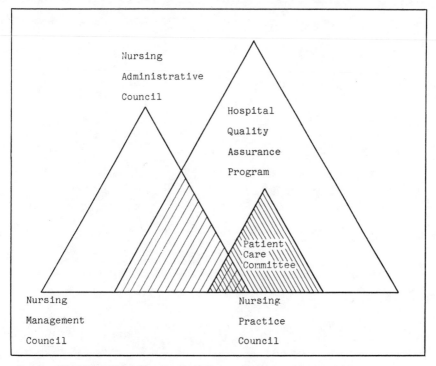

Source: Eitel Hospital, Minneapolis, Minnesota. Used with permission.

As part of the integrated quality assurance plan, performance standards were developed for each job category within the department. The format for these standards is an extension of the job performance description advocated by Joan and Warren Ganong in their book *Nursing Management*. A third column was added that further defines the quality aspects or expectations. Figure 11-4 is an excerpt from a performance standard description for a registered professional nurse. It exemplifies quality control incorporated into a job performance description.

This format clarified the nurses' responsibilities in using nursing process. Any aspect of the standards in the third column could be audited concurrently or retrospectively, by either the nursing unit or the individual care giver. Ultimately these standards will be used by staff nurses for peer review.

This comprehensive quality assurance program emphasizes a synthesis of activities which were already occurring. However, the problem-solving capabilities of the department personnel continue to expand because PRESEARCH was incorporated into quality assurance efforts.

Figure 11-4 Eitel Hospital *Performance Standards* General Duty Registered Nurse

MAJOR PERFORMANCE RESPONSIBILITIES	PERFORMANCE IS SATISFACTORY WHEN	STANDARDS AND/OR COMPONENTS
A. Demonstrates an understanding of and ability to use the nursing process.	Uses an orderly, systematic approach to determine the patient's care needs, makes plans to solve them, initiates the plan or assigns other to implement it, evaluates the extent to which the nursing plan of care was effective in meeting the patient's care needs, evaluates the patient's response to the medical regime, and reassesses needs based on the patient's changing condition.	Assesses each patient's condition at the time of admission.
		Completes admission data sheet for each patient admitted.
		Rationale for exceptions must be acceptable to the Head Nurse.
		Initiates an individualized care plan; reviews and updates it daily or as needed; revises it according to the change in patient's condition.
		Reviews and approves patient care plans written by an LPN.
		Obtains input into the care plan from the patient and/or family. (Patient should have the opportunity to make an informed decision about his/her care).
		Provides reassurance and support to families.
		Initiates patient care conferences.
		Uses recognized standards when developing patient care plans.
	Recognizes the difference between the dependent nursing activities (physician ordered) and the independent nursing activities (nursing directives for patient care) and practices accordingly.	Initiates appropriate nursing directives.
	Initiates a discharge plan for each patient within the first 24 hours of hospitalization.	Assures that discharge planning assistance is provided to the patient during the hospital stay and prior to the day of discharge.

Figure 11-4 continued

MAJOR PERFORMANCE RESPONSIBILITIES	PERFORMANCE IS SATISFACTORY WHEN	STANDARDS AND/OR COMPONENTS
		Involves appropriate interdisciplinary personnel in discharge planning.
	Provides appropriate patient education.	Identifies the patient's learning needs. Assesses the patient's learning readiness. Designs an individualized patient teaching plan which is compatible with the medical plan of care.
B. Demonstrates an ability to apply theory to practice.	Practices clinical nursing based on a sound knowledge of nursing practice.	Plans, assesses, and performs daily patient cares. Assists the patient with activities of daily living. Carries out medical order for patient treatment. Performs nursing routines. Asks for clarification on physicians' order when appropriate.
C. Is familiar with hospital and nursing policies and procedures.	Upholds departmental and hospital policies and practices nursing according to recognized standards and procedures.	Prepares and administers medications according to established policy and physician's orders. Assesses the patient's response to the effect of medications. Follows standard medication procedures. Takes initiative to familiarize self with new equipment and products. Has a working knowledge of the principles involved in operating hospital equipment and products.

Figure 11-4 continued

MAJOR PERFORMANCE RESPONSIBILITIES	PERFORMANCE IS SATISFACTORY WHEN	STANDARDS AND/OR COMPONENTS
D. Participates in the hospital Risk Management Program.	Contributes to a safe environment for patient care.	Knows and observes the hospital and nursing department safety, fire, and disaster policies and procedures. Participates in fire and disaster drills. Reports and documents incidents involving patients, staff, and visitors. Knows and practices proper body mechanics. Practices aseptic and isolation techniques.
E. Respects the individual right of each patient.	Uses a patient centered approach when providing direct nursing care.	Prives for patient's personal privacy. Introduces self and accompanying others who enter a patient's room. Allows time (if only a few seconds) to establish human contact and develops rapport with the patient before beginning any task or procedure. Talks with the patient; not at, around, or above him. Explains to the patient and family the procedure which is to be performed; includes teaching if appropriate. Allows the patient to make choices about his care whenever possible. (i.e., blood transfusions, diet etc.) When it is not possible to give the patient a choice, or the patient is unable to make a choice, provides the patient or family with a logical, compassionate, yet scientifically sound (within the realm of nursing) explanation why the treatment or procedure is being done.
	Respects the confidentiality of privileged information and the patient's medical record.	Refrains from disclosing information about the patient's condition or care except to the patient's immediate family or health care team.

Figure 11-4 continued

MAJOR PERFORMANCE RESPONSIBILITIES	PERFORMANCE IS SATISFACTORY WHEN	STANDARDS AND/OR COMPONENTS
F. Contributes to an environment in which the patient care team can work cooperatively to accomplish unit objectives.	Supervises ancillary and outside agency personnel.	Accepts responsibility for professional assessment of patients of co-assigned nursing assistants.
		Accepts responsibility for professional care (i.e., medications, speical treatments, etc.) of co-assigned nursing assistants.
		Evaluates care provided by outside agency personnel.
		Uses "Pool" Personnel Evaluation Forms.
		Intervenes when nursing action is deemed to be unsafe or inappropriate.
	Cooperates with the nursing staff, Head Nurse, Clinical Coordinator and/or Supervisor.	Assists with orientation of personnel on the unit.
		Keeps head nurse informed of unit activity, personnel problems, and patients' conditions.
		Seeks assistance from co-workers and/or head nurse in problem solving.
		Informs head nurse and/or supervisor of abilities and limitations when functioning in the capactty of a "float" nurse.
		Cooperates in approved studies and research programs conducted on the unit.
G. Acts as unit charge nurse after orientation to charge responsibilities.	Accepts responsibility for running the unit in the absence of the head nurse.	Makes sound nursing judgements and clinical assignments.
		Provides support for the staff members during the given shift.
	Serves as a resource to other staff members.	Assists staff as necessary.

Figure 11-4 continued

MAJOR PERFORMANCE RESPONSIBILITIES	PERFORMANCE IS SATISFACTORY WHEN	STANDARDS AND/OR COMPONENTS
H. Communicates appropriate information to members of the health care team verbally and in writing.	Communicates in a professional and timely manner.	Gives pertinent patient reports at the change of shift.
		Keeps co-workers, head/charge nurse, supervisor, clinical coordinator, patient/family, and physician informed of changes in patient condition.
		Makes rounds with the physician to clarify orders and to provide patient care information.
		Documents care provided to the patients according to the hospital system of record-keeping.
		Familiarizes self with normal lab values and reports pertinent findings to appropriate persons.
	Acts as a liaison between the physician and the patient care team.	Communicates appropriate information and obtains feedback from co-workers.
		Participates in discharge planning conferences.
I. Assumes responsibility for own personal and professional growth.	Is knowledgeable of current trends in the nursing profession.	Sets personal and professional goals to meet the expectations of the staff nurse position.
		Attends clinical conferences, inservice education offerings, unit meetings and RN staff meetings.
		Reads and uses current literature for updating clinical knowledge.

Source: Eitel Hospital, Minneapolis, Minnesota. Used with permission.

Figure 11-5 Quality Assurance Definitions

I. Quality of Care
   A. Technical Care
   B. Art of Care

Includes two basic concepts: technical care and the art of care. The adequacy of the diagnostic and therapeutic process. The milieu, manner, and behavior of the provider in delivering care to and communicating with clients.

II. Quality Assessment

Measures the levels of quality provided at a point in time; it connotes no effort to change or improve that level of care. Some quality assessment techniques are:

1. Audit
   a. Chart Audit: a review of charts for content and evaluation of care as applied to a previously existing set of criteria for care. A chart audit may be internal or external; retrospective or concurrent.
   b. Internal Chart Audit: an audit performed by those within an organization.
   c. External Chart Audit: an audit performed by those outside an organization, which thus has additional assurance of objectivity.
   d. Retrospective Chart Audit: an audit performed after treatment or management is concluded, in order to evaluate the care given. This is usually done in a health care facility after discharge.
   e. Concurrent Chart Audit: an audit performed at set times during on-going treatment or management to evaluate care being given.
2. Problem-solving Models
3. Surveys, Opinion Polls, etc.
4. Interviews
5. Educational Needs Assessment
6. Evaluation of Learning
7. Trend Studies
8. Observation
9. Methods Analysis
10. Time and Motion Studies
11. Employee Evaluation
12. Peer Review
13. Critical Incident Technique
14. Morbidity and Mortality Studies
15. Tissue Review

III. Quality Assurance

A guarantee that on-going evaluations of direct and/or indirect client/patient care occur. Evaluation in this context means a comparison of existing practice against:

Figure 11-5 continued

1. the client's perceptions and expectations of the total experience within an acute, intermediate or long-term care facility. This includes what the client and/or significant others would or should expect if adequately informed.
2. predetermined criteria that qualify and quantify expected levels of practice,
3. the health care provider's philosophy or policies, and/or
4. the department's policies and procedures.

The purpose of evaluative monitoring is to improve or maintain a defined level of practice for the benefit of the client.

IV. Criteria

Predetermined standards against which aspects of the quality of care to be given, or being given, are compared.

There are four types of criteria: structure, process, outcome, and prospective. Structure, process, and outcome criteria refer to three different variables that can be used to assess or measure quality of care. The conceptual distinction among these three measures is important to maintain, since in essence they measure three different things: the resources necessary to solve a problem, the way the problem is solved, and the results of the problem-solving, respectively.

A. Structure Criteria

The descriptive, innate characteristics of facilities or providers (e.g., the soundness of a building, whether a poison control chart is posted in an emergency room, or the age and board certification status of the physicians).

Structure encompasses the setting, instrumentalities, and conditions where and under which the provider-client relationship occurs. Structure includes the philosophy and objectives of an institution, agency, program, or department; organizational characteristics; fiscal resources; equipment and physical facilities; legal authority for the mission of the agency; management structure; licensure, accreditation, and certification status; qualification, characteristics (values), and goals of (all) professional, paraprofessional, and technical employees; the expectations and

Figure 11-5 continued

	attitudes, and values of clients and providers; and the client's biopsychosocial condition on entry into the system.
B. Process Criteria	Measures that evaluate what a provider (nurse/physician) does to and for a client (e.g., ordering a cardiogram for a client with chest pains). They can also mean how well a person is moved through the health care system, either in a "macro" sense (e.g., from first symptom, to seeking care, to obtaining care) or in a "micro" sense (e.g., from arrival to departure at an emergency room or out-patient clinic).
	Process focuses on the activities, pursuits, and behaviors of the health care provider. Because it encompasses the totality of provider behavior in interaction with the client, it includes both behavior and lack of behavior, either of which may be judged as appropriate or inappropriate. In other words, the process domain includes that which is done and should be done by the provider; that which is done and should not be done; that which is not done but should be done; and that which is not done and should not be done.
C. Outcome Criteria	Measures the results obtained by the patient, in terms of palliation treatment, cure, or rehabilitation. Outcome criteria are used to measure change in client behavior. Change in client behavior can include any alternation in health status and/or knowledge of or compliance with, specific disease control behaviors.
D. Prospective Criteria	Predetermined guidelines for the provider to follow when completing a form, performing a procedure (as in a department procedure manual).
V. Peer Review	Evaluation of clinical management of specific patients as judged by fellow practitioners.

Sources: Richard H. Egdahl and Paul M. Gertman, *Quality Assurance In Health Care* (Germantown, Md.: Aspen Systems Corp., 1976), pp. 4–6; Mary C. Brucker and Nancy Jo Reedy, "Quality Assurance—An Overview," *Journal of Obstetric, Gynecologic and Neonatal Nursing,* May-June 1977, p. 13; and John Charles Schmadl, "Quality Assurance: Examination of a Concept," *Nursing Outlook,* July 1979, p. 463.

NOTES

1. Mary C. Brucker and Nancy Jo Reedy, "Quality Assurance—An Overview," *Journal of Obstetric, Gynecologic and Neonatal Nursing,* May-June 1977, pp. 9–13.
2. Daniel J. O'Regan, "Quality Assurance: Consensus Reached on Assessment But Not on Assurance," *Hospitals, JAHA,* April 1, 1978, pp. 150–155.
3. Julie Hover and Marie Zimmer, "Nursing Quality Assurance: The Wisconsin System," *Nursing Outlook,* April 1978, pp. 242–248.
4. Robert H. Brook and Allyson D. Avery, "Quality Assurance Today and Tomorrow: Forecast for the Future," *Annals of Internal Medicine,* December 1976, pp. 809–817.
5. Richard H. Egdahl and Paul M. Gertman, *Quality Assurance in Health Care* (Germantown, Md.: Aspen Systems Corp., 1976), p. 8.
6. Egdahl and Gertman, p. 4.
7. "New JCAH Quality Assurance Standard," *Hospital Peer Review,* May 1979, pp. 67–69.
8. Hover and Zimmer, *op. cit.*
9. *Accreditation Manual for Hospitals* (Chicago, Ill.: Joint Commission on Accreditation of Hospitals, 1980), pp. 120–121.
10. *Accreditation Manual for Hospitals,* JCAH, p. 121.

Chapter 12

Situational Interviewing

Situational interviewing is a method of assessing how an applicant will respond to commonly encountered job situations. This technique expands the traditional interview with the perspective employee. It is especially useful when there are several highly qualified individuals applying for the same position.

When searching for a candidate to fill a key position, part of the field of uncertainty is not knowing how the individual will perform in the actual job setting. The formal data gathering for situational interviewing occurs in three phases. The manager must: (1) identify the expectations of an acceptable candidate, (2) prepare a position application questionnaire with which to conduct a face-to-face interview, and (3) develop case studies to which each candidate responds in writing.

PREPARING FOR THE INTERVIEW PROCESS

In order to develop the interviewing tools, the manager must identify the following:

- the most important aspects of the job,
- the performance expectations of the person filling the position, and
- the essential qualifications of the applicant.

To identify the most important aspects of the job, it is important to review the job description and ask yourself, "What do I really want this person to do?" For example, if you are interviewing applicants for a position of an executive secretary and the job description states that good interpersonal and communication skills are required, translate that into what you actually expect in terms of those skills. Do you expect the person to answer the telephone in a polite manner, to function as a receptionist, to schedule your appointments, to compose letters, and to collect information from external and internal sources? With the scant amount of information that former employers are allowed to submit, based upon Equal Employment Opportunity regulations, there is no way for you to determine from a reference check how the person performed in the last job situation. Yet, as a perspective employer you have certain performance expectations of the individual whom you select for the position. In all fairness to yourself and the applicant, you should identify major expectations prior to interviewing the candidates.

Identifying essential qualifications for a position sounds fairly simple and straightforward. In reality, interviewers often find themselves considering trade-offs. For example, your advertisement for an emergency room head nurse may state, "Three years of emergency room experience plus demonstrated leaderships skills." However, you may interview ten people and not find in any of the candidates the exact qualifications that you had specified. At some point you must stop advertising and make a selection. When this happens you must weigh the importance of emergency room nursing experience versus management experience. If management training is available within your institution (or in the local community) you probably will select a person who is highly skilled in emergency room nursing and has the ability and willingness to take management training courses.

FACE-TO-FACE INTERVIEWING

In this process, a list of well planned questions is an essential data-gathering instrument. The interview can be compared to an informational survey. All applicants must be interviewed in a like manner and with the same questions. Applicants should be informed that you are recording their responses during the interview process. When applicants are being interviewed for a position that requires an individual to work interdepartmentally, there may be two or more interviewers. One interviewer actually asks the questions and the other records the information. This type of interview, while extremely stressful to the candidate, can be most helpful in eliminating the personal bias of one interviewer.

An example of a position application questionnaire which was developed for a medical head nurse position at Eitel Hospital, Minneapolis, Minnesota follows. Figure 12-1 is the oral interview form.

In order to be impartial to each person applying for this key position, it is advantageous to interview all applicants in like manner. Therefore, the same information is collected from each applicant, both those from within

Figure 12-1 Eitel Hospital Position Application Questionnaire

Applicant _____ Date _____

1. What attracted you to this position?
2. How does your application for this position fit into your long-term career goals?
3. How can you build on past experiences in this position?
4. Think about the various positions you have held.
   a. From what types of situations did you receive the greatest job satisfaction? Give one example.
   b. From what types of situations did you receive the least job satisfaction? Give one example.
5. State your philosophy of nursing.
6. Describe a stressful situation from your own personal work experience and the steps you took to resolve it.
7. Describe how (in behavioral terms) you most frequently cope with stress.
8. What would be your top priorities if you were the candidate selected for the position?

Comments:

Action:

Interviewer/s _____

Source: Eitel Hospital, Minneapolis, Minnesota. Used with permission.

the organization and those applying in response to advertisement. It should be noted that the position application form included questions about career goals, positions held in the past, job satisfaction, and philosophy of nursing.

During the interview, time must be allocated for and spent reviewing the person's job description. The candidate must have an opportunity to ask questions and clarify the expectations and requirements of the position. It is essential that the person have this type of exposure prior to responding to the written interview questionnaire. Needless to say, a well written job description will facilitate the applicants' understanding of the situations to which they must respond in writing.

If a methodical data-gathering process is used during the interview, why is additional written information from the candidate necessary? In many situations candidates apply from within the organization. In fact, most organizations encourage this. The external applicant, on the other hand, usually responds to some type of advertisement. External candidates may spend a considerable amount of time preparing resumés and application letters that state why they believe they are qualified for the desired position. How then do you equate or compare the external, formal application to the informal, internal request for an interview? Face-to-face interviewing allows you to assess the person's oral communication skills. When written communication skills are also a requirement of the job, each candidate should be given the opportunity to respond in writing as well. Applicants should be informed of the written portion that will follow the interview. The interviewer should be able to approximate the amount of time the applicant will spend responding to the questionnaire.

SITUATIONAL QUESTIONNAIRE

A team approach works well when developing a situational questionnaire. Two people who are thoroughly familiar with the job requirements of the vacant position can work effectively together to identify typical situations regularly encountered. One case study and one representative situation will usually suffice to collect adequate data. The case studies or situations should be clearly stated and succinctly written. The developers of the questionnaire should know precisely which aspects of the job are being addressed through the case example. As with other questionnaires, examples that have been formulated must be pretested. Your directions must be clear to the pretest audience before you ask a perspective employee to fill out the situational questionnaire. Figure 12-2 is an instrument that includes a clinical case study and a managerial situation. Each applicant for the medical head nurse position was asked to complete this form as part of the selection (data-gathering) process.

THE SELECTION PROCESS

Prior to any of the applicants being interviewed, a team approach again can be used to identify the important factors that will be weighed. Each significant item should be listed in a columnar fashion to form a rating grid. In order to rank each of the applicants, the interviewers must know in advance which answers are acceptable ones. "Acceptable answers" are those that indicate that the applicant will:

- meet the requirements of the job performance description,
- meet the written and unwritten expected standards of practice of the department,
- have a philosophy of nursing that is compatible with that of the institution,
- bring professional and personal assets to the job that will complement those of the existing management team members,

Figure 12-2 Situational Interview Questionnaire

Head Nurse Position/Medical Unit

Applicant_____ Date_____

Situation I—Mrs. Smith is a 72-year-old woman admitted at 9:00 a.m. to a medical nursing unit with a diagnosis of congestive heart failure. Her physician arranged for her admission to the hospital based on her past medical history and information obtained from the patient who called him early this same morning. There is no history and physical examination record available for you to review. Her previous hospitalizations have been elsewhere so a past medical record is not available either.

From the patient you learn that she lives alone in a senior citizens' complex. She told you that she has been feeling tired and short of breath for about one week prior to her admission. During the night she was awakened by a severe cough and felt that she just "couldn't catch her breath."

Directions:

Describe the essential components of the nursing assessment for this diagnosis.

Describe the content of your telephone conversation with the physician after the physical assessment has been made.

During your conversation with the physician, he gave you the following medical orders:

DOCTOR'S ORDERS

1. Bedrest with BRP
2. 2 gram low-sodium diet
3. Daily weights
4. Elastic stockings
5. Arterial blood gases, call to MD
6. EEG, chest x-ray
7. SMA_{12}, electrolytes, CBC/UA
8. Lanoxin 1.0 mgm po (loading dose)
9. Lasix 40 mgm po daily
10. KCl 20 meq BID

Directions:

Given this medical plan, write your initial patient care plan based on the presenting symptoms. The care plan should be initiated within the first 12 hours of the patient's admission.

Situation II—A decision was made at Nursing Management Council that nursing personnel would be expected to float from their assigned unit when their unit's census was low. The expectation of the director of nursing and the clinical coordinator is that all head nurses demonstrate their support of this decision through their verbal and nonverbal behavior. Although the plan looks reasonable on paper, you personally feel

Figure 12-2 continued

uncomfortable supporting this decision. You anticipate that your staff will be extremely upset at the mention of floating. Your feelings are based on the fact that three of your nursing staff were hired during the past year and have since shared with you individually that one of their primary reasons for experiencing a high level of dissatisfaction in their other positions was the expectation to float from their assigned units.

Directions:

Describe in three steps, your plan of action.

If you did not submit a resume, please list in reverse order the nursing positions which you have held in the past.

Source: Eitel Hospital, Minneapolis, Minnesota. Used with permission.

- be acceptable as a leader of the work group,
- view the position as an important milestone in a career path,
- indicate that the applicant perceives role modeling as an important factor and can teach by example,
- have a sound knowledge of medical nursing,
- be able to individualize patient care through a patient care plan,
- be able to support nursing management decisions under duress, and
- have skills in managing the personnel aspects of a busy nursing unit.

An example of a rating grid which was used for the head nurse interview is shown in Figure 12-3.

When more than one variation on a theme is acceptable, that fact must be acknowledged by the interviewer in advance. There should be a fairly clear cut "yes" (adequate) or "no" (inadequate) response to each item being rated. The applicants' responses are recorded on the rating grid with a plus for an acceptable reply and a minus for an unacceptable one. The scoring method is simply totalling the number of positive and negative responses for each applicant. In addition to being a selection instrument, the situational questionnaire can also be an extremely useful conference tool. Occasionally an applicant will ask for information about not being selected for a particular position. The interviewer can use the data-gathering instruments, which the applicant has completed, to provide constructive feedback to the interviewee. This is helpful for the person who desires to apply for a similar job in the future. Constructive criticism can help that person know which skills to develop in order to be considered an outstanding applicant. In our experience, as we developed rating

Figure 12-3 Interview Rating Grid

Applicant's name _____

Interviewer's name _____

Criteria for the head nurse position	YES	NO
Minimum of five years medical nursing experience		
Prior head nurse experience		
Formal management training		
Reason for wanting to change jobs acceptable		
Long term career goals satisfactorily explained		
Described ways to build on experience within scope of job description		
Described job satisfiers within scope of job description		
Described job dissatisfiers infrequently encountered in head nurse position		
Personal philosophy of nursing compatible with department philosophy		
Described means of coping with stress acceptable		
Personal stress coping behaviors acceptable		
Stated priorities are deemed acceptable		
Nursing assessment appropriate for patient diagnosis		
Described communication with physician regarding patient information in a professional and timely manner		
Initial nursing care plan meets established department standards		
Staff meeting described demonstrates:		
a. sensitivity to the feelings of staff members		
b. skill with small groups		
c. support of nursing management decision		
TOTALS:		

Comments:

Source: Eitel Hospital, Minneapolis, Minnesota. Used with permission.

grids for each key position, one person always surpassed the rest of the candidates. There was also an interesting and unexpected finding: a candidate who excelled in the oral interview was not consistently the person who had the best comprehension of the job (as indicated by the completion of the written form). This was a startling revelation when we considered how people had been interviewed for key positions in the past.

The *pre*search emphasis during the preemployment process for candidates for key positions has many beneficial features. Among these are:

- the employer identifying expectations of the person's performance in that position,
- a systematic and fair information gathering from all applicants,
- an opportunity for each applicant to respond orally and in writing, and
- the manager identifying areas of needed improvement prior to the person being put into the job situation.

A good example of this is a candidate who had an excellent overall comprehension of the job requirement as well as the ability to set priorities within those requirements, but who was a poor speller. This "upfront" information was discussed candidly by the manager and the applicant. Poor spelling therefore, did not become a deterrent for the person's future performance. Had this not been the case, several months after the person was hired the secretary who was doing her typing could have come in utter dismay to the new employee's supervisor and expounded, "When is dingbat ever going to learn to spell correctly?" Instead, the applicant was encouraged to use a dictionary and other resources when preparing written information. Hence, poor spelling did not become a source of anger or frustration and a dilemma for coworkers six months after employment of the new person. Rather, it was dealt with in the very beginning.

CONCLUSION

In summary, the manager who uses systematic interviewing as described in this chapter has adopted PRESEARCH to a problem prevention model. Indeed, situational interviewing requires more time spent during the interview and preselection process than traditional methods. In our experience, the time expenditure resulted in these benefits:

- unpleasant surprises about the candidate's performance in the new job setting were minimized,

- the interviewer used an objective selection process,
- each applicant's qualifications for the position were equitably weighed, and
- the employer was satisfied that the best presenting candidate was selected.

These were benefits both for the employer and the new employee.

Chapter 13

A Tool for Administrative Decision Making

The purpose of this chapter is to illustrate the effectiveness of systematic data gathering as a base for administrative decision making. In this case a system that works well for the accounting and personnel departments is creating a large volume of tedious paper work for the nursing department. An investigation of the field of uncertainty was prompted by a computer programming delay. The program in question was one for recording and calculating accrued employee benefits such as vacation, holiday, and sick time. This example was chosen because it is a very fundamental one and exemplifies the kinds of problems that are encountered frequently by people at the administrative level.

Although the hospital was fairly small in size, the employees used time clocks to record working hours on a daily basis. This information was hand calculated, converted to number of hours worked, and entered on the time cards by designated nursing department personnel. The time cards were sorted and batched in the accounting office to be processed by a centralized computer payroll service. This service generated the individual employee paychecks which were distributed later at the hospital. After the time cards were processed at the computer center, the daily time card information was transferred by nursing personnel to individual employee work records. This was a permanent file card retained in the personnel office.

The nursing department had undergone many personnel changes. Several individuals who were accustomed to completing the burdensome time recording task were no longer assigned to process payroll information because of position transfers both in and out of the department. The new nursing administrator was troubled by the amount of time that several people on her administrative staff were spending with payroll related items. She observed her staff recording numbers into massive record-keeping volumes. She noted that a large portion of their work time was also spent transferring information from one volume to another. This was a case where a system had evolved over the years. The people involved had become so integrated into the process that they did not question the duplicate recording. Precisely, they had become victims of a system without realizing it. The field of uncertainty was discovered when new individuals were introduced to the procedure and began to question its inefficiency. When the nurse director explored the topic with the hospital administrator, she was informed that the hospital's long-range plan included computerizing the payroll system. This answer sufficed temporarily. However, as the weeks passed and the computer programming was delayed, it was apparent that there was more to the situation than had first appeared.

The intradepartmental course of events went something like this: two clinical coordinators who were responsible for monitoring overtime remarked that they believed an honor system would be more cost effective than using the time clock. They had observed that employees frequently had one-tenth of an hour overtime. They related this to the distance from the nurses' station to the time clock. They proposed piloting an honor system for recording time worked on one nursing unit. Their plan included a concurrent audit of overtime and comparing that to historical data using old time cards punched on the time clock.

The director's secretary expressed frustration at having to do payroll clerk duties. She was experiencing a loss of job satisfaction because she was spending an increasing amount of time recording payroll information. This conscientious lady was concerned about the margin for human error in the existing manual system. She suggested purchasing calculators for each person who worked on the time cards. She felt that replacing the old adding machine with more up-to-date equipment would facilitate the process and increase accuracy.

The staffing secretary, who was being introduced gradually to the payroll recording components of her position, could not envision managing this additional workload. The idea of the payroll related tasks becoming part of her workload was almost overwhelming. In all seriousness she believed that she would need an assistant if her job expanded.

The unit manager was uncomfortable spending large blocks of time away from the nursing units. Her priority was supporting the unit secretaries and trouble shooting where needed throughout the hospital rather than spending eight hours every two weeks assisting with time card calculations. She asked if we couldn't just delegate the whole task to someone else in another department.

The administrative assistant was the only person in the group who had worked with the system for many years. She too felt stressed by the amount of time that the process required. However, she had difficulty understanding how the department could relinquish control of any part of the payroll information flow.

The symptoms of an interdepartmental conflict were emerging. It is interesting to note that as personnel from the nursing department were identifying what they termed to be "the problem" they were also bringing with them a solution. This is an extremely common occurrence. It highlights the value of a systematic data-gathering process in complex problem identification. It is easy, in the busy work world, to agree with the person who comes to you, not only with an identified problem, but with a solution. Whenever this happens, approach the proposed solution cautiously in a questioning framework. Try to determine if the entire scope of the problem has been addressed; otherwise a solution to part of the problem may not produce a noticeable effect.

In this example the hospital administrator, the controller, the personnel director and the nursing administrator shared a common concern. As discussed in earlier chapters, the nursing administrator was the one who, because of the number of people in her department, dramatically felt the impact of a seemingly inefficient system. The other two department heads, the personnel director and the controller, saw this as a problem in terms of: "How can we get a manual benefit accrual system on the computer?"; however, the director of nursing saw the problem from the standpoint of: "How can I minimize the amount of time spent by nursing personnel getting payroll information ready for the keypunch operator?" Hence, the personnel director and the controller were speaking in terms of computer memory technology, while the director of nursing was seeking a more efficient system for processing information before it left the department.

In any interdepartmental problem-solving effort, one should remember that each department has its own vocabulary. In formal and informal meetings, statements like the following had been tossed around by various members of this administrative group.

The controller was saying, "Our auditors have said we have to put sick time and vacation accrual on the computer."

The personnel director cautiously added, "We have to have a double check mechanism to be sure that the computer input is accurate."

The nursing director was saying, "The payroll input system is inefficient and something has to be done about it."

She felt uneasy because she sensed that even after the proposed computer programming, the system would continue to consume large amounts of administrative staff time. Computer programming would not alleviate this stress factor within the administrative office. When the personnel director wanted the nursing department to continue manual recording for at least one year as a double check mechanism, the nurse director restated, "Entirely too much nursing administrative time is being spent manually recording payroll information."

The controller explained, "Well, even if we establish a payroll department, a certain amount of manual computation has to go on in the nursing department."

Each administrative person was approaching the situation from a slightly different viewpoint and suddenly the nursing director realized that there were four distinct parts to the system under discussion. These were:

- processing of time cards
- maintaining individual employment records
- administering wage and salary programs
- compiling individual accrued benefits at the end of each pay period and at the completion of the fiscal year.

Computerization of accrued benefits was a step in the right direction but it was not going to address the greatest portion of processing time in the nursing department. Without additional data she could not adequately explain to the three gentlemen why the system was awkward for her department. Consequently, she decided to conduct a method analysis of the payroll system as it affected the nursing department. From experience, she realized that she needed concrete information to present to the administrative group. She needed facts to explain her point.

A METHODS ANALYSIS

Methods (or systems) analysis is a systematic examination of a process. The process can involve an entire system or be a single procedure. In the context discussed here, methods analysis is the questioning procedure described by A. C. Bennett in *Methods Improvement in Hospitals.*[1]

When evaluating the details of the job that is being studied, one should try to discover what is wrong and how it can be improved. This task requires an open mind, and it can be accomplished most easily by making use of a well-established pattern of questioning which examines each detail in terms of:

1. The purpose for doing it.
2. The place where the detail is being done.
3. The sequence in which it is done.

4. The person doing it.
5. The means by which it is done.

After the over-all job has been reviewed to make certain that the activity itself is necessary, each detail of the job should be challenged through the use of the questions shown in Figure 13-1. These questions appear in a definite order and should be applied systematically to each detail in that order.

Figure 13-1 shows the proper sequence and scope of questions to be answered in a methods analysis procedure. The methods analysis questions can be used as the survey instrument to collect information in a variety of circumstances. In the case described earlier in this chapter, the director of nursing addressed these questions to the process of preparing payroll information for the keypunch operator. She asked the controller and each of the nursing department members who worked with the system to answer the Methods Analysis Questions independently. Their collective responses to those questions produced the following facts, givens and issues:

Figure 13-1 Methods Analysis Questions

1. Purpose	What is being done? Why is it being done? What else might be done?	The answers to questions such as these help us to eliminate unnecessary parts of the job.
2. Place	Where it is being done? Why is it being done there? Does it need to be done at that particular place? Where else might it be done?	The answers to these questions often suggest that two or more details can be combined or the sequence, the place or the person can be changed.
3. Sequence	When is it done? Why is it done then? Does it need to be done at that particular time? When might it be done?	
4. Person	Who is doing it? Why does that person do it? Could it be done better by someone else? Who else might do it?	
5. Means	How is it being done? Why is it done this way? How else might it be done?	Finally, these questions are asked with a view toward improving or simplifying the necessary details.

Source: A. C. Bennett, *Methods Improvements in Hospitals* (New York, N.Y.: J. B. Lippincott). Reprinted with permission.

Recording Time Worked for Payroll Purposes
Facts, Givens, and Issues

1. Preparing the time cards for the controller's office takes at least 32 hours every two weeks of nursing administrative staff time (four people working eight hours each).
2. The combined cost for their 32 hours of work is $215.00.
3. A time clock is used for recording "time in" and "time out" for each staff member. The employees do not punch in and out for lunch breaks.
4. Any time an employee from one nursing station has floated to another, the floated hours should be coded on the back of the time card. There is no place for the individual (the staff nurse punching in or out) to record floated hours on the time card. Therefore, the recording of the floated hours on the time card from a master staffing sheet is done by the nursing administration personnel (one of the four above-mentioned people) every two weeks.
5. There are frequent interruptions during the compilation of data onto the time cards. Most especially for the: secretary—answering the nursing office telephone; unit manager—answering pages from the nursing units; and staffing assistant—answering staffing requests and sick call-ins.
6. Four people have only one electric adding machine on which to figure employees' individual salary amounts. These amounts are calculated and entered on the time card. Therefore, a large amount of hand figuring is done. This is not only tedious and time consuming, it also allows for a wide margin of human calculating error.
7. There is a table used to convert numbers of minutes worked to tenths of an hour.
8. Mental calculation is necessary for every "punch in" and "punch out" time. For example: on the first shift if the employee punches in at 06:45, and out at 15:15, that is considered an eight-hour shift. If, however, the employee punches in at 06:45 and out at 15:43 those working on the time card must mentally calculate that the person has worked 28 minutes beyond the eight-hour shift and then convert that amount of time to five-tenths of an hour and calculate that the person has worked eight and one-half hours for that particular day. On the other hand, if the employee punches in at 07:02 and out at 15:15, someone working on the time cards must mentally subtract seventeen minutes from the eight hours, convert that seventeen minutes into three-tenths of an hour and subtract it from

the eight-hour shift and conclude that this individual for this particular day has worked 7.7 hours.

9. Charge pay has to be paid for each nurse who is designated as the person in charge on any given shift. This information has to be transferred from the master schedule to the time card and the dollar amount due to each individual for each eight hours of charge time is calculated from a table.

10. When an employee has marked "sick pay" on his or her time card, it has to be verified on the master staffing sheet. Thereafter, the employee record has to be checked to verify that the employee is eligible for sick time pay. There is some guess work in this process, because employees accumulate sick pay at the rate of one day per month.

11. The employee record notebook (which is 3½ inches deep by 8½ by 11 inches) contains approximately 225 employees' record cards and weighs 7½ pounds. This book is passed from person to person each time an employee claims vacation, sick, or holiday time. The people working on the time cards have to look up the employee's record individually and determine if the person claiming the vacation, sick time, or holiday is eligible to be paid for it.

12. "On call" pay has to be calculated separately when the employee remains on the premises, is off the premises, or is called in to work.

13. After the procedure for calculating and recording the information on the time cards is completed, there is a recheck procedure. The time cards are redivided among the four individuals compiling the records and they manually recheck each other's work. If there have been interruptions during the day and time does not permit the recheck procedure to occur, it is omitted. Due to calculation errors it is not uncommon for a few of the time cards to be returned to the nursing office the following morning by someone in the controller's office.

14. On the Thursday afternoon or Friday morning following pay day there are several calls to the nursing office questioning how their pay was figured for the previous two weeks. Often there were mistakes that must be corrected and a separate check generated from the controller's office to adjust the person's salary amount due. Other times the error is corrected in the next pay period's check.

From the above information they formulated the following problem statement: How can we actively involve the individual employee in calculating and manually recording their hours worked and reduce the

amount of processing time spent every two weeks by the nursing administrative staff yet maintain at minimum the present level of accuracy?

The nursing administrator recalled that Maier had stated in *Problem-
solving Discussions and Conferences* that

> Problem solving is successful only when the solution reached is
> one which can be put into practice. If a person or group lacks the
> ability to put a solution into effect, the problem remains un-
> solved. It follows, therefore, that a supervisor should locate
> problems that fall within his jurisdiction for taking action. This
> region over which he has such control is his "area of freedom."
> Each level of supervision has an area of freedom, and its bound-
> aries may be clear or vague, large or small.[2]

At this point the nursing director was unsure about her decision-making
boundaries as they related to this portion of the payroll preparation.
However, she decided to ask the staff members and the controller to offer
alternative solutions to the problem as stated.

Before proceeding, they defined their problem goal as: To develop a
cost-effective payroll processing system for the nursing department as
evidenced by maintaining the present level of accuracy and reducing the
number of concentrated hours spent recording information.

They used a solution analysis grid like the one discussed in Chapter 7 to
record the goal and defined problem. They then listed possible solutions
on the same form. Figure 13-2 shows the grid as it was developed for use
in solving this problem.

The nurse director was certain that purchasing calculators fell within
her area of decision-making freedom. Without hesitation she requisitioned
those items. Not only was her area of freedom about the rest of the
alternatives vague, she was also unsure of the organizational decision-
making constraints. Therefore, she requested another meeting with the
hospital administrator, the controller, and the personnel director to determine the feasibility of the other six proposed alternatives. Because the
material was presented in this manner and the administrative people present had decision-making responsibility as well as knowledge of the constraints, the following decisions were made collectively. The group decided that:

- The employees could indicate the unit to which they floated on the
  front of the time card.
- A volunteer would be recruited to answer the nursing department
  telephone while the time cards were being processed.

Figure 13-2 Solution Analysis Grid

Problem Solving Objective: to develop a cost effective payroll processing system for the nursing department as evidenced by maintaining the present level of accuracy and reducing the number of concentrated hours spent recording information.

Problem Statement: How can we actively involve the individual employee in calculating and manually recording their hours worked and reduce the amount of processing time spent every two weeks by the nursing administrative staff yet maintain at minimum the present level of accuracy?

LIST OF ALTERNATIVE SOLUTIONS	CONTRIBUTION TO OBJECTIVE	COST IN DOLLARS	TIME FRAME	FEASIBILITY
a space on time card for employees				
1. to record floated hours				
decentralize the completion of				
2. time card information				
3. change the design of the time card				
calculate the time clocks to				
4. record in tenths of an hour				
5. replace time clocks with an honor system				
purchase four calculators to				
6. replace one adding machine	High	$	Immediate	Yes
replace employee record book				
7. with computer print-out				
8.				
9.				
10.				

Best Acceptable Solution:

Source: Eitel Hospital, Minneapolis, Minnesota. Used with permission.

- Calculators would be ordered.
- The personnel director agreed to explore the possibility of converting the time clocks to record in tenths of an hour rather than in minutes.
- The controller would provide a code number for in-hospital and a separate code number for call when the employee was out of the building.
- The three-color recording system in the employee record book was eliminated.
- The personnel director gave the nursing department top priority in the computer programming sequence.
- The personnel director explained his rationale for opposition to an honor system and to decentralizing of the recording. An honor system had been used at this hospital in the past. Unfortunately, the privilege had been abused by some department members. Therefore, based on historical data, it was deemed to be too high risk. He contended that teaching people to complete the time cards on the individual nursing units (whether it was the unit secretaries or the individual employees) would be extremely time consuming. The potential for a wider margin of error was believed to be great. The personnel director agreed that after the computer print-out sheets were accurate for two consecutive months, the manual recording could be discontinued. This was a compromise, for at first he had requested a one-year dual record-keeping process. The controller, the hospital administrator, and the personnel director all agreed that the large payroll in the nursing department deserved the amount of time and salary which was being spent by the nursing administrative staff.

The best acceptable solution in this case simply was to make minor adjustments within the system. Those adjustments were possible only after data had been collected and presented in such a way that those at the administrative meeting could focus on the same aspects of the problem. Heretofore, the controller, the hospital administrator, the director of nursing, and the personnel director were all talking around and about "the problem" as viewed from their own perspectives. In prior meetings they were simply engaged in verbal ping-pong. In the group meeting that lasted no more than an hour, decisions were made and explanations given that helped to accomplish the goal as stated. Due to the adjustments that were made, the nursing administrative staff had better equipment with which to work and the number of hours spent every two weeks in time card processing was reduced from 32 to 24. Eventually the computer print-out for vacation, sick time, and holiday accrual replaced the employee record book.

CONCLUSION

This example shows how the solution analysis grid can be used to present information for administrative decision making. In this case it occurred as a group process by those who had decision-making authority. The nurse administrator thereafter understood the historical as well as the current rationale for the existing systems. She was able to explain the decision-making constraints to her staff. The explanations and the minor adjustments that were instituted made the procedure more tolerable.

The action plans that resulted were procedural and investigative. At the time of this writing they had neither been implemented nor evaluated. Even so, it was believed that this example showed a valuable use of the PRESEARCH process in defining one's area of freedom. It also demonstrates the process for collective decision making.

NOTES

1. Addison C. Bennett, *Methods Improvement in Hospitals* (Maspeth, N.Y.: Metromedia Analearn: J. B. Lippincott, 1964), pp. 24–25.
2. Norman R. F. Maier, *Problem-solving Discussions and Conferences: Leadership Methods and Skills* (New York, N.Y.: McGraw-Hill, 1963), p. 70.

Chapter 14

A Student's Nonthesis Project Paper

During the 1978–1979 academic year, Martyann Penberth taught an undergraduate course entitled "Introduction to Hospital and Health Care Administration" at St. Joseph's College in Maine. All of the students were registered nurses and the majority of them were in a management position, from director of nursing to head nurse. This created a very challenging environment. The students may not have had a great deal of management theory, but their years of experience enhanced the theoretical content presented and allowed them to bridge the theory/practice gap quickly. One of the major goals of the course was a written assignment that would fulfill the course requirements and at the same time have relevance and meaning for their everyday work situation.

Problem solving seemed the common element in all the managers' positions. It is an unavoidable activity that can only be effective when carried out systematically. The PRESEARCH model provided both a framework to work through a problem situation and guidelines for writing the paper. Since the model can be used by any nurse in any problem situation, it was well suited to the variety of nursing positions in the group.

The paper that follows was written by Adriane Weaver and is just one example of how a student applied the PRESEARCH process in her setting to solve a very real problem.

TELEPHONE APPOINTMENT SYSTEM IN THE INTERNAL MEDICINE DEPARTMENT: CENTRALIZATION VERSUS DECENTRALIZATION

I. **Field of Uncertainty**
   A. *Background*
   B. *Current Environment of Uncertainty*

II.   Purpose of Exploring Field of Uncertainty
III. Use of Data Collected
IV.   Identification of Target Population
V.   Method of Data Collection
VI.   Time Frame for Collection of Data
VII. Interviews and Responses
VIII. Issues Extracted from Similar Responses
IX.   Desired Outcome Goal
X.   Construction of a Problem Statement
XI.   Exploration of Alternatives
XII. Plan for Action
XIII. Strategy for Implementation
XIV. Expected Date of Implementation
XV.   Evaluation

I. Field of Uncertainty

A. Background

Over the past three to four years, I have met with various telephone company representatives to discuss the problem that exists because of the way our telephone system operates. In most instances, all of the suggestions submitted for change by the telephone representatives were basically the same. They proposed to delete the many telephone numbers that are in use by the department and change the numbers, publishing only one or two telephone numbers for consumers to use. Also, they recommended separating the department's telephone lines from the main switchboard except for intradepartmental extension lines that are a necessity.

The physicians in the department object to these suggestions because they would have to give up their private appointment clerks and have little control over the appointment books.

Many years ago when the entire medical plan was in the early stages of development, a centralized appointment system was used. All medical services at that time had one telephone number listed for appointments. Four appointment secretaries, with no medical background, scheduled appointments for all departments in the facility. Problems such as allocating identical time frames for different patient appointments; placing ten-year-olds on internists' schedules; and scheduling surgical patients with internists surfaced. Also, specialists were called in for problems that did not relate to their specialties because the secretaries did not know enough about the practice of internal medicine. As a result, the centralized appointment system did not last very long.

I believe that some of the same internists who were present during the time of the previously mentioned centralized appointment phase are still fearful that this type of poor scheduling will recur if we change from the current decentralized system to a new central appointment system. Patient education is easy, but physician reeducation is difficult.

B. Current Environment of Uncertainty

There is increasing concern, shared by the consumers of the medical plan as well as some staff members, that telephone access into the internal medicine department is awkward and confusing. Ideally, the consumers should be able to call the department for future appointments and resolve other health care problems. However, the consumers are being put on hold for long periods of time, or are asked to dial the private number of their personal physician.

Currently, there is no direct dial telephone system for internal medicine. All calls come through the main switchboard, and the operator routes the calls to one of the six internal medicine extensions. When an extension is busy, the calls are automatically routed sequentially to the next open line. In addition, each of the five full-time physicians in the department has two private telephone numbers to accommodate incoming calls. An appointment secretary is assigned to each physician for purposes of maintaining schedules and answering the telephone.

Incoming telephone traffic for the department can be classified as: (1) same day appointments and other business—prescription refills, messages, and general information; and (2) future appointments. An intradepartmental intercom system connects all the telephones in internal medicine. This allows the doctors to communicate with each other, their appointment secretaries, and other staff members. Each appointment secretary has a console telephone with the two private numbers listed for the appropriate physician served by her, the six extensions, and the intercom to dial other internal medicine staff members.

Example: Appointment secretary A makes appointments exclusively for Dr. S. Her telephone console looks like this:

private numbers: 997-0180; 997-0181
extensions: 230, 231, 232, 233, 234, 235
intercom numbers: 1–20

This secretary is required to answer telephone calls coming in on 997-0180 and 997-0181 only. These calls will be coming in for Dr. S., the physician with whom she works. However, if the extensions ring, she is expected to answer any of them if she is not tied up with the private lines. The extensions are employed for both incoming and outgoing calls. Private lines are used solely for incoming calls. Each of the other four appointment secretaries' telephone consoles are set up identically except for the different private numbers. There is one large console used by the receptionist in the department. This console has all the department telephone numbers listed, as well as all the extensions and intercom numbers. An example follows:

Internal Medicine Receptionist's telephone console layout:

Dr. S: 997-0180, 997-0181
Dr. R: 997-5305, 997-5306
Dr. D: 730-2611, 730-2612
Dr. T: 730-5542, 730-5543
Dr. P: 997-0044, 997-0045
extensions: 230, 231, 232, 233, 234, 235
intercom numbers: 1–20

If a patient wanted to contact her or his private physician in the department of internal medicine and could not remember the doctor's telephone number, this is what happens. The patient calls the medical plan on 997-8500, the telephone listed for all departments. The switchboard operator for the entire medical plan will answer, "Medical Plan, may I help you?" The patient replies, "Yes, I would like to speak to Dr. S." The switchboard operator immediately puts the call through on one of the internal medicine extensions. An appointment secretary picks up and answers "Internal medicine, Ms. H., may I help you?" The patient states "I'd like to speak with Dr. S." The appointment secretary states that the telephone number is 997-0180, that his secretary is on another line now, and she has another call waiting. She further tells the patient that it would be easier to hang up and redial the private number so that the patient could talk directly with the doctor's secretary, or if the patient would like, he or she might hold. If the patient does not wish to redial, she or he might be left on hold indefinitely because the appointment secretary's main interest is to answer the doctor's two private incoming lines. At times, the secretary becomes confused as both private lines and the extension lines ring. Four calls may come in for the same physician, and the secretary cannot remember the proper sequence of calls. Some patients report secretaries to administration after being left on hold for long periods of time.

II. Purpose of Exploring Field of Uncertainty

The purpose in exploring this field of uncertainty is to find alternative methods for better telephone communications with consumers of the medical plan. If patients' complaints continue to rise with the present telephone system, the plan membership may decline because of dissatisfied consumers.

III. Use of Data Collected

The collected data will be used:

1. To correct an already existing problem;
2. To gain additional information and suggestions for alternative telephone systems; and
3. To determine if some of the appointment secretaries can be used more efficiently elsewhere in the department.

IV. Identification of Target Population

People involved in the target population are physicians, nurses, appointment secretaries, and consumers of the medical plan. I shall consult with a telephone representative in the area who is familiar with similar problems in other health care facilities.

V. Method of Data Collection

1. Interviews with some internal medicine staff members and appointment secretaries in other departments of the medical plan.
2. Consultations with a telephone communications representative, and consumers.

VI. Time Frame for Collection of Data

It will take approximately three weeks to collect the data. During that time, I will personally interview individuals as well as groups. The telephone representative will come to the medical plan, make observations, talk with staff members and offer suggestions for changes in the telephone operations of the department.

VII. Interviews and Responses

A. Interview with appointment secretary in the department of internal medicine.

Questions: How do you feel about our present telephone system? Do you have any suggestions for change?

Response: "It's terrible. As membership in the plan increases, service seems to get worse. There are not enough people to answer the number of incoming calls that we receive. Patients become angry and hang up after being put on 'hold.' I can't blame them. My suggestion would be to have only one or two published telephone numbers to give out for the entire department. One number should be for general information, and the other should be for appointments. I don't believe physicians need individual private lines. That's what makes the system ineffective."

B. Interview with an internist in department of internal medicine.

Questions: What do you think of our present telephone system? Do you have any suggestions for change?

Response: "Really, is there a problem? I think it's okay. However, I might add, it would be nice for me to have an additional private line, nonpublished, so that when I'm in the office after hours dictating and reviewing charts and the phone rings I can pick it up and know it's not a patient calling. This would be for my personal use, of course. Oh yes, one problem I see is when the clinic is closed, my telephone rings incessantly. Don't the patients know our hours of operation? I would suggest an answering device or an answering service for after office hours. But I think each physician should leave individual messages if we decide on an answering service. While you are asking for suggestions, I need a 3–4 ft extension cord for my telephone!"

C. Interview with receptionist–transcriptionist.

Questions: What do you think of our present telephone system? Do you have any suggestions for change?

Response: "It's quite frustrating. There are too many published telephone numbers for this department. Patients are really confused. I often help out by answering phones because I can't stand to hear them ringing. This interrupts my work. We need more people to answer phones or we must change the system so that there is only one number to call for general information and appointments for the department."

D. *Interview with all five internists at an internal medicine physicians' meeting.*

Questions: What do you think of our present telephone system? Any suggestions for change?

Response: Consensus of opinion was that each of the internists prefer having his own private telephone lines; and they also want to maintain their individual private appointment secretaries. The physicians feel they have some control of the appointment books by retaining their individual secretaries. An additional suggestion (overwhelmingly) was to have an answering service or answering device for after clinic hours.

E. *Interview with appointment clerk in pediatrics department.*

Questions: How do you like your telephone system? Do you get many patient complaints? How does your system work?

Response: "Our system is quite simple and it works. We have very few patient complaints about setting appointments or obtaining information. We have only two published numbers for patients. These are for (1) same day appointments and other business, and (2) future appointments. These duties are split between two appointment clerks. When the volume of calls becomes too heavy, there is an additional clerk to help. We have had very few problems with this system. We have four pediatricians and four nurse practitioners in the department, and we have a high volume of telephone calls."

F. *Interview with a consumer who has been a plan member for six years.*

Questions: Do you encounter any problems when calling internal medicine? Do you have any suggestions for improvement?

Response: "Yes, all I ever get is—'Is this an emergency?' or 'Can you hold?' Thankfully, it's never been an emergency. However, I get tired of being put on hold. There are too many telephone numbers in that department to call for this doctor and that doctor. One must always remember to dial

the correct number of her physician. Otherwise you'd be
on the telephone all morning. It's just too much. It should
be made easier, especially for older folks like me. I'd like to
call the internal medicine department one time and have all
my health care needs attended to by dialing one number
only and not have to redial and hold and all the other non-
sense they put me through if I call an incorrect number."

G. Interview with C&P telephone communications representative.

Ms. D. visited our facility several times. She has made observations,
had the secretaries do stroke counts, busy studies, and keep telephone
logs for the various types of problems about which patients telephone.
The telephone representative's report follows:

"The major problem appears to be a direct result of the multitude of
telephone numbers that the internal medicine department utilizes for
incoming telephone calls. The many numbers result in confusion to
the calling party and is also an inefficient use of telephone lines as
well as personnel. The primary reason for the use of many different
telephone numbers is that each doctor has his own private telephone
numbers. This arrangement may have been useful when the internal
medicine department was much smaller, but this arrangement has
outlived its usefulness. I recognize the reason for this arrangement is
that each doctor's appointment book is maintained by his own secretary; and the doctors want calls to come directly to their appointment
secretary. What happens in reality is that almost any time a call is on
hold for a particular doctor the patient calling hangs up, and then
redials internal medicine through the main switchboard number. This
is a very poor arrangement since it results in busy lines and severely
limits your call handling capacity.
"The most efficient manner to handle and process incoming calls to
the department would be for only one telephone number to be listed
for all the doctors and for future appointments. You may wish to
maintain a number for same day appointments of emergencies, but I
would suggest having these calls go to the same main number. One
person should be assigned the dedicated task of answering incoming
calls and then passing them to the appropriate secretary for processing. A second person should be assigned as a backup.
"I hope these suggestions will be of benefit to you. If you have
further questions, please don't hesitate to call."

VIII. Issues Extracted from Similar Responses

A. Publish two telephone numbers for internal medicine.

1. Same day appointments and other business
2. Future appointments

B. List all physicians under one number for appointments.
C. Adopt telephone system similar to that in the pediatrics department.
D. Install answering service or similar device for use when internal medicine department is closed.
E. Retain existing system.

IX. Desired Outcome Goal

A telephone communication system that is acceptable to the clinic practitioners and that provides the consumer with access to physician without lengthy waiting periods.

X. Construction of a Problem Statement

Can the appointment system in internal medicine be changed without creating more problems and confusion for consumers? Will this new system be difficult for the physicians to accept?

XI. Exploration of Alternatives

A. Keep present telephone system.

Pro—physicians only would be satisfied.
Con—inefficient use of personnel. Patient complaints will continue to rise and eventually plan membership may decrease.
Opinion—poor alternative.

B. Change system to accommodate two published numbers.

Pro—will require less staff to perform this function. Patients can dial one number to either make an appointment or a different number to take care of other patient needs. Less confusing.
Con—some patients may miss or lose the personal rapport established with individual private appointment secretaries.
Opinion—good alternative.

C. Installation of computerized appointment system.

Pro—more efficient use of staff.
Con—investigation of this system proves it is too costly to consider installing at the present time.
Opinion—poor alternative.

Alternative "B" is the best alternative because fewer staff will be needed to accommodate the two published numbers and the remaining two secretaries can be trained to do other office procedures. They can also be used as backup personnel in the case of illness or vacations.

XII. Plan for Action

The action plan is to implement a two telephone line system proposed by one of the telephone company consultants.

XIII. Strategy for Implementation

A. Arrange a meeting with chief of service, business manager of the medical plan, and the telephone representative. Discuss the proposed changes in the telephone system. Arrangements will be made for each internist to visit the pediatrics department and talk with the appointment secretaries as well as pediatricians. This will enable them to see the telephone appointment system in operation and they will then be better able to understand how the new internal medicine system will operate.

B. Call a general staff meeting to review the changes that are scheduled to take place in the appointment by telephone system.

C. Set up in-service training program for the secretaries who will be making appointments for same day and the future. Also schedule in-service training for the remaining two appointment secretaries that will now be required to perform other office duties.

D. Send a memo to the medical plan public relations person. Inform this person of the changes in the telephone system for internal medicine so that the general public will be aware of the change.

E. Publish an article in the medical plan's monthly newsletter to consumers. The article should state that there will soon be a change in the telephone appointment system in internal medicine, and all consumers will be notified when the change will actually take place.

XIV. Expected Date of Implementation

The expected date for implementing a change in the telephone appointment system is October 15, 1979.

XV. Evaluation

The change project will be evaluated by:
1. A 50% decrease in patient complaints about being inconvenienced when "calling in" to speak with a professional practitioner about a health related problem.
2. Clinic staff expressing satisfaction with the telephone communication system.
3. No patient's having dissatisfaction with telephone access to the clinic as a reason for discontinuing participation in the group health plan.

CONCLUSION

There are several educational advantages to utilizing the PRE-SEARCH process as a requirement with a group of students, whether prospective nurses or registered nurses. First, it forces the individual to work through the problem in a systematic manner. How many times have we seen managers listen to a few comments about a problem situation and then begin implementing a solution to the "perceived problem?" Second, the emphasis on data collection is crucial to defining a problem and gives the nurse some exposure to the research process. The process utilizes others in developing alternative solutions that increase organizational communication between different members of the health care team and different departments and should create a more workable solution. A last advantage is the time saving factor. The initial investment in time to define the "real" problem to be solved prevents the manager from dealing with the same problem situation time and again.

Chapter 15

Interdepartmental Problem Solving

Care of Valuables/Important Change!!!
Effective Thursday, the care of valuables procedure will be
simplified. New procedure cards have been sent to all nursing
units. Please take time to review the new procedures as a great
deal of time and effort have been invested in this simplification.
We need everyone's support and cooperation to make the new
procedure work well.

The above announcement appeared in a weekly newsletter from the
nursing office in a large metropolitan hospital. Work simplification—can
that really be true? What prompted this announcement?

In this hospital the two associate directors of nursing felt they qualified
for detective badges. Week after week they were tracking down lost
pajamas, missing nighties, misplaced slippers, disappearing dentures,
vanishing jewelry, and mislaid eyeglasses. Their detective duties were
consuming valuable time that should have been spent on other requirements of their jobs. Their frustrations magnified with the discovery
that JC Penney nighties became Christian Dior originals once placed on
the missing list.

The problem of missing patient valuables was an old problem and had
nagged at the nursing directors for many years. A rather elaborate and
involved documentation procedure had been developed in an effort to
minimize the losses. The procedure, however, was so intricate that it was
seldom followed. As a result the documentation was worsening and the
claims were continuing.

The director of nursing initiated a city-wide survey of hospitals to
determine their policies about the care of patients' valuables. The majority of the hospitals surveyed indicated that they initiated a preadmission
telephone call to the patient. At that time someone asked patients to bring

no more than $5.00 in cash to the hospital with them. Any valuables that the patient brought to the nursing unit were sent to the business office in a container. Then a receipt was returned to the patient. At the time of discharge, the patients collected their valuables. After obtaining this information the nursing administrative group, exhausted with the amount of time being spent on detective work, recommended the following: "The hospital should take the position of assuming no responsibility for the care of patient valuables and/or personal belongings."

This approach was not acceptable to the hospital administrator and therefore another approach was necessary. At that time one person was designated to be in charge of this project. The project director walked through the procedures, as a patient, from the time of admission to the time of discharge. By doing so, the project director discovered that an informal procedure had been developed in lieu of the complex one that was intended to solve the problem previously.

The informal procedure had several subparts. The procedure between the admitting office and the cashier was effective and working well. However, due to lack of control over patient valuables during their hospital stay, the nurses, for the most part, had chosen to disregard the procedure completely. Interviews with key informants in the admitting office, the cashier's office, and nurses on the nursing unit revealed the following facts, givens, and issues:

- A hospital management policy exists for lost, damaged or stolen items.
- Loss, misplacement, damage, or theft of patient valuables and/or personal articles continue to occur causing:
  —distress to the patient/family,
  —frustration to the nursing staff who try to locate the missing items,
  —disruption to the associate directors of nursing and other administrative staff who are called away from other duties to spend time investigating claims, and
  —time-consuming yet necessary public relations followup letters and phone calls by the director of public relations department.
- The elaborate "valuables and personal belongings" (Form #S702-41) is not being used by the nurses.
- Nurses on general med/surg, OB, and intensive care units have no means of control over articles the patient's family and friends take home or bring to the patient during hospitalization.
- The practice of storing patient valuables temporarily (in a locked drawer or cabinet on the nursing units) using valuables envelope (Form #P-140) is reported to be working and effective. It should be

noted that the practice does not correspond to the approved procedure.

- The face sheet (Form #S702-40) is printed with a space for each patient to sign a waiver of responsibility for valuables and personal equipment which are not placed in the hospital's safe.
- Form #S702-41, "Valuables and Personal Belongings," also provides a space for each patient to sign a waiver of responsibility for valuables and personal equipment not placed in the hospital safe.
- A double logging procedure for the admitting clerk and the cashier reportedly has reduced incidents of items missing between those two departments.
- The admitting clerk is responsible for having the patient sign Form #S702-41 at the time of admission. If for some reason this is not done, it becomes the responsibility of the nurse on the unit receiving the patient to obtain a patient's signature that releases the hospital of responsibility for articles the patient chooses to retain.
- An audit of 161 claims over a period of four years showed a total of 37 claims with reimbursement and 124 claims without reimbursement. Total retrievable cost of reimbursement was $1,258.72.
- Nurses are not completing the care of valuables chart form during the patient's hospital stay.

Although it sounds simple, this process of arriving at a workable procedure took a lot of patience and involved negotiations and compromises between the admitting office, the safety officer, the business office, the medical records librarian, the public relations officer and the nursing units. The best acceptable solution was to streamline the complex forms and salvage the parts of the system being used. The resulting action plan was as follows:

1. Retain the "logging in" procedure performed by the admitting clerks and the cashier.
2. Redesign the valuables and personal belongings form.
3. Rewrite the "Care of Valuables" and "Personal Belongings" procedure cards to reflect the new accepted practice.
4. Rewrite the "Temporary Storage of Valuables" procedure card to reflect the acceptable practice.
5. Present the above to the hospital administrator for approval; thereafter to the departments involved.
6. Present the revisions to the appropriate assistant administrators, department heads, and committees.

7. Inform the admitting office, cashier's office, and nursing staff of the new form and educate them to use the revised system.
8. Retain the existing policies and procedures for handling patient and staff claims of lost, stolen or damaged articles.

Although the plan seems fairly straightforward, the intricacies of the procedures were quite involved. The plan included presenting the patient with printed information about the hospital's position on care of valuables at the time of admission. An internal control of valuables also had to be devised. Because of the number of people who needed to accept and implement this project, as well as the various interdisciplinary groups represented, it was decided that the system revision project warranted PERT charting. (Refer to Chapter 8 for details of PERT charting.) That chart is reproduced in Figure 15-1 to point out the number of events that were essential to implement the new simplified system.

The events in the PERT flow chart are numbered in the order which they were scheduled to occur. A corresponding key lists the events in their sequential order. This PERT chart does not show the number of weeks between the events. However, during the actual experience the time required between the events was calculated. An implementation date was determined from the PERT flow chart.

Once all of the printed materials were obtained, meetings were scheduled to inform the staff of each department concerned about the changes and the system was implemented.

Audits were designed to monitor the key points of this multifaceted system. Audit I was developed to evaluate retrospectively the subsystems procedures between the admitting officer, the cashier's office, and the medical records department. Representatives from those departments conducted the audits. That audit tool is reproduced in Figure 15-2.

Audit II was designed to assess the awareness of patients and nursing staff of the revised procedure. The midsection of this concurrent tool addresses the use of CARE cards. The person conducting the audit on a designated day randomly visited patients, interviewed nurses, and observed for the use of CARE cards in information card racks above the beds. CARE was the code word that signaled staff to take special precautions for such items as eyeglasses or dentures because of the patient's consciousness level or mental status. An example of Audit II is shown in Figure 15-3.

Audit III was constructed as a retrospective or concurrent assessment tool for correct use of the procedure "temporary storage of patient valuables." This chart audit, shown in Figure 15-4, was conducted by nurses working mainly on surgical units to assess pre- and post-operative documentation.

Audit IV, Figure 15-5, was a concurrent audit tool to assess the nurses correct use of the Kardex and nursing data base as the entries related to patient valuables. A nurse from one unit conducted the audit on another unit to minimize biasing of the samplings.

These audits were conducted at three- and six-month intervals after implementation. The design of the audit tools made it possible to discover the weak links and take corrective action. The noncompliance factor was so minimal within six months that the procedure was considered successfully institutionalized. The people involved in this project learned by experience that getting the most accomplished with the least effort requires a great deal of thought, planning, and effort.

Through this experience, they discovered that it was quite an undertaking to simplify an existing complicated system. Needless to say, the work spent arriving at a functional process paid off as revealed by the audit results.

CONCLUSION

In summary, careful planning produced an implementable procedure. The outcome was a simplified system. The new version eradicated unwarranted reimbursement and eliminated the associate directors from being bombarded with nagging claims. Planning replaced putting out brushfires. Important patient care matters rightfully took precedence over the urgent detective work interruptions.

The investment in time in the PRESEARCH process is in data gathering and planning. Success stories such as this one demonstrate the benefit of preliminary time expenditure. It pays off in the end and, truly, is cost effective.

Figure 15-1 PERT Chart for Revision of Care of Valuables Form and Procedures

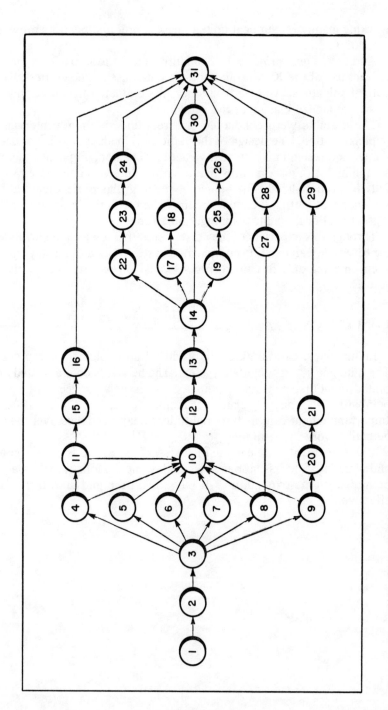

Source: St. Joseph's Hospital, St. Paul, Minnesota. Used with permission.

Key for PERT Chart for Revision of Care of Valuables Form and Procedures

1. Data gathered about the existing system in a three-year audit regarding valuables lost, damaged, or stolen.
2. Draft No. 1 of revised procedure developed.
3. Draft No. 1 approved by director of nursing.
4. Draft No. 1 presented to public relations director for input.
5. Draft No. 1 presented to head nurses for input.
6. Draft No. 1 presented to safety officer for input.
7. Draft No. 1 presented to medical records librarian for input.
8. Draft No. 1 presented to chief cashier for input.
9. Draft No. 1 presented to director of admitting for input.
10. Draft No. 2 of revised procedure developed and presented to hospital administrator for approval.
11. Patient information sheet rewritten.
12. Draft No. 2 presented to assistant administrators and department heads who were directly affected by the change.
13. Three new procedures written.
14. New procedures approved by head nurse council.
15. Patient information sheets printed.
16. Patient information booklets stuffed with printed sheets.
17. Procedure cards ordered.
18. Procedure cards printed and ready to be distributed to the units.
19. Old forms (S702-41) cut in half and ready for use by admitting office.
20. New 2–part forms (S702-41) ordered (½ sheets).
21. New forms (S701-71) ordered (changed release of responsibility statement).
22. New procedure presented to continuing education staff.
23. New procedure presented to unit coordinators.
24. New employee orientation on care of patient valuables revised.
25. CARE cards, overbed inserts ordered.
26. Rubber stamp for charts ordered.
27. Interdepartmental procedure between cashier/medical records revised.
28. Orientation to new procedure for cashier.
29. Orientation to new procedure for admitting clerks.
30. Announcement to nursing units of revised procedure in weekly memo and separate memos to all other departments involved.
31. New system implemented.

Figure 15-2 Care of Valuables Audit I

Care of Valuables Audit I

Conducted by_____ Date_____

Date: _____Pt. Census:_____ Time: _____	
Cashier's copy of Form #S702-41, Number complete _____	
Number incomplete_____	
Number missing_____	
Total _____	

Number of incomplete Forms #S702-41 returned to
 admitting office_____
Admitting clerks not completing forms:_____

_____
_____

Medical records clerk receiving cashier's copies of Form
#702-41 on designated days post patient's discharged date.
      yes /‾7   no /‾7

Lost items claims made by patients from   to

Patient	Unit	Nature of claim	Reimbursement yes no

Source: St. Joseph's Hospital, St. Paul, Minnesota. Used with permission.

Figure 15-3 Care of Valuables Audit II—Awareness Survey

Care of Valuables Audit II - Awareness Survey

Conducted by_____ Date_____

Patient	Room#	Patient's comments indicating an awareness or lack of awareness of the hospital's policy on the care of valuables.
1.		
2.		
3.		
4.		
5.		
6.		
7.		
8.		
9.		
10.		

Confused or Comatose Patient	Room#	Indicate use or lack of use of the "CARE" cards at the pts. bedside.
1.		
2.		
3.		
4.		
5.		

Staff Member	Unit	Staff members comments indicating an awareness of or lack of awareness of the revised procedure concerning the care of patient's valuables.
1.		
2.		
3.		
4.		
5.		
6.		
7.		
8.		
9.		
10.		

Source: St. Joseph's Hospital, St. Paul, Minnesota. Used with permission.

Figure 15-4 Care of Valuables Audit III—Temporary Storage

Care of Valuables Audit III - Temporary Storage

Conducted by_____ Date_____

Patient	Room#	Valuables for temporary storage yes no	Stamp used-valuables received by (name) valuables listed - before & after surgery	pre-op nurse	post-op nurse

Source: St. Joseph's Hospital, St. Paul, Minnesota. Used with permission.

Figure 15-5 Care of Valuables Audit IV—Use of Data Base and Kardex

Care of Valuables Audit IV - Use of data base & kardex

Conducted by_____ Date_____

Room#	Personal belongings noted on data base	Dentures/eyeglasses noted on kardex	Room#	Personal belongings noted on data base	Dentures/eyeglasses noted on kardex
2N			2A		
2C			3B		
3C			4A		
4C			5A		
CCU			5B		
4B			ICU		

Key: OK=noted appropriately   NO=not indicated appropriately   NA=not applicable/Admitting
Nurse Name

Source: St. Joseph's Hospital, St. Paul, Minnesota. Used with permission.

Part III

The Theory Base, Models, and Concepts

Chapter 16

Research within
PRESEARCH

PRESEARCH is an eclectic approach to creative problem solving. Problem solving is not the aim of research. However, elements of scientific research are built into the problem-solving process, PRESEARCH. Research concepts enhance this problem-solving process by adding systematic data gathering and analysis before defining the problems to be solved.

PROCESS DIFFERENTIATION BETWEEN RESEARCH AND PROBLEM SOLVING

An understanding of the difference between research and problem solving guides the users to the appropriate application of each separately or collectively within the PRESEARCH framework. A forthright distinction is made between research and problem solving in *A Guide for the Beginning Researcher* written by Mabel Wandelt.[1] The introductory section of her book makes the points extremely well:

> Problem solving and research are frequently compared, sometimes to the extent that they are purported to be one and the same thing. Nonetheless, if the researcher and the problem solver keep in mind the fundamental difference between the two, they will avoid many pitfalls along the paths to their different goals.
>
> The fundamental difference is that of purpose. *The purpose of research is to reveal new knowledge; the purpose of problem solving is to solve an immediate problem in a particular setting.* The fact that knowledge obtained through research may contribute to the solution of a problem, or that an exercise in problem

solving may reveal a new knowledge applicable beyond the immediate problem, does not alter the validity of this fundamental difference. Many process differences between research and problem solving may be noted, but these vary with each situation cited, whereas the fundamental difference is constant and applies in all situations.

Some of the process differences may be identified by considering the elements essential to research and noting the nature and degree of differences of parallel elements in problem solving.

RESEARCH

All elements of a scientific inquiry must be explicitly and precisely described.

Where research data are quantitative or quantifiable, they are analyzed with appropriate statistical procedures.

Elaborate pains are taken to control for factors other than the variable under study.

A primary aim is to ensure that findings are generalizable to a population larger than the one subject to study.

The search for new knowledge through

PROBLEM SOLVING

The same explicitness and precision, though they may be utilized, are not usually demanded of problem solving.

Detailed statistical analyses are seldom done, and quantitative data are usually limited to simple frequency counts.

Such controls are not imposed.

The primary aim is the solution of a problem existing in the population being studied; addresses little or no attention to whether findings may be expected to apply to a larger population.

The facts for the investigation are always

hypothesis testing must be done in a setting and with study subjects different from those which gave rise to the observations that prompted the study and hypotheses (lest there be circularity: from problem, to evidence, to "proof").	gathered in the same setting and from many of the same subjects that gave rise to the proposal that the study be done.
Entails a plan written in sufficient detail and explicitness that the study may be replicated and the findings verified.	Entails no such requirements.

Research adds the dimension of discovery to PRESEARCH. Discovering unknown factors that contribute to a problem situation is extremely helpful to the problem solver. This dimension often simplifies, facilitates, or guides the solution-seeking process. While it is unnecessary for every complex problem-solving situation, there are times when the problem solver needs the kind of information that only research can produce. Two examples follow, one hypothetical and one actual, to illustrate the use of research within the problem-solving framework.

HYPOTHETICAL CASE: POSTOPERATIVE RESPIRATORY INFECTIONS

A journal article entitled "Research, a logical problem-solving method" by Bradley J. Manuel demonstrates how investigative research provides information for the problem solver.[2] Manuel's article offers a hypothetical case where an increasing number of patients experience postoperative respiratory infections. The infection control nurse has eliminated all variables except inhalation anesthesia with intubation. She determines that all of the anesthesia equipment is sterile and disposable except the laryngoscopes and blades. These are cleaned with a germicidal solution. After reviewing the literature this nurse sets up a research study, dividing the patients into an experimental and a control group. The patients in each group are assumed to be "basically healthy and free from infections preoperatively." For the experimental group the laryngoscopes and blades are terminally sterilized before use. For the control group the existing cleaning procedure is used. The methodology includes culturing the laryngoscope blades and examining the patients in both groups for signs of respiratory infections at 48 and 72 hours postoperatively. The patients with respiratory infections are cultured and the results compared with the laryngoscope cultures. The bacterial counts on the sterilized and clean laryngoscopes are compared also. The results are reported in numbers of postoperative respiratory infection cases, the infection rate, and comparable colony counts.

This hypothetical case represents preliminary data gathering in a problem-solving effort. Should such a study reveal a significant association between the "clean" laryngoscope blades and the incidence of postoperative respiratory infections in the control group, further investigation would be needed. PRESEARCH would require additional data gathering by:

- monitoring the instrument washing techniques of the workers,
- determining if the germicide is being used according to the manufacturer's recommendations, and
- determining how the instruments are being processed and where they are placed after washing until the time of use.

If there is a decision to use terminal sterilization for these instruments, examples of questions that will need to be addressed before instituting the revised procedure are:

Who will be responsible for writing the new procedure, obtaining interdepartmental cooperation and getting the new procedure approved?

Who will determine the number of laryngoscopes and blades needed to implement the new procedure?

Who will be responsible for proposing a budget revision?

Who will be responsible for revising the cost analysis of the operating room charges?

Who will be responsible for conducting a followup study or audit as a quality assurance measure?

These questions are examples that demonstrate that there are multiple components to consider in a problem-solving action plan. Although the research findings may form the base from which an action plan is launched, the research does not solve the problem by itself.

AN ACTUAL RESEARCH PROJECT

The following project was conducted by Catherine Marienau, director, University Without Walls, University of Minnesota, and Karla M. Klinger, program director, Morris Learning Center/UWW, University of Minnesota. It demonstrates the effective use of bonafide research to gather data within the PRESEARCH model. The remainder of this chapter is a reproduction of their paper which was presented to an adult education research conference on April 20 through 22, 1977 in Minneapolis, Minnesota. This research on educational barriers of adults at the postsecondary level focused on the perceptions of an adult population in west central Minnesota. The authors used an anthropological research approach in their investigation. The application of anthropological methodology is illustrated through a description of the research, an interpretation of the findings, and the application of these findings within a specific postsecondary program. Their paper represents their joint authorship throughout.

AN ANTHROPOLOGICAL APPROACH TO THE STUDY OF EDUCATIONAL BARRIERS OF ADULTS AT THE POSTSECONDARY LEVEL

Conceptual Framework

By way of providing a conceptual framework for the barrier research, we wish to first view educational barriers of adults in relationship to the broader scope of adults' access to education. Hence we briefly considered certain conditions influencing adults' access to education and the attention which had been given to research in this area.

American society supports the notions that education is the privilege and obligation of youth; that work and family management are the responsibilities of adulthood; and that retirement and leisure are events withheld for the aged. Educationally minded adults often confront this "segmented life"[3] phenomenon in their attempts to gain access to educational institutions that respond only minimally to the needs of society's age and role–defined populations.

Education has even more challenging responsibilities with regard to providing access for an adult population. Today's generation of adults is faced with managing a culture that is different *in kind* from the one originally transmitted to them.[4]

Adults who seek access to education as a means of responding and adapting to cultural changes experience serious institutional restrictions. They confront educational systems that are confining in time, space, and youth-oriented traditions. The personal, professional, and social needs adults bring to educational institutions differ from those of the favored youth population; yet their needs are often peripheral to the main functions of the institution. The complex, dynamic culture in which we live continues, however, to exert great pressures on education to develop a capacity within each individual to learn, to change, and to create a new culture throughout his or her lifespan.[5]

These dominating conditions pose complex problems concerning adults' access to education that need to be investigated from a variety of perspectives and methodologies. The most prevalent approach to the access question has been to investigate the ways in which adults participate in institution-sponsored educational offerings. Various studies have produced findings concerning adults' subject interests, their preferred modes of study, and their selection of institutional settings.

While continued research in this area was needed, the issue of adults' access to education also needed to be investigated with respect to those conditions that prohibit adults from participating in postsecondary education. The question of educational barriers has typically been a minor factor under investigation within quantitative studies primarily concerned with the adult participation issue. Thus, the findings concerning educational barriers have been limited to defining categories of barriers.

In the well-known 1965 national study of adult learners, Johnstone and Rivera identified two main categories of barriers: (1) situational (influences external to the individual's control) and, (2) dispositional (individual's personal attitudes toward participation).[6] Another national study in 1974, sponsored by the Educational Testing Service, explored what reasons respondents "felt were important in keeping them from learning what they want to learn."[7] Using Johnstone's taxonomy, this study identified primarily situational barriers. Geographically restricted surveys of adults' participation in postsecondary education in Wisconsin (1973)[8] and in California (1975)[9] also reported situational and dispositional types of barriers.

While evidence of this type supports the existence of educational barriers of adults, it is limited in its application to understanding the needs of an adult population and ways in which institutions might effectively respond. The research presented here on educational barriers stemmed from our attempts to extend university offerings to adults in a particular geographic area.

Barrier Research Context

The Morris Learning Center (MLC), located 150 miles due west of Minneapolis in west central Minnesota farmland is the University of Minnesota's response to adult learners who are often geographically isolated both from the Morris campus and from access to educational opportunities at the undergraduate level. The Center offers the University Without Walls (UWW) external baccalaureate degree option, and, since 1975, has also sought to provide course opportunities through other external delivery systems.

Most of the people who responded in 1974 to the publicity about the pilot UWW program had educational barriers such as jobs and family responsibilities. We were able to identify their barriers and to categorize them. However, we soon found that knowing what the barriers were did not tell us what the barriers meant, or how barriers functioned in peoples' lives, or under what circumstances they might be overcome. We wondered why two students with seemingly identical barriers made opposite programmatic decisions. We also were puzzled about how the adult's own perceptions of barriers contributed to determining whether that adult decided to participate in educational opportunities.

As the Morris Learning Center proposed to broaden its services, it became increasingly important to explore the field of uncertainty. We believed that understanding the range and function of barriers from the adult perspective would help us (at the MLC) make long-range plans to serve the same adults more effectively. We were interested in obtaining data that would give us an indication of how we might design the program further to make it more responsive to adult students. Therefore we designed a research project because we believed it was necessary to continue to rely only on our perceptions formed by our experiences with adult students. While we had intended to use the data from the research to feed into the on-going operations of the program, it did prove useful in the summative evaluations of the main UWW program. As is often the case, the data resulting from research into a particular problem also had utility within a broader context.

Methodology

While previous studies provided data concerning the types of educational barriers adults face, the data did not address the kinds of questions we were asking about adults' perceptions of the range and functions of barriers to continuing education. We determined that the commonly used quantitative, standard-response approach was not suited for investigating this field of uncertainty.

We applied several criteria in selecting methodology that would be compatible with the aims of the research. The first criterion was that the data should be influenced as little as possible by our biases as adult educators and, instead, should reflect the perspectives of the adult population. Second, the data should be analyzed not only to define categories of barriers, but also to identify the relationships of their variables and the influences of those variables upon the adult learner's participation in education. Finally, the data should be communicated in a form to provide direction for programming possibilities for adult learners in the Morris Learning Center region.

We selected methods often used in anthropological fieldwork as meeting these basic criteria. Three anthropological fieldwork methods were applied in the study, involving selection of the research sample, data collection, and data analysis. Our basic approach was to explore a range of questions with the research population concerning barriers to education and to allow patterns to emerge which would increase our understanding of the problems as experienced by the adult learner.

Research Sample Selection

The first anthropological fieldwork method used was to establish a referral network through which we identified the research population. We wanted the research population to include two main groups of adult learners: (1) those who were already engaged in educational pursuits, and (2) those who were interested in continuing their education but who were not yet participants.

We chose students enrolled in the University Without Walls program to represent the group of adults who had faced barriers to continuing their education and had overcome the barriers to participate in a degree program. The UWW students served as primary informants by providing names and addresses of people in their respective communities whom they knew to have expressed interest in continuing their education in some way beyond the high school level.

These secondary informant referrals, in turn, provided us with additional contacts, through which we eventually established four referral networks. The secondary informants identified through the referral networks were formally requested to participate in the study and were selected according to their availability for interviews and their geographic representation of the area.

The total research population consisted of 12 primary informants who were engaged in a degree program and 30 secondary informants who were interested in participating in educational activities. While the number of secondary informants was somewhat arbitrarily determined, we could have enlarged the sample had preliminary data analysis not revealed consistent patterns of responses.

Data Collection

The second method drawn from anthropological fieldwork was the ethnographic collection of data through in-depth personal interviews. We designed an interview schedule for primary informants that included seven open-ended questions. Each main question was followed by a series of five to ten probe questions that were used to assist the informant in expanding upon his or her responses to the open-ended question. The primary informant interviews were conducted by either the principal investigator or the MLC director.

Based on our experiences in using the interview schedule on a preliminary analysis of the informant's responses, we designed an adapted interview schedule for the secondary informants. The majority of these interviews were conducted by three university undergraduates, each of whom first participated in a week-long training session.

The majority of the interviews with both informant groups occurred some 60 miles from main headquarters in the informant's home or work place. In order to reduce time and travel expenses, we often traveled in pairs to a given community, each scheduled with a full day of interviewing. The interviews lasted from 1–1½ hours, during which time the interviewer hand recorded the informant's responses using the "key word or key phrase" method. This technique requires the interviewer to selectively record the informant's main expressions concerning an attitude, idea, action, event, or person in response to a given question. Since the interview notes were the only data source, the interviewer had to allow time immediately after each interview to add full detail to the notes.

Data Analysis

The third anthropological technique was drawn from ethnoscience[10] and applied during the phase of data analysis. Through this technique, the raw data from the informant interview notes were manipulated through a complex process involving data organization and content analysis. For purposes of clarity, the process will be presented as consisting of six stages, with each stage representing an increased level of meaning from the data.

It should be recognized that the data remain basically in control of the informants during all stages of the analysis process. It should also be noted that the data move from increasing levels of specification to a level of generalization during the six-stage process. For example, in stages one, two, and three, the raw data are being worked toward specification; in stage four, the data from both informant groups are integrated, promoting a move toward generalization in stage five. Finally, in stage six, the data are formed into the final level of generalization.

The first stage involved organizing the raw data within a very general organizational framework. The 42 sets of interview notes were separated into primary and secondary informant groups. Each set of interview notes was studied to identify key words and key phrases expressed by the informant. These data were organized under the general headings of the open-ended interview questions.

The second stage involved working with the data as organized under very general headings to form natural categories of responses. During this process, similar key responses were identified and grouped together to form response patterns. Categories were derived from the general theme expressed in each grouping. For example, from the open-ended question concerning the informant's "process of deciding about continuing his or her education," two categories were formed: "How barriers are perceived" and "How barriers might be overcome."

The third stage involved establishing subcategories of responses. The data within the preceding response categories were analyzed further to uncover specific patterns of responses. These response patterns were then analyzed to form specific subcategories of responses. The general category of "How barriers are perceived" was further specified into such categories as "family responsibilities," "time," "finances," "access," and so forth.

The data from the primary and secondary informant groups were analyzed separately during the first three stages. In order to establish relationships between the two groups and to discover their similarities and dissimilarities, a fourth stage was added to the process. In this stage, both general and specific categories of responses were compared between informant groups and were found to be nearly identical. At this point, the categories were integrated to represent the total research population.

During the fifth stage, the process began to move out of the specification level to a more general level. In this process, the specific response patterns under each category were analyzed to uncover relationships between categories. For example, the responses in the categories of "family responsibilities" and "time" were found to contain similar variables, thus forming a relationship between the two categories. Based on the relationships identified between categories, it was then possible to draw inferences with respect to the informants' perceptions of various issues addressed in the interviews.

In the sixth and final stage, generalizations were formulated concerning the nature of the barriers adult learners face in continuing their education and the circumstances through which these barriers can be overcome.

One such generalization, for example, was that barriers are derived from two sources: from the situations people face and from the particular value orientations held by individuals.

While this particular method of data analysis requires painstaking attention to detail and permits no short cuts with respect to time, it has proven highly effective as a means to elicit how participants in a given culture structure their own meanings of critical issues.

By using an anthropologically based approach to the barrier research, adult learners were allowed to participate actively in all key aspects of the research. They were engaged in the selection of the research population, in the identification of the important research issues, and in the interpretation of the data which they directly supplied. In addition, the voices of the adults were distinctly conveyed in the final research results. In the barrier research report, each pattern or significant finding was accompanied by representative verbatim responses from the informants. In this way, adult learners were able to speak to a wide audience about issues directly influencing their access to continuing education. In the following section of this paper, we will present the main findings of the research and their application to programs serving an adult clientele.

Research Findings

The Participants

The research population derived through the network sampling technique included 42 adults who had already expressed an interest in continuing their education. Most of them had completed nearly two years of prior postsecondary education and had participated in frequent informal learning experiences. All had faced barriers to continuing their education.

The 12 primary informants in Group I were engaged in a degree program. Eleven were enrolled in UWW/Morris, a program specifically designed to overcome barriers. The 30 secondary informants in Group II were not currently enrolled in a program but had expressed an interest either in nondegree options or in obtaining a baccalaureate degree.[11]

Biographic data obtained as an initial part of the interview process showed that most of the 42 research participants were town dwellers, Minnesota born, and long-time residents of the region. Most were married with children living at home. Over half were between 25 and 34 years old, with the age span extending from 20 through the late 50s. With two exceptions from Group II, all participants were Caucasian.[12] Because the referrals made through the network sampling technique were predominantly female, the participation of adult learners in this study was 80 percent female and 20 percent male.[13]

The participants themselves provided data directly about their educational goals and about the circumstances that made them difficult to achieve. The seven main discussion questions[14] focused on the subjects' formal and informal educational involvement and goals, the decision-making process affecting their educational participation, their membership-making process affecting their educational participation, their membership in families and larger social groups, their familiarity with existing educational institutions and opportunities, and their perspectives toward education and learning.

The Barrier Components

The chart following[15] lists the barriers identified by the people interviewed in the order of the frequency with which each was discussed by the two groups. The barriers identified by Group I (those engaged in a degree program) and Group II (those interested in, but not pursuing, learning options) were found to be identical in name, nearly identical in makeup, and to differ only slightly in the ordering of their significance.[16]

Barriers Identified by Sample Population	Frequency of Response	
	Group I	Group II
1) Access to Educational Facilities	all group	+ ½ group
2) Family Responsibilities	½ group	½ group
3) Finances	¾ group	− ½ group
4) Time	¾ group	+ ⅓ group
5) Motivation	⅓ group	+ ⅓ group

In the sections that follow, the components of the barriers identified by the people interviewed, together with their reports of how barriers functioned within their lives, are discussed. In addition, generalizations will be drawn from the data with their implications for adult educators including the Morris Learning Center staff. As in the original report, the adult learners will, as far as it is possible, speak for themselves.

In an attempt to suggest the process of data analysis used throughout this research, representative sample responses from the interviews will be presented that illustrate how categories and relationships emerged.

Barrier No. 1: Access to Educational Facilities. West Central Minnesota hosts some 17 postsecondary educational institutions. Seven grant the baccalaureate degree, two grant the associate of arts degree, and eight are vocational-technical schools.

All of Group I and slightly more than half of Group II identified access as a barrier. Sample responses from the interviews[17] included the follow-

ing: "The schools don't offer courses on what I need to take." . . .
"There are not really that many classes available around here. Those we
get have to be brought here by a college." . . . "In order to enter the
special RN program for a BS in nursing, I must first complete 45 college
credits, but they won't accept my nursing credits. How do I do this at my
age? The opportunities to do it aren't available here. I'd have to sell my
home, give up a good job—that's what I see as a barrier."

Based on statements like these, the lack of access to educational
facilities was found to have two meanings to the people interviewed: first,
that the institutions within the area did not offer the type of curriculum,
course, or program that was needed; or second, that access to the kinds of
programs desired was at too great a distance.

Barrier No. 2: Family Responsibilities. Those members of the population with families usually functioned within the family as parents. Respondents said: "My children are too small and until they go to nursery
school they must have babysitters. I can't ask my husband regularly to
care for the children." . . . "My family is very important—they come
first." . . . "If I did go to school, how would I support myself and the kids
and maintain a house?"

For half of each group, family responsibilities function as a barrier to
educational participation (1) because of the age of the children, (2) because the family was placed at a higher priority than education, and (3)
because money required for education was felt to be needed for the support of the family.[18]

Barrier No. 3: Finances. For three-fourths of Group I and slightly less
than half of Group II, finances presented a barrier to continuing education. We were told: "Going to school is financially inhibiting. I would
need a grant." . . . "I must keep employed. I have a wife and four kids. I
can't stop everything and go back to school." and "I had never spent too
much money on myself before. I had to be pretty certain it would pay for
itself."

Responses such as these revealed that to the population sampled, a
financial barrier included: (1) money for tuition, (2) the need to maintain
employment, and (3) the use of finances for the benefit of the family.[19]

Barrier No. 4: Time. Time as a barrier to continuing education was
referred to by three-fourths of Group I and by slightly more than one-third
of Group II. For example, a woman in Group I said, "I really had to
consider the time factor—I knew I'd still be doing all the housework and
be responsible for the kids. I really didn't feel I could manage the time to
attend classes." A Group II woman said, "Kids need the security of
having family around. You must learn to sacrifice when you have kids."

Both groups needed "time to devote to school" and "time to spend with family" and spoke about the problem of scheduling between the two.

Group II members identified a third factor—the need to spend time on the job. "My job requires a great deal of attention. I don't want to spread myself too thin."[20]

Barrier No. 5: Motivation. One-third of both groups identified motivation as a problem. Group I, most of whom were pursuing degrees, saw motivation as a potential barrier rather than as an actual deterrent. One said, "You need a high degree of self-motivation. You have to seriously question—is it just a whim? You must have the discipline to keep at it, speaking from experience. You figure out your priorities and you stick to them."

Group II spoke of a lack of self-discipline and an inability to set priorities. For example: "I'm not sure I could adapt. I'm not sure I have the study skills to cope with that. I'm groping and I really need direction." . . . "I've put things off because I felt other things were priority."[21] Motivation functioned as a barrier because of a lack of self-discipline or because of an inability to set priorities.

Relationships among the Barriers

The people interviewed had identified and defined five educational barriers along with those factors that contributed to their functioning. The data had been ordered into groups and the responses had been integrated to establish the barrier categories. The first phase of data organization was complete. The second phase, that of data content analysis, involved identifying relationships among the patterns of responses. Through this analysis two distinct relationships among the barriers emerged which added to the complexity of each individual's situation.

First, we found that over two-thirds of the participants reported the presence of two or more barriers. The two barriers that each participant was likely to face at a minimum were "access to educational facilities" and "family responsibilities." Second, we found that the barriers were intricately related to one another. While each barrier had distinguishable characteristics, the characteristics were sometimes indistinct because of the close relationships between the barriers.

For example, the most frequently mentioned barrier, "access to educational facilities," was found to be linked with "finances" and/or "family responsibilities." Gaining access to educational offerings at a distance might take time away from the family or require someone to "give up a good job."

Similarly, "family responsibilities" was not only a barrier in itself, but appeared as a subpoint of both the "finances" and "time" barriers. The barrier "family responsibilities" was found to be linked with *all* of the other barriers. Families were found to influence the use of time, make demands on the use of finances, affect motivation, and act as a major force of support for or hindrance to access to educational facilities.[22]

The financial barrier was linked to family responsibilities because money used for educational purposes might mean "no bike for Christmas" or "my wife having to work." The "time" barrier was linked with finances because time must be spent "on the job" in order to "support myself and my family."

Generalizations

Once the intricate relationships between the barriers were clear, it was possible to formulate generalizations based upon the patterns that had emerged. We had set out to explore how the adults' own perceptions of barriers contributed to the decisions they made about educational participation. The generalizations, based on the data, explained the derivation of barriers and the circumstances in which they might be overcome.

Generalization I: *Barriers are derived from two sources: they are derived from the situations people face and from the particular value orientations of the people themselves.*

" 'Values' are viewed as those elements of one's life which have high priority, i.e., the important things in life as perceived by the population studied."[23]

Although none of the barriers could be isolated as being solely situational or solely value-related, the "access" barrier and "financial" barrier stood out as highly situational.

For example, access is determined in part by where someone lives and in part by the availability of programs at the appropriate level in that geographic region. Attendance at educational institutions costs tuition money at a minimum. "Most people are not in the position to give up their full-time jobs to return to school."[24]

The barrier of "time" involved both situational and value-related elements. A certain amount of time is controlled by employment, child care, and other commitments. The problem of deciding to devote time to school or of scheduling between the demands of home and school is influenced by values.

Both "family responsibilities" and "motivation" were barriers containing strong value orientations. For example, a woman in Group I who "for years put my family first" had finally decided to pursue a degree because

"I need to set priorities for myself. The family can adjust to me this time."
In direct contrast were several women in Group II who were not pursuing
their education because of family priorities. "My family is very
important—they come first." Their allegiance to their families is such
that other things—an education—are viewed as something less than first
priority.[25]

Generalization II: *Value-related barriers require personal readjustments by the adult learner.*

The decision of whether or not a barrier can be overcome is often a
matter of individual value. The adult female who has determined that she
may not go back to school until the children are in school is not likely to
enroll until her situation changes and her children are in school. A person
in need of greater self-discipline, reordered priorities, or a sense of security about her goals will not enroll until those problems can be solved.
Group I enrolled students spoke of having to "put my family on a tighter
schedule," having "less time for my family," and asking them "to help
around the house." They had made readjustments in their personal family
lives in order to work toward a degree.[26]

Most Group II people, though also valuing education, were not yet
ready to make readjustments either because other competing values held
a higher priority or because their situations had not been changed.

Generalization III: *Situational barriers have the potential to be overcome by external sources.*

The barrier research had established that barriers can be created potentially from both external and internal sources and are likely to contain
elements from both sources. External sources would be situational factors
such as those represented in the barriers "access to educational facilities"
and "finances."[27] Barriers that are largely situational hold the greatest
promise of being overcome by external sources.

For Group I students "access to educational facilities" was overcome
through the structure of the UWW program which made it possible for
them to pursue a baccalaureate program in their home or job environment
without moving away from either. For many Group II students the UWW
program was not found to be appropriate, either because of the type of
degree program they hoped to pursue, the level of the program desired, or
because they sought nondegree options. Therefore the barrier remained.

Implications for Adult Educators

"External sources" capable of overcoming educational barriers clearly
include the educational institutions which offer programs to adults. The
adult learners, through in-depth interviews, revealed their educational

needs, interests, and barriers, offered direction to educational institutions serving adults.

Following are characteristics of the adult learners we interviewed and a corresponding problem list which was considered by the adult educators:

Characteristics	Problem Statements
1. Most of the population studied had interests that were professionally related.[28]	How can the educators develop and offer accessible courses and degree routes that relate educational resources to professional interests?
2. Because of their commitment to their families, jobs, and home ownership, adult learners need classes provided within their communities at convenient times.	How can educators bring educational resources to the community rather than requiring adult learners primarily to come on campus?[29]
3. Adult learners distinguish between learning—an internal occurrence—and education, which they link to external sources.[30] They typically have educational experiences gained through both formal and experiential settings.[31]	How can educators acknowledge the range of experiences adults bring to the formal academic setting while providing programs and courses that merge informal learning with a formal education?[32]
4. Adult learners assign similar values to an educated person and to a successful person. They are interested in application of education to their daily lives.[33]	How can educators provide education so that it is more readily consumed within the course of daily living?[34]
5. Adult learners, even those with clearly expressed educational goals, conduct limited investigations into edu-	How can educators evaluate existing publicity and promotional efforts while establishing communication links among sources of

Characteristics	Problem Statements
cational opportunities and have limited knowledge of existing area educational institutions.[35]	educational information within the community?[36]
6. Value barriers are the most difficult for adults to overcome.	How can educators provide services that assist adults to establish educational goals and set priorities?[37]

In designing the barrier research, we had sought to use methodology which would supply information that could be applied to actual programming problem solving for adult learners in West Central Minnesota. In this final section, we would like to comment briefly on the application of the barrier research to the programs offered through the Morris Learning Center.

For the Morris Learning Center staff, the barrier research provided a conceptual framework for programmatic decisions and the setting of priorities. We have made a greater effort to publicize available short-term external learning options such as independent correspondence study. We have also designed new ways to make on-campus courses available to off-campus students, such as audio taping course lectures while they are given. Whenever possible, we now take information sessions about educational opportunities to outlying areas rather than holding them only on campus, and our publicity efforts are on-going. We have established communication links with other postsecondary schools in the area and hope within the near future to coordinate our services regionally.

Perhaps the most significant contribution of the barrier research has been the greater understanding that we now bring to our advising. Within the context of the barrier research, we view each request for information as an important event. We no longer are surprised that adults know so little about the learning options available to them. We provide whatever assistance we can with on-campus procedures.

It is not unusual for our staff to talk with prospective students infrequently over a period of years about what they might do "someday." With the help of the barrier research, we have come to understand why there is so often a time gap between the interest that is expressed in educational opportunities and registration in a specific learning option. Statements by adults introduced by "When my youngest goes to school . . ." or "Maybe the year after next . . ." are projections rather than statements of evasion. The time gap is explained by values and in no way diminishes that adult's commitment to education. Given the responsibilities of adults and the inaccessibility of programs for them, the adult commitment to learning often extending over a period of years is indeed impressive. In planning college programs with individual adults, discussing their values provides a time frame in which to plan or delineates a period of waiting in which to provide support.

The 42 participants in the barrier research shared with us their educational aspirations. Within the context of their individual situations, they are proponents of lifelong learning. All of them faced obstacles which either prevented them or slowed them down in their efforts to obtain an education. Their commitment to education, like that of many others who contact the Learning Center, is high enough to warrant belief in their willingness to carry out their goals given the opportunity to do so.[38] We see our role as adult advocates who try to locate or to provide that opportunity.

The barrier research raised other questions of access in addition to those that it helped us answer. It has told us about a special group of adults in a rural setting in west central Minnesota. How representative of this region are the 42 people with whom we spoke? What are the differences in access problems between degree and nondegree seekers? To what extent does what we learned apply in other geographic regions or in urban settings? What especially are women's perceptions of the patterns, goals, and barriers they face as they re-enter postsecondary education? These are some of the unanswered questions that call for further exploration.

CONCLUSION

Although the research raised other unanswered questions, it helped us state our immediate problems in such a way that we were able to take action. It gave us direction and a data base from which to operate. Thus, we were able to deal with the immediate problems from a position of strength. Our strength was knowledge of perceptions about educational barriers from an adult population sample in west central Minnesota.

NOTES

1. Mabel Wandelt, *A Guide for the Beginning Researcher* (New York: Appleton-Century-Crofts, 1970), pp. xvii–xviii.
2. Bradley J. Manuel, "Research, A Logical Problem-solving Method," *Association of Operating Room Nurses Journal,* January 1978, pp. 56–61.

3. James O'Toole, "Education, Work and Quality of Life," in Dyckman Vermile, ed., *Lifelong Learners—A New Clientele for Higher Education* (San Francisco, Calif.: Jossey-Bass, 1974), p. 13.

4. Gale Jensen, A. A. Liveright, and Wilbur Hallenbeck, eds., *Adult Education: Outlines of an Emerging Field of University Study* (Adult Education Association of the U.S.A., 1964), p. iv.

5. Malcom Knowles, *Higher Adult Education in the United States* (Washington, D.C.: American Council on Education, 1969), p. 23.

6. John W. C. Johnstone and Ramon J. Rivera, *Volunteers for Learning* (Chicago, Ill.: Aldine Publishing Company, 1965), p. 214.

7. See, supra note 4, pp. 214–215.

8. *Southeast Adult Education Study*, Survey Report No. 1 (May) and No. 6 (June) (Division of Program and Staff Development, University of Wisconsin, 1973).

9. Richard E. Peterson and J. B. Lon Hefferlin, *Postsecondary Alternatives to Meet the Educational Needs of California's Adults*, Final Report, Prepared for the California State Legislature (Sacramento, California, 1975).

10. Ethnoscience is defined as "a mode of eliciting, in a rigorous way, the means by which a culture structures meaning for the participants in that culture," in Raoul Naroll and Ronald Cohen, eds., *A Handbook of Method in Cultural Anthropology* (New York: Columbia University Press, 1970), p. 11.

11. Catherine Marienau, Unpublished report, "Study of Barriers to Participation in Postsecondary Education as Perceived by Adults In West Central Minnesota" (Morris Learning Center, Continuing Education and Regional Programs, University of Minnesota, Morris, January 1976), p. 12.

12. See, supra note 9, p. 14.

13. See, supra note 9, pp. 75–77.

14. See, supra note 9, p. iv–ix.

15. See, supra note 9, p. 25.

16. See, supra note 9, p. 24.

17. See, supra note 9, pp. 25–26.

18. See, supra note 9, pp. 27–28.

19. See, supra note 9, pp. 28–30.

20. See, supra note 9, pp. 30–32.

21. See, supra note 9, pp. 32, 33.

22. See, supra note 9, pp. 59–60.

23. See, supra note 9, p. 61.

24. See, supra note 9, p. 63.

25. See, supra note 9, p. 62.

26. See, supra note 9, pp. 67–68.

27. See, supra note 9, p. 69.

28. See, supra note 9, p. 70.

29. See, supra note 9, p. 88.

30. See, supra note 9, p. 79.

31. See, supra note 9, p. 73.

32. See, supra note 9, p. 87.

33. See, supra note 9, pp. 71–73.

34. See, supra note 9, p. 87.

35. See, supra note 9, p. 82.

36. See, supra note 9, p. 86.

37. See, supra note 9, p. 87.

38. See, supra note 9, p. 83.

Planned Change Theory in PRESEARCH

The purpose of this chapter is to discuss the integration of *planned change theory in PRESEARCH*. In an earlier chapter research was compared to problem solving. The theory of planned change will not be compared to problem solving; quite the contrary, for it permeates the entire process. In PRESEARCH, planned change theory is analogous to the warp on a weaver's loom. In a sense, the problem solver weaves the fabric of solution. Each weaver chooses color and texture based on prior experiences, level of expertise, perceived use of the finished product, and available resources. The fabric produced by the novice weaver can be beautiful, interesting, and utilitarian. As the expertise of the weaver increases, the predictability of a useful finished product increases also. As the weaver learns to use the loom, the weaver and the loom become partners in a process. So it is with problem solvers who learn to use the tools of planned change theory. They too, enter a partnership.

One of the reasons for emphasizing planned change in health care administration is to equip the manager with useful theoretical tools. For change is indeed present in any work environment. As an observer and a consultant, I became keenly aware that health care managers can become inundated with problems. They may neither have the time nor energy to plan thoroughly the change that will result from a significant action. Because planned change theory infiltrates PRESEARCH, it offers the practicing manager a vehicle for involving others. Involvement of the work group is essential in planned change. PRESEARCH provides a framework that actively involves the client system. It permits the change agent (manager) to include the client system (work group) as an intricate part of the entire change process. With this concept, the change agent expands and multiplies the ability to influence the total client system. In essence, a select portion of the client system becomes an extension of the change agent. Together they are involved in a problem-solving process.

In an article entitled "Managing Change Creatively" Barbara Spradley presents a brief discussion of change theory and principles.[1] Within the theoretical perspective she identified the chief principles of planned change as:

- interdependence of systems and subsystems,
- homeostasis, the maintenance of equilibrium,
- opposing forces, the constraints and capabilities of an organization, and
- resistance to accept change.

Each of these principles is highlighted in chapters within this volume. Interdependency of systems and subsystems exists in all health care institutions. Chapter 18 describes conceptual models that depict the interrelatedness of systems within an organization. The change agent can use these graphic illustrations to explain relationships of systems and subsystems. An understanding of systems theory and the ability to create line drawings that depict a concept can be extremely useful in problem solving. Figure 18-1 offers a clear explanation of how internal and external decisions affect direct patient care.

Throughout Part I of this book the field of uncertainty was described as an out-of-balance situation. Homeostasis is the tendency of an organization to restore equilibrium. It is reasonable to conclude that when disequilibrium exists the timing is right for introducing change. When the manager does not intercede as a change agent, the organization will find its own equilibrium. An example of a system within which informal procedures replaced the formal ones can be found in the first portion of Chapter 15. In this instance the subsystems replaced an overly complex procedure with what they viewed as "workable." One of the crucial aspects of evaluation and followup is to assure that homeostasis has occurred and that acceptable practices are being followed.

A discussion of planned change theory is hardly complete without Kurt Lewin's classic model that shows an organization's driving forces in opposition to the restraining forces. When the driving and resisting forces have stabilized in undesirable practice, it may be necessary for the change agent to create disequilibrium in order to introduce change.

In Chapter 13, which discussed administrative decision making, an example was given that showed the interdependence of systems and subsystems. It also exemplified a situation that is viewed as a problem for one department and that works quite well for two others. In order for beneficial change to occur for the department experiencing difficulty, the driving forces from the nursing department were increased and the resisting forces from the personnel and accounting departments were decreased. This resulted in a few slight changes that allowed system equilibrium to be restored. Although the change was not of great magnitude, it converted several time consuming tasks to more efficient ones.

Resistance to change is presented by every author who discusses planned change theory. In *Nursing Management*, the Ganongs state that "People don't resist change as much as they resist being changed by others."[2] A typical example of people resisting change was presented in Chapter 14. The interview responses obtained by Adriane Weaver reflect how the various members of the client system were reacting to a proposed change.

Aside from change itself, there are two other major aspects of planned change theory:

- the change agent—the manager
- the client system—those affected by change.

A positive trusting relationship between the change agent and the system is the single most important factor for successful implementation of the desired change. PRESEARCH is people centered; it stresses client system involvement early in the process. It emphasizes a helping relationship between the change agent and the client system; the problem statements all begin, "How can we (management) help facilitate return to balance?"

Donald Klein has emphasized the importance of involving members of the client system:

> Few expert planners in any field are prepared to believe that their clients can be equipped to collaborate with them as equals. What can the lay person add to the knowledge and the rationality of the technical expert? And is it not true that the process of involving the client would only serve to slow down if not derail the entire undertaking? The result is that each planning project proceeds without taking the time to involve those who will be affected by the planning until such a point when it is necessary to gain the client's consent. And if decisions can be made and implementation secured without involving his public, the planner's job is greatly simplified.
>
> It is little wonder, therefore, that planners typically do not engage in collaborative planning with clients on specific projects. It is costly, time consuming, irritating, frustrating, and even risky.

However, the failure of planners to work collaboratively with those for whom they plan contributes to a well-known American mistrust of the highly trained, academically grounded expert. Under the most benign circumstances, the client may be skeptical of the planner's recommendations. Given any real threat to livelihood or position, or given any feared reduction in integrity, clients' skepticism may be replaced by mistrust of the planners' motives and open hostility towards them.

The motives of the innovators are especially apt to be suspect when the planning process has been kept secret up until the time of unveiling the plans and action recommendations. By this time the innovators usually have worked up a considerable investment in their plans, and are often far more committed to defending them than to attempting to understand objections to them. They are not prepared to go through once again with the newcomers the long process of planning which finally led them to their conclusions. And they are hardly in the most favorable position to entertain consideration of new social data or of alternative solutions which might be recommended on the basis of such information. The result often is that opposition to the recommended change hardens and even grows as the ultimate clients sense that their reactions will not materially influence the outcome in any way short of defeating the plan in open conflict.[3]

Undoubtedly, Donald Klein's comments address experiences each of us has had in the innovator role. A change, no matter how clever, creative, or beneficial can meet abrupt resistance. This is more likely to occur when a representative sample of the client system has not been included in the planning. Granted it does take more time, more patience, and involves risk. Nevertheless, when members of the client system are involved they develop a sense of ownership and have a vested interest in the outcome. This is much less risky than trying to sell a plan into which the work group had no input. Lippitt writes in *The Dynamics of Planned Change:*

One of the most discouraging moments in many a process of change comes when resistance to change suddenly appears in an important subpart of the system. Usually the initiating subpart responds by being intensely angry or painfully disheartened. Often it seems incomprehensible to the proponents of change that this kind of resistance should occur. "Why are they resisting something that will benefit them as much as it does us?" "Can't they see that this will be an advantage to the whole community even if they have to give up a little bit?'' At such times these and similar statements are what one is likely to hear.[4]

CONCLUSION

Planned change is the purposeful effort to affect improvement. The PRESEARCH framework gives the practicing manager a way to incorporate basic principles of planned change into everyday operations. Within the PRESEARCH framework, you can delegate and expand the scope of your problem-solving capabilities. You can greatly increase your problem-solving effectiveness when your subordinates learn to use the principles of planned change theory also. This process helps you to eliminate people delivering problems to your doorstep. Instead, teach them to use PRESEARCH and they will provide you with solution proposals.

NOTES

1. Barbara W. Spradley, "Managing Change Creatively," *Journal of Nursing Administration,* May 1980, pp. 32–37.
2. Joan Ganong and Warren Ganong, *Nursing Management* (Rockville, Md.: Aspen Systems Corp., 1980), p. 278.
3. Donald Klein, "Some Notes on the Dynamics of Resistance to Change: The Defender Role," in *Concepts for Social Change* (Union, N.J.: National Training Laboratories Institute for Applied Behavioral Science, National Education Association, 1969), pp. 29–30.
4. Ronald Lippitt, Jeanne Watson, and Bruce Westley, *The Dynamics of Planned Change* (New York, N.Y.: Harcourt, Brace, Jovanovich, 1958), p. 232.

Suggested Reading List

Bennis, W. G. et al. *The Planning of Change* 3d ed. New York: Holt, Rinehart and Winston, 1976.
Claus, K., and Bailey, J. *Power and Influence in Health Care: A New Approach to Leadership.* St. Louis, Mo.: C. V. Mosby, 1977.
Lewis, K. *Field Theory in Social Science.* New York: Harper and Row Publishers, 1951.
Stevens, B. "Effecting Change," *Journal of Nursing Administration,* May 1974.
Welch, L. Ed. "The Nurse As Change Agent," *Nursing Clinics of North America,* June 1979.
Zaltman, G., and Duncan, R. *Strategies for Planned Change.* New York: John Wiley, 1977.

Chapter 18

The Use of Conceptual Models in Problem Solving

Developing a conceptual model is frequently viewed as a difficult academic exercise. When teaching PRESEARCH workshops, I have observed participants groan and indicate resistance through nonverbal communications such as squirming and exchanging bewildered glances. These responses were overcome after the audience understood that a conceptual model could help them define problems.

A conceptual model shows relationships of the various components, disciplines, and/or systems that are interrelated in the complex problem. A conceptual model helps the problem solvers to put the situation into its proper perspective. In other words, it helps the manager to allocate equitable amounts of problem-solving effort to the various components of the problem. Without a conceptual model, it is not uncommon to get trapped into placing great emphasis on the part of the problem that is making the most noise. However, the silent underlying components can later surface, if not given sufficient attention, and pose very difficult situations.

A model supplies a graphic image that can be used to stimulate discussion. Several examples are included in this chapter to demonstrate how line drawings can clarify a large volume of information and provide direction for group problem-solving process.

The first example concerns the community served by St. Joseph's Hospital, St. Paul, Minnesota.

For several years, the nursing administrative group had seriously considered studying the systems and subsystems within the hospital that related to nursing care. It was their dream to obtain a grant for a systems study in order to redefine the scope of nursing practice within that institution. In order to convey their philosophy, definitions, and project proposals, conceptual models were developed. Figure 18-1 is one of those conceptual models. It is included here as an example for it had multiple uses, including orientation of new nursing personnel. The instructors used it to

Figure 18-1 Community Served by St. Joseph's Hospital

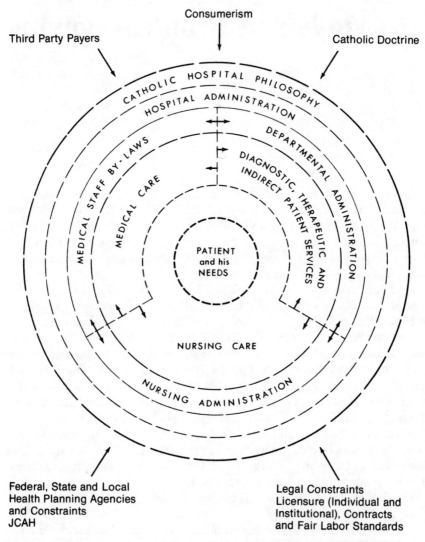

Consumerism

Third Party Payers

Catholic Doctrine

Federal, State and Local
Health Planning Agencies
and Constraints
JCAH

Legal Constraints
Licensure (Individual and
Institutional), Contracts
and Fair Labor Standards

Source: St. Joseph's Hospital, St. Paul, Minnesota. Used with permission.

supplement their explanation of the nursing and hospital philosophies. It was used with introductory remarks whenever there was need to explain significant changes occurring within the organization. It served as a reminder to the management group that both internal and external changes in the health care delivery system affect how each staff nurse delivers care to the patient.

The explanation that was provided went something like this:

This is an open systems model. The openness is represented by the broken lines. In an open system model, information from one area flows freely to the other areas. You will notice that the openness is not limited to the internal organization; external factors also impact on how care is given in any institution. At the center of the model is the patient and his needs, for truly the patient is the reason for our existence. Nursing care surrounds the patient; the nurses are with the patient 24 hours a day.

The next portion of the model signifies the physicians rendering medical care. They are in and out of the hospital, yet they influence how the nurses render care to a large degree. Diagnostic, therapeutic, and indirect patient services come in contact with the patient episodically.

The next layer is an administrative one. Medical staff bylaws, decisions made by nursing administration and other departments' administration all indirectly affect the care being rendered at the bedside. Likewise, decisions made at the hospital administration level impact all of the preceding. The Catholic hospital philosophy encompasses and pervades the organization. Beyond the walls of the hospital many factors influence the health care provided within. Among the external factors affecting patient care at St. Joseph's Hospital are:

- Third party payers: These include Medicare, Medicaid, Blue Cross–Blue Shield, Health Maintenance Organizations, and private insurance carriers. Each of these organizations has an impact on patient care because each imposes limitations in terms of reimbursement to the health care provider.
- Consumerism: Today's consumer is better informed. The Patient's Bill of Rights is posted in prominent places in the building and it is given to each patient at the time of admission. Consumers want to know more about their condition and the care being rendered to them. They have a right to make informed decisions about their health care.
- Catholic doctrine: As a member of the Catholic Hospital Association and an extension of the Catholic Church, this hospital upholds Catholic doctrine and its philosophy and day to day operation.
- Legal constraints: Included here are licensures—individual and institutional—labor contracts and fair labor standards. Certain criteria must be met in order for an institution to be licensed to operate. Each hospital has a certain number of licensed beds. A large portion of the individuals who staff a hospital must be licensed to

practice their profession. Many organizations have groups of employees who are included in union contracts and those contracts must
be honored. In addition, there are fair labor standards that govern the
number of hours per week that an individual can work, after which
overtime must be paid.

• Voluntary accreditation: The Joint Commission on Accreditation of
  Hospitals has minimal standards which must be met by each institution that chooses to participate in a voluntary accreditation process.

• Government regulations: Included here are federal, state, and local
  health planning agencies that directly and indirectly limit and control
  services provided by individual institutions.

This conceptual model serves as a gentle reminder that health care
providers have limitations. When planning for change, one must acknowledge both internal and external constraints and develop the best acceptable solutions within a given institution. This model was instrumental in
improving interdepartmental communication. After it was presented at a
department head meeting, those in attendance had a better understanding
of how decisions made in each part of the hospital influence patient care.

Another example is a model which is often referred to as a pie chart.
Figure 18-2 exemplifies percentages of activity within one hospital's
emergency room/outpatient department.

This chart was developed from factual data about an outpatient/
emergency service. A series of meetings was scheduled to determine if the
hospital should expand its emergency services aggressively to the community. In this instance the volume of unscheduled, walk-in cases had
steadily increased over a five-year period. In spite of the volume increases
in nonscheduled cases, the greatest proportion of the nurses' time on the
day shift was spent with scheduled minor surgical and endoscopy procedures. Therefore, a nurse supervisor was faced with the difficult task of
convincing a group of staff nurses that their skill levels in emergency
nursing needed to be upgraded.

Prior to the development of this conceptual model, the staff had not
been able to internalize the direction of volume expansion. They simply
felt busier and knew that they were spending large blocks of time with
scheduled cases. The model was shown on a screen with an overhead
projector in the staff nurse meeting. Although it conveyed the same message that the manager had attempted to communicate in other ways, the
graphic visual clarified a point that heretofore had been evasive. As a
result they were more willing to participate in the activities necessary to
upgrade their skills and the emergency services of that department.

Figure 18-2 Emergency Room/Outpatient Department Activities

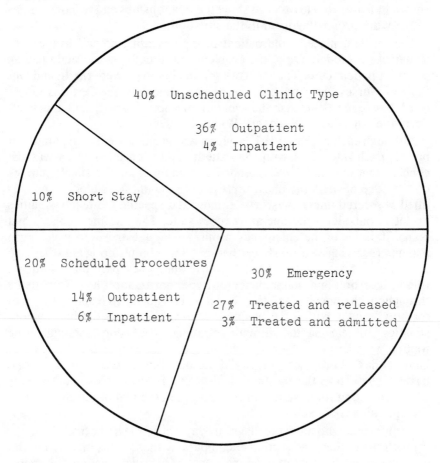

40% Unscheduled Clinic Type

36% Outpatient
4% Inpatient

10% Short Stay

20% Scheduled Procedures

14% Outpatient
6% Inpatient

30% Emergency

27% Treated and released
3% Treated and admitted

Six months of data

December 1979 through May 1980

Source: Eitel Hospital, Minneapolis, Minnesota. Used with permission.

In another hospital, a hospital administration resident was collecting information about the department of anesthesiology and anesthesia-related problems. Numerous symptomatic types of complaints were surfacing. This indicated to the hospital administrator that there were underlying problems. After collecting facts and conducting interviews with an interdisciplinary sampling, the overlapping and separation of responsibilities were still unclear. A resident constructed the conceptual model shown in figure 18-3 in order to show the relationships and responsibilities of the work groups involved in the situation.

The resident placed "the patient in the operating arena" in the very center of the model. Truly, the problems all directly or indirectly had an effect on patient care. The six work groups involved were the In and Out Surgery Nurses, the Surgeons, the Anesthesiologists, the Certified Registered Nurse Anesthetists, the Operating Room Nurses, and the Postoperative Anesthesia (Recovery Room) Nurses.

Although each of these work groups was not exactly equal in number or power, each interfaced with the patients and each other. This was the concept that the model was intended to demonstrate. The smaller circles on the edge of the large ones, representing the anesthesiologist and certified registered nurse anesthetists, indicated specific job responsibilities or duties outside of the operating room suite. The anesthesiologists had responsibilities in the emergency room, giving anesthesia to psychiatric patients receiving electric shock therapy, and administering anesthesia to cesarean section patients in the obstetric anit. They played a significant role in insertion and maintenance of hyperalimentation lines to patients throughout the hospital and they had a responsibility to respond to "doctor blue" codes within the hospital. The nurse anesthetist had responsibilities for starting the difficult intravenous infusions, administering routine anesthesia in the obstetric unit, and for responding to "doctor blue" codes. While these duties did not occur every day or on a routine basis, they did take the anesthesiologists and the nurse anesthetist outside of the operating room suite and thus had the potential of interfering with the operating room schedule.

The resident who drew the diagram symbolized the department of nursing with the broken line section encompassing those areas included in the organizational structure of the department of nursing. A larger box represented the hospital. This included both the department of nursing as well as the in and out surgery nurses who had line responsibilities elsewhere. The surgeons who used the hospital operating room suite and the anesthesiologist who had a commitment to deliver anesthesia in that hospital were also encompassed within the hospital.

In this instance the anesthesiologists were creating the biggest stir. Consequently a disproportionate amount of emphasis was being placed on problems as they were perceived by that work group. This conceptual model had a settling effect on the problem solvers who were trying to sort out the facts. Again, the graphic visual helped the hospital administrator and the resident to get a better grasp of the situation that confronted them. It showed the interrelatedness of the work group and the problems they

Figure 18-3 Complex Overlapping Problems Related to the Department of Anesthesiology

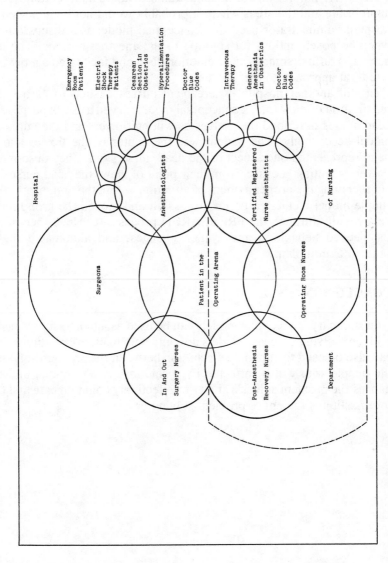

shared. It also showed where responsibilities overlapped and interfaced. It drew attention to the fact that a decision reached by one group would impact significantly on the rest of the work group. The model clarified the areas where nursing and/or hospital administrative intervention would be appropriate and the areas where it probably would not be indicated. The hospital administrator used this conceptual model as a discussion point when he posed options for solution to the anesthesiologists. The model helped to diffuse some of their emotionalism and facilitated a more objective total approach to the situation.

In still another hospital where head nurses desired to participate in redefinition of their role, a conceptual model served a useful purpose. The head nurses described themselves as wilting flowers and they drew their model accordingly. The patient was the center of the flower and each petal represented one aspect of the head nurse's job. They described the flower as wilting because, from their point of view, the head nurses were not receiving the proper amount of attention within the organization. This simple model facilitated group discussion and moved the group forward very rapidly through the PRESEARCH process. It helped them identify the needed behavioral and system changes, and illuminated the subsequent action plan.

CONCLUSION

In summary, conceptual models can be used as a tool to supplement the problem-solving process. Models not only help to clarify relationships but can also be used to stimulate discussion between the problem solvers and the people who will be affected by a solution. A conceptual model enhances the problem solver's ability to effectively communicate and therefore facilitates the entire problem-solving process.

Chapter 19

A Comparison of Problem-Solving Models

The purpose of this chapter is to compare and discuss several well-known managerial and health care problem-solving methods. Much of this chapter is an exerpt from an article "Managerial Problem Solving Models: A Review and a Proposal" by Lang, Dittrich and White. The portion of that paper which first appeared in the *Academy of Management Review* is reprinted here with permission.[1] A list of the problem-solving models discussed by these authors is included at the end of the chapter.

SIMILARITIES AND DIFFERENCES IN PROBLEM-SOLVING CONCEPTUALIZATIONS

The literature on problem solving exhibits a high degree of basic consistency in conceptualization of the problem-solving process. Most models of the problem-solving process schematically depict broad areas of cognitive and/or behavioral activities which are linked in continuous (or continuing) sequence. Beyond this basic process similarity, conceptualizations of problem solving show considerable variation. Some writers envision problem solving as a broad process that includes decision making.[2] Other authors depict the opposite—problem solving as an element in the decision-making process.[3, 4] A third set of authors treat decision making and problem solving as synonymous and use both terms to describe a general process of information gathering, analysis, and choice behavior.[5, 6] This fundamental confusion about the relationship between problem solving and decision making has led to difficulty in identifying what is or is not pertinent literature. The models reviewed for this article have been broadly defined by their authors as problem-solving models rather than more narrowly defined as depictions of the decision-making process.

Levels of Problem Solving

Research and discussion of problem solving can be partitioned conveniently into three levels of complexity, depending upon who is involved in the problem solving:

1. An individual level that involves a single manager,
2. A group level that involves the small group or task force, and
3. A larger organizational level that involves more than a single group.

Problem Solving as an Individual Process

At the individual level, a number of problem-solving models have been suggested that reveal similar underlying process structures. Most models incorporate a feedback loop to denote a cyclical process. All seem to account for problem finding, choice, and action behaviors with varying degrees of precision, ranging from the simple models suggested by Norton, Gustafson, and Foster[7] through Jackson[8] and Pounds[9] to more complex systemic models of Dill, Hilton, and Reitman[10] and Newell and Simon.[11]

Beyond the level of model development Shaw and Simon[12] refined the cognitive aspects of the process, but did not incorporate action steps. Reitman[13] and MacCrimmon[14] developed more detailed statements of conditions necessary for problem solving, a topic to be discussed later. Frequently cited, is Maier's simple two element conceptualization of problem solving that includes an idea getting process and an idea evaluation process.[15]

Problem Solving as a Group Process

While the use of groups for some forms of problem solving has been extensive,[16] conceptual frameworks of general managerial problem solving at the group level have received less attention. Similarities among the models are again noticeable. All models include sequences of problem finding and choice, but only one[17] explicitly includes a feedback loop and only one[18] incorporates an action step.

Two possible reasons may account for these omissions: (a) concentration on the additional complexities of the group processes in the analysis and choice phases, or (b) emphasis on special purpose groups problem solving, such as conflict resolution.[19] Two examples of special purpose models are the conflict resolution models of Filley, House, and Kerr[20] and of Blake, Shepard, and Mouton.[21] These two models differ from the individual level models in their greater emphasis on the search for alternatives. Delbecq, Van de Ven, and Gustafson[22] and Vroom and Yetton[23] are among authors who have addressed the added complexity of problem solving in groups and assessed positive and negative effects on problem solving arising from forces within the group. Delbecq, Van de Ven, and Gustafson[24] explored the advantages of the Nominal Group and Delphi problem-solving methods for reducing negative influences and enhancing the creative potential of groups and also proposed a five-step group planning process and a two-phased problem-solving process. Vroom and Yetton[25] identified three factors arising from group participation that affect problem-solving effectiveness: (a) the problem information held by the group, (b) the extent to which acceptance is needed for implementation, and (c) the extent to which there is congruence between organizational objectives and member goals.

Thus, with some adjustments in emphasis, owing possibly to the added complexity of multiple actors and to specialized research interests, basic similarities among the models and basic commonalities of components between group and individual processes remain.

Problem Solving as an Organization-Wide Process

At the organizational level, problem solving is more complex than group problem solving because of the range of resources available, the increased potential for conflict, the wider variety of environmental variables, the number of actors, and the magnitude of consequences.

The organizational-level models indicate closed loop processes of problem solving and all but one,[26] an explicit action step. Models of the top level management strategy making process use problem-solving approaches as a fundamental element in developing organization-wide strategies.[27,28] These models show a more explicit consideration of objectives than do the individual or group models, probably owing to the necessity for goal directed behavior and goal congruence when larger numbers of participants are involved.

Some organization-level authors have accounted for a nesting or an aggregation of individual problem-solving activities in their descriptions. Kast and Rosenzweig[29] described planned change as a process whereby the organization as a whole moves toward improvement. A component of the planned change model is problem solving, a process which is broken down into an eight-step sequence. The steps of both models are similar and represent a "systems within systems" arrangement similar to the authors' view of organization in general. Consistent with Kast and Rosenzweig, Kolb[30] postulated that the organization "learns" through problem solving and that the entire organization is a problem-solving system. In this view, an organizational system is a framework within which differing individual problem-solving (learning) styles serve multiple organizational problem-solving needs.

While apparently not proposing an explicit process model, Lawrence and Lorsch[31] also viewed the organization in an adaptive problem-solving entity. In their terms, the successful organization will "differentiate" to solve increasingly specialized problems and informational loads but will continually address itself to the problem of maintaining cross functional interrelationships by "integration" of the differentiated units.

In this same paper the authors propose a new model that focuses on the individual's ability and motivation to solve problems.[32] Their discussion includes the variables that affect problem perception, motivation, individual cognitive ability, and problem-solving skills. They also include mathematical formulas that can be used to predict outcome based on the previously mentioned factors. They conclude that their proposal will require carefully controlled laboratory research.

Lang, Dittrich, and White[33] did not include notable models such as the Kepner-Tregoe[34] method because these authors present a dual emphasis on problem solving and decision making. Likewise, "The Minnesota Way," developed by Bright M. Dornblaser[35] at the University of Minnesota is excluded for the same reasons.

Souder and Ziegler[36] present a synopsis of 20 creative and problem-solving techniques in an article entitled "A Review of Creativity and

Problem Solving Techniques.'' Within the body of their article a table is included which suggests appropriate techniques for particular types of problems depending on the desired outcome.

Two of the most familiar problem-solving models in health care are the problem-oriented medical record and the nursing process. Both of these models focus on patient "problems"—one from the medical perspective and the other from the nursing perspective. Each is designed to stimulate professionals to use a logical problem-solving process. These models include an evaluation of the effectiveness of the patient plan of care. Both are individual (patient-illness focused) models. These patient-focused models provide health professionals with a way to organize thoughts and subsequently to document observations, actions taken, and the patient's response to care giver intervention. According to the classifications of Lang, Dittrich, and White, problem oriented medical records and nursing process are individual level models.[37]

THE PRESEARCH MODEL

PRESEARCH is appropriate for use at both group and large organizational levels. This model is unique in two major respects: data are collected systematically prior to problem definition and planned change theory permeates the entire process. It differs from the Kast and Rosenzweig model that includes problem solving as part of planned change.[38]

The following list shows which of the many problem-solving models described in the literature and discussed in this book may be grouped based on situational level usage.

Problem-Solving Models—Three Levels:

- Individual Level
  - Norton, Gustafson and Foster
  - Jackson
  - Pounds
  - Dill, Hilton and Reitman
  - Newell and Simon
- Group Level
  - Delbecq, Van de Ven, and Gustafson
  - Filley
  - Filley, House and Kerr
  - Blake, Shepard and Mouton

● Organizational Level
—Kast and Rosenzweig
—Kolb
—Gleuck
—Johnson[39]

Group and/or Organizational Level

● Golightly, PRESEARCH

A primary goal in presenting the PRESEARCH process is to augment an individual's cognitive ability and problem-solving skills as described in the previously cited "Managerial Problem-Solving Models: A Review and a Proposal." No single model is right for all occasions. Just as leadership requires the manager to use a leadership style appropriate to the situation and the followers, so must the manager be able to select the problem-solving model most appropriate for a specific need.

NOTES

1. James R. Lange, John E. Dittrich, and Sam E. White, "Managerial Problem Solving Models: A Review and a Proposal," *Academy of Management Review,* October 1978, pp. 855–859.
2. W. F. Pounds, "The Process of Problem Finding," MIT Working Paper, *Psychological Review,* January 1953, pp. 55–63.
3. W. R. Dill, T. L. Hilton, and W. R. Reitman, *The New Managers: Patterns of Behavior and Development* (Englewood Cliffs, N.J.: Prentice-Hall, 1962).
4. R. F. Maier, "Maximizing Personal Creativity Through Better Problem Solving," *Personnel Administration,* January-February 1964, pp. 14–18.
5. F. E. Kast and J. E. Rosenzweig, *Organization and Management.* 2d ed. (New York, N.Y.: McGraw-Hill, 1974).
6. K. R. MacCrimmon and R. N. Taylor, "Decision Making and Problem Solving" in M. D. Dunnette, ed. *Handbook of Industrial and Organizational Psychology* (Chicago, Ill.: Rand McNally, 1976), pp. 1397–1453.
7. S. D. Norton, D. P. Gustafson, and C. E. Foster, "Assessment for Management Potential: Scale Design and Development, Training Effects and Rater/Ratee Sex Effects," *Academy of Management Journal,* March 1977, pp. 117–131.
8. K. R. Jackson, *The Art of Solving Problems* (New York, N.Y.: St. Martin's Press, 1975).
9. See, supra note 2.
10. See, supra note 3.
11. A. Newell and H. A. Simon, *Human Problem Solving* (Englewood Cliffs, N.J.: Prentice-Hall, 1972).
12. A.Newell, J. C. Shaw, and H. A. Simon, "Elements of a Theory of Human Problem Solving," *Psychological Review,* May 1958, pp. 151–166.

13. W. Reitman, "Heuristic Decision Procedures, Open Constraints and the Structure of Ill-Defined Problems," in M. Shelby and G. Bryan, eds. *Human Judgment and Optimality* (New York, N.Y.: Wiley, 1964), pp. 282–315.
14. K. R. MacCrimmon, "Managerial Decision-Making," in Joseph W. McGuire (Ed.) *Contemporary Management* (Englewood Cliffs, N.J.: Prentice-Hall, 1973).
15. See, supra note 4.
16. A. F. Osborn, *Applied Imagination*, 3rd ed. (New York, N.Y.: Charles Scribner's Sons, 1963).
17. A. C. Filley, *Interpersonal Conflict Resolution* (Glenview, Ill.: Scott Foresman, 1975).
18. A. L. Delbecq, A. H. Van de Ven, and D. H. Gustafson, *Group Techniques for Program Planning* (Glenview, Ill.: Scott Foresman, 1975).
19. R. I. Walton and R. B. McKeisie, *A Behavioral Theory of Negotiation* (New York, N.Y.: McGraw-Hill, 1965).
20. A. C. Filley, R. J. House, and S. Kerr, *Managerial Process and Organizational Behavior* (Glenview, Ill.: Scott Foresman, 1976).
21. R. R. Blake, H. A. Shepard, and J. S. Mouton, *Managing Intergroup Conflict in Industry* (Houston, Texas: Gulf Publishing Co., 1964).
22. See, supra note 18.
23. V. H. Vroom and P. W. Yetton, "Leadership and Decision Making: Basic Considerations Underlying the Normative Model," in W. R. Nord (Ed.) *Concepts and Controversy in Organizational Behavior*, Second ed. (Pacific Palisades, Calif.: Goodyear Publishing Co., 1976), pp. 626–643.
24. See, supra note 18.
25. See, supra note 23.
26. R. J. Johnson, *Executive Decisions*, Second ed. (Cincinnati, Ohio: South Western Publishing Co., 1970).
27. W. I. Glueck, *Business Policy: Strategy Formation and Management Action*, Second ed. (New York, N.Y.: McGraw-Hill, 1976).
28. See, supra note 26.
29. See, supra note 5.
30. D. A. Kolb, "On Management and the Learning Process," in D. A. Kolb, I. M. Rubin and J. M. Macintyre (eds.) *Organizational Psychology*, 2d ed. (Englewood Cliffs, N.J.: Prentice-Hall, 1974), pp. 27–42.
31. P. R. Lawrence and J. W. Lorsch, *Organization and Environment* (Homewood, Ill.: R. D. Irwin, 1969).
32. See, supra note 1.
33. See, supra note 1.
34. C. H. Kepner and B. B. Tregoe, *The Rational Manager* (New York, N.Y.: McGraw-Hill, 1965).
35. B. M. Dornblaser, *Problem Solving and Decision Making: A Philosophy and a Technique* (Minneapolis, Minn.: University of Minnesota, 1977).
36. W. E. Souder and R. W. Ziegler, "A Review of Creativity and Problem Solving Techniques," *Research Management*, July 1977, p. 40.
37. See, supra note 1.
38. See, supra note 5.
39. See, supra note 1, pp. 855, 857–858.

Index

A

Ability One (cognitive problem-solving ability), 82
Ability Two (possession of skills), 82
Academy of Management Review, 223
Access to educational facilities as barrier to adult education, 200-201, 202
Accommodation as mode of coping, 20
Action plan, 11-12, 71, 73-83, 92, 96, 109-114, 224, 225
Administrative backing, 63
Administrative decision making, 151, 154, 161, 210
Allen, Myron, 64
Alternative survey questions, 33, 34
Alternative(s)
  exploration of, 63-73, 109
  generation of, 64-66, 92, 109
  piecing together of, 70

American Nurses Association (ANA), 119
Analysis of data, case study in, 102-104
Anonymity and survey response, 32
Applicant Rating Grid, 95
Area of freedom, defined, 13, 14
Audit(s)
  and care of patient valuables, 178-179, *182, 183, 184, 185*
  as component of quality assurance, 124
  individual chart, 86
  joint, 119
  nursing, 119
Authority, lack of, 23
Avery, Allyson D., 121
Avoidance as mode of coping, 20

B

Barrier research
  conceptual framework, 193-194
  data collection and analysis, 197-199
  findings, 199-203

Note: Page numbers in *italic* indicate a figure or table.

implications, 204-207
methodology, 195-196
relationships among barriers,
    202-203
sample selection, 196-197
Behavioral change, process factors
    of, 81-82
Bell-ringing technique, 66
Bennett, Addison C., 154, *155*
Best acceptable alternative, 67
Best acceptable solution, 11, 66, 67,
    68, 69-71, 73, 82, 92
Best fit. *See* best acceptable solution
Bias in surveys, 30, 32, 37
Blake, R. R., 225, 227
Blue Cross, 217
Blue Shield, 217
Brain Mind Bulletin, 24
Brainstorming
    rules for, 65
    time limits for, 66
Brainstorming, 66
Brooke, Robert H., 121
Brucker, Mary C., 119, *138*
Budget (and best acceptable
    solution), 67
Bush Leadership Fellows, 231

C

Calendar
    MBO, 73, 75
    Programmed Planning and
        Implementation, 73-74
Campbell, David, 65, 71
CARE cards and patient valuables,
    178
Care givers. *See* health care
    providers
Catholic Hospital Association, 217
Center for Creative Leadership
    (Greensboro, N.C.), 70
Change
    implementation of, 211
    organizational effects of, 80-81
    ownership of, 61

planning for, 218
resistance to, 211-213
staff concurrence with, 108-109
Change agents. *See* health care
    manager
Change impact monitoring, 85
Change theory, planned, 62
Choice in problem-solving models,
    224, 225
Clark, Charles, 65, 66
Client system in planned change
    theory, 209, 211-212
Closed-ended survey questions, 39,
    40, 41, 48, 51, 105
Cognitive problem-solving ability
    (Ability One), 82
Collaboration as mode of coping, 20
Command of resources, 82
Committee(s)
    and group dynamics, 53-54
    role in problem-solving, 61
Communication channel bypass, 23
Communication networks and
    managerial role, 15-16
Community service determination,
    29
Community surveys, 31
Competition as mode of coping, 20
Complex conflict situations, 22-23
Complex problems, identification of,
    59
Complex projects, flow chart for, 94
Comprehensive approach to
    problem-solving, 4
Compromise as mode of coping, 20
Concentration phase of creativity, 65
Conceptual framework for barrier
    research, 193-194
Conceptual models, 215, *216,* 217,
    218, *219,* 220, *221,* 222
    and interdependence of systems,
        210
Conflict
    benefits of, 16, 25
    complex, 22-23
    and entropy, 24-25

and goal-directed behavior, 17-19
occurrences of, 16
and the organization's energy,
   24-25
potential for, 22-23
reasons for, 17-22
resolution in problem-solving
   models, 225
simple, 22-23
and work groups, 23
and work relationships, 16-22
Conflict of interest, *19*
Consumers and consumerism, 122,
   217
Content, clustering of, 58
Content analysis, 39, 49-51, 55, 58
   as approach to data gathering, 10
Continuing education, 97, 100-101
Cooperation, role of in problem-
   solving, 63
Coping abilities and mechanisms,
   14-15, 20, 22
Cover letter(s) for surveys, 103
CPM. *See* Critical Path Method
Creative Growth Center (Los Gatos,
   Calif.), 64
Creativity, phases of, 65
Crisis intervention, 21, 22, 28
Crisis prevention efforts, 8
Critical Path Method (CPM), 75

D

Data
   objective, 10
   and PRESEARCH process, 90
   and problem solving, 57-62
   data sorting, 41-42, 43, 48
   subjective, 10
   tabulation, 39, 51
   uses of, 9, 29, 164, 167
Data analysis, 10, 39
   for barrier research, 197-199
   case study in, 102-104
Data display possibilities, 41, 43, 48

Data gathering, 3, 4, 6, 7, 8-9, 27-38,
   59
   for barrier research, 197
   and field of uncertainty, 27-29, 30
   and interviewing, 141-142
   and librarians, 27
   methods of, 90, 99-102, 164, 167
   practical hints for, 34-37
   and PRESEARCH, 27, 29, 193
   and problem-solving effort, 192
   process of, 3, 4, 6, 7, 8-9, 27-30, 59,
      63
   time frames for, 32-33, 34, 164, 167
   and unanticipated information, 53
Decision-making, 67
   boundaries of, 13
   and problem-solving, 223-224, 226
Delbeq, A. L., 225, 227
Delphi problem-solving method, 225
Departmental reorganization,
   97-117
Dill, W. R., 224, 227
Disequilibrium (in problem
   statements), 57
Disturbance handling as managerial
   role, 15-16
Dittrich, John E., 82, 226, 227
Dornblaser, Bright M., 226
The Dynamics of Planned Change,
   212-213

E

Education department
   reorganization (case study),
   97-117
Eductional barriers of adults,
   research in, 193-207
Educational Testing Service (ETS),
   194
Egdahl, Richard H., 121, 138
Eitel Hospital (Minneapolis, Minn.),
   95, *159*, 231
   and conceptual models, *219*
   position application
      questionnaire, 142, *143*

and protocol, *125*
and quality assurance (case
    example), 126, *127*, 128, *129*,
    130, *131*, 132, *133*, *134*, *135*
Emergency service, 218, *219*
Emotional release and crisis
    intervention, 21-22
Employee orientation, 97
Entropy, 24
    and organizational conflict, 24-25
    and PRESEARCH problem-
        solving, 25
Equal Employment Opportunity
    Commission (EEOC), 143
Equilibrium (in problem
    statements), 57
Ethnoscience, 197
Evaluation, 85-94
    case study application for, 114-117
    and followup, 12, 56
    and quality assurance, 120, 122
Evaluative monitoring. *See* followup
Excellence in Leadership, 64
External factors (and best
    acceptable solution), 67

F

Facts (as element in defining
    problems), 57-59
Fair labor standards, 217-218
Family responsibilities as barrier to
    adult education, 201, 202, 203
Feasibility, 68, 69
Feedback, 91, 92, 97
    to interviewee, 146
    in problem-solving models, 224,
        225
    and quality assurance, 120
Field of uncertainty, 6, 8-9, 10, 13-25,
    55, 57, 90
    and data gathering, 27-29, 30
    identification of (case study), 98
    as out-of-balance situation, 210
    and PRESEARCH, 125, 163-167
    and problem-solving, 163-167

in situational interviewing, 141
Filley, A. C., 225, 227
Finances as barrier to adult
    education, 201, 202, 203
Fixed alternative survey questions,
    90-91
Fixed survey questions, 33
Flexible scheduling, 58-59
Flow chart for complex project, *94*
Followup, 12, 56, 85-94
    amount necessary, 85-86
    defined, 86
    workforce view of, 85
Foster, C. E., 224, 227
Friedman, William, 81
Funnel analogy, 59, 60

G

Ganong, Joan, 80, 130, 211
Ganong, W. L., Health Care Man-
    agement Team, 231
Ganong, Warren, 80, 130, 211
Gertman, Paul M., 121, *138*
"Givens" (existing facts, traditions
    and restraints)
    and data gathering, 27, 29, 33, 55
    as factor in defining problems,
        57-59
Gleuck, W. I., 228
Goal Analysis, 54-55
Goals, 85, 91, 104-105
    case study in, 104-105
    and conflict, 17-19
Goble, Frank, 64, 65, 71
Golightly, Cecilia, 228, 231
Government regulation and patient
    care, 218
Grid, solution analysis, 67-68, 70, 71
Group facilitator for problem-solv-
    ing, 11
Group process, 11, 53-54
Guide for the Beginning Researcher,
    5, 189-191
Gustafson, D. H., 225, 227
Gustafson, D. P., 224, 227

H

Hawthorne Study, 21, 22
Health care managers
and conceptual models, 215, 218, 228
and disturbance handling, 15-16
and effects of problem-solving, 53
and followup, 85
and monitoring, 15
in planned change theory, 209, 210, 211, 213
planning time for, 89
and problem-solving, 13, 163
and response to crisis, 13-15
responsibilities, 82
in situational interviewing, 141, 148
Health care providers
and conceptual models, 217, 218
and quality assurance, 119-120, 122, 123. *See also* hospitals; nurses; physicians
Health care trends, 67
Health Maintenance Organizations, 217
Hearsay interpretation, 22
Help with Career Planning: A Workbook for Nurses, 231
Hilton, T. L., 224, 225
Hirschowitz, R. J., 81
Homeostasis, 210
Hospitals
and quality assurance, 119, 121, 122-123
in sample conceptual model, 220, *221,* 222 *See also* health care providers; nurses; physicians
House, R. J., 225, 227
Hover, Julie, 120, 123

I

"Icebreakers" as survey information collection technique, 34
Ideas, group ownership of, 61

Illumination phase of creativity, 65
Implementation of problem-solving efforts, 11-12
Incubation phase of creativity, 65, 66
Indirect response to survey questions, 36, 37
Information. *See* data
In-service education, 97, 98
Institute of Medicine (IOM) and quality assurance, 120
Interviews
face-to-face, 142-144
facilitating, 36-37
personal, 9, 31-32, 33, 35-37
and responses (case example), 164, 168-170
situational, 141-149
as written process, 95
Involvement
group ownership of, 61
importance of, 59-62, 89
Issues
clustering of, 91
definition of, 49
as factor in defining problems, 57-59
goals based upon, 104-105

J

Jackson, K. R., 224, 227
Job description in situational interviewing, 141-142, 143
Job performance expectations and standards, 22, 86, 141-142
Johnson, R. J., 228
Johnstone, John W. C., 194
Joint Committee on Accreditation of Hospitals (JCAH), 218
and quality assurance, 121-123, *125,* 127
standards, 119, 123-124
Journal of Obstetric, Gynecologic and Neonatal Nursing, 138

K

Kast, F. E., 226, 227, 228
Kepner, C. H., 226
Kepner-Tregoe method, 226
Kerr, S., 225, 227
"Killer phrases," 65-66
Klein, Donald, 211, 212
Klinger, Kalia M., 193
Kolb, D. A., 226, 228

L

Lange, James R. 82, 223, 226, 227
Lawrence, P. R., 226
Learning needs assessment, 29
Legal constraints and patient care, 217-218
Level of practice and quality assurance, 120, 122
Lewin, Kurt, 210
Librarians and data gathering, 27
Licensures, 217-218
Lippitt, Ronald, 212
Literature research and review, 27, 95
Long-range planning, 8, 28
Lorsch, J. W., 226

M

MacCrimmon, K. R., 224
Maier, Norman R. F., 158, 224
Mail questionnaire, 32, 34
Malpractice, 123
Management by Objectives (MBO), 73-74, 75
Manager. See health care manager
Manuel, Bradley J., 191
Marienau, Catherine, 193
Mayo, Elton, 21-22
MBO. See Management by Objectives
Measurable outcome goals, 85, 91
Medicaid, 217
Medicare, 217

Methodology
anthropological, 193-207
for barrier research, 195-196
Methods analysis, 9
defined, 154-155
questions, 155
Methods Improvement in Hospitals, 154-155, 155
"Minnesota Way," method, 226
Mintzberg, Henry, 15
Mission statement (and best acceptable solutions), 67
Models, conceptual, and interdependence of systems, 210
Monitoring, 15
systems and quality assurance, 120, 125
Morris Learning Center (MLC), 193, 194-195, 196, 197, 199, 200, 206, 207
Motivation, 82, 202
Mouton, J. S., 225, 229

N

National League for Nursing, 77, 78, 80
Negativity, emotional, 20
Negotiation as coping, 20
Network, simple PERT, 75-77
Neutral persons as data gatherers, 35, 36-37
Newall, A., 224, 227
Nominal Group problem-solving method, 225
Nonspecific response to survey questions, 36, 37
Nonverbal messages, 15, 16
Norton, S. D., 224, 227
Nurses
in conceptual models, 217, 220, 221, 222
and JCAH standards, 123-124
and performance standards, 131, 132, 133, 134, 135. See also

health care providers; nursing departments; physicians
Nursing Administrative Council, *127*-129
Nursing departments
  in conceptual models, 220-221, *222*
  and interdepartmental problem-solving efforts, 151-161
  and JCAH standards, 123-124
  quality assurance development in, 126-127, *127*, 128-129, *129*, 130-132, *132*, *133-135*. *See also* nurses
Nursing Management, 80, 130, 211
Nursing Management Council (Eitel Hospital), 127, 128-129
Nursing Outlook, 138
Nursing Practice Council (Eitel Hospital), 127, 128-129

O

Objective(s) for problem solving, 67
Open-ended survey questions, 9, 30, 33, 34, 39, 40, 49, 50, 51, 90-91
Open systems model, 217
Oral interview process, 95
O'Regan, Daniel J., 120
Organizational problems and survey response, 35
Osborne, Alex, 65, 66
Outcome
  charted, 93
  criteria, 12, 95
  and goal statements, 53, 54, 55, 56, 85
Outpatient service, 218-*219*
Ownership
  of change, 61
  of ideas, 61
  of involvement, 61
  of problems, 11, 63, 92
  of solutions, 62

P

Patient, 123-124, 217, 220, *221,* 222
Patient care, 119-120, 121, 124, 217-218, 220
Patient Care Committee (Eitel Hospital), 129
Patient education, 102
Patient valuables, care of, 96, 175-185
Patient's Bill of Rights, the, 217
Peer review, 86, 95
Penberth, Martyann, 96, 163
People-centeredness, 62, 71
  approach, step-by-step procedures for, 89, 90-92
  definitional process of, 57-62
  and evaluation and followup, 89
  and the problem, 64
  another problem, 86
Performance evaluation, 29
Performance Evaluation Review Technique (PERT), 73, 75-77, 96, 109, 112, 178, *180, 181*
Performance Evaluative Tool, *87-88*
Performance standard, 86, *87-88*
PERT. *See* Performance Evaluation Review Technique
Phi Kappa Phi, 231
Physicians
  in conceptual models, 217
  and quality assurance, 119, 121
  usage patterns as problem indicators, 8, 9. *See also* health care providers; hospitals; nurses
Plan of action. *See* action plan
Planned change, 226
  theory of, 62, 209, 210, 211, 213
Planning, 89
Policy interpretations, 22
Population sampling, 31
Position application
  form, 143
  oral questionnaire, 142, *143,* 148
Position description, 101-102
Positive reinforcement, 35

Possession of skills (Ability Two), 82
Pounds, W. F., 224, 227
Power: Use It or Lose It, 77
Preparation phase of creativity, 65
Presbyterian Hospital School of Nursing, 231
PRESEARCH
  action plans in, 11-12, 71, 73-83, 92, 96, 109-114, 224, 225
  application, 95-96
  case study of, 95, 97-117
  chart for, 93, 94
  and collective decision making, 161
  as compared with other problem-solving methods and research, 6-7
  in conceptual models, 163-173, 222, 227, 228, 231
  and data gathering, 3, 4, 6, 7, 8-10, 27, 29, 191, 192, 193
  defined, 3-7
  educational advantages of, 173
  and entropy, 25
  in interdepartmental problem solving, 179
  and JCAH standards, 123-125, *125*
  and multidisciplinary approach, 8
  as people-centered, 8-12
  planned change theory in, 209, 211, 213
  planning in, 89
  in preemployment process, 148-149
  process, summary of, 90-92
  as provider of group work structure, 11
  as provider of process framework, 4
  and quality assurance programs, 124-125, 126-130
Prigogine, Illya, 24-25
Principles and Application of PERT/CPM, 75
Priorities, 8, 22

Privacy, 35
Private insurance, 217
Problem(s)
  analysis of, 77-82
  awareness of, 7
  definition of, 49, 57-59
  importance, departmental differences in, 64
  ownership, 11, 63, 92
  potential identification of, 16
  prevention, 95, 148
  strategy, 77-82
  symptoms of, 3-4, 8, 9
Problem-solver(s)
  and conceptual models, 222
  responsibility of, 89, 93
  as role of health care manager, 3, 4, 11, 163
  selection of, 11
Problem-solving
  as art, 3, 5
  aspects of, 90-93
  compared to research, 5, 6, 7
  comprehensive approach, 4
  conceptual models, 5, 6, 7, 215, 222, 223-228
  and data collection, 6, 7, 8-10, 191-207
  and decision-making, 223-224, 226
  delegation of responsibility for, 89, 93
  and goal statements, 10
  as group process, 224-225
  and health care managers, 3, 4, 11, 163
  as individual process, 224, 227
  interdepartmental, 175-185
  levels of, 224, 227-228
  models, 215, 222, 223-228
  as organization-wide process, 225-226
  as people-centered, 61-62
  and planned change model, 209, 226, 227
  PRESEARCH approach to 189
  priorities, establishment of, 29

project documentation and evaluation, 124, *125*, 126
and quality assurance, 124
and research, 189-207
symptomatic view, 3-4
and systems theory, 210
Problem-solving Discussions and Conferences, 158
Problem statements, 39, 49, 54, 57-62, 91
case study in, 105-109
and data, 7, 10-11
formula for, 57-59
Process criteria, 95
Production-verification phase of creativity, 65
Professional Standards Review Organization (PSRO), 119, 121
Programmed Planning and Implementation Calendar, 73-74
Progress reports, 12
Protocol and quality assurance programs, 124, *125*, 126

Q

Quality assurance, 95, 119-138
defined, 119, *120*, 136-138
and health care consumers, 121-122
and health care providers, 119
and hospitals, 122-123
and PRESEARCH, 125
programs for, 12, 120-124, 126-130
Quality Assurance and Health Care, 121, *138*
Questionnaire(s)
development of, 29-30, 32, 33-34, 59
evaluation, 34
flexible scheduling, *40*
mail, 32, 34
response rates, 41-48
situational, 144, *145*, 146

R

Reedy, Nancy Jo, 119, 138
Reitman, W. R., 224, 227
Research
barrier, 196, 199-204
compared with PRESEARCH, 6, 191, 193
compared with problem-solving, *5*, 6, 7, 189-191
models, characteristics of, 6
and problem-solving, 191-207
Respect, lack of, 21
Rivera, Ramon J., 194
Riley, Mary, 115-117
Roach, Margaret, 17-22
Role clarification, 101
Role conflict as organizational problem, 97-117
Rosenberg, Pearl, 15
Rosenzweig, J. E., 226, 227, 228

S

St. Joseph's College, 163
St. Joseph's Hospital (St. Paul, Minn.), *180-185*, 215, *216*, 217-218, 231
Salk, Dr. Jonas, 28
Satir, Virginia
Schaefer, Marguerite, 16, 25
Schmadl, John Charles, *138*
self-interest groups, involvement of, 80
Shaw, J. C., 224
Shepard, H. A., 225, 227
Sigma Delta Tau, 231
Simon, H. A., 224, 227
Solution(s)
and alternatives, 63-73
determination of, 66-69, 71, 72
ownership of, 62
Solution Analysis Grid, 67-68, 70, 71
case study example, 110
and decision-making, 158, *159*, 161
procedures for, 68-69

Souder, W. E., 226
Spradley, Barbara W., 210
Staff development, 29
Staff education, 29
Structure criteria, 95
Subjective responses, 39
Support systems and solsution-seek-
    ing process, 23
Survey(s)
  appropriateness, 91
  and bias, 30, 32, 37
  methods of, 31-37
  participants, rights of, 37
  questions, types of, 29-30, 33, 34
  response examination, 39-51
  and response patterns, 37, 49
Survey instrument(s)
  development of, 9, 29-30, 33-34
  evaluation of, 34
  examples of, 100-101, 103
  and PRESEARCH process, 90-91
  pretest of, 30, 34
  and target population, 30-31, 32,
    33, 34

T

Take the Road to Creativity, 65
Target population
  and PRESEARCH process, 90
  and survey instruments, 30-31, 32,
    33, 34
Task force, role in problem defini-
    tion, 61
Telephone surveys, 9, 32, 34
  territorial rights, 22
  time as barrier to adult education,
    201-202, 203
Time frames, 69, 91, 96
  for data gathering, 32-33, 34
Timing and best acceptable solution,
    67
Transactional analysis (TA), 17

Tregoe, B. B., 226
Trend studies, 16, 17
Trust
  lack of, 23
  role of in group work, 82

U

University Without Walls (UWW),
    193, 195, 196, 199, 204
Unstructured survey questions, 32

V

Van de Ven, A. H., 225, 227
Verification-production phase of
    creativity, 65
Voluntary accreditation, 218
Vroom, V. H., 225

W

Wandelt, Mabel, 189
Wassenaar, Dirk J., 75
Weaver, Adriane, 163, 211
White, Sam E., 82, 223, 226, 227
Work groups, 220, 221, 222
  and quality assurance, 120
Work relationships and conflict,
    16-22, 23
Written interview questionnaire,
    143-144
Written messages as data, 16

Y

Yetton, P. W., 225

Z

Ziegler, R. W., 226
Zimmer, Marie, 120, 123

ABOUT THE AUTHOR

CECELIA GOLIGHTLY is an assistant administrator at Eitel Hospital, Minneapolis, Minnesota. She is also an associate member of the W. L. Ganong Health Care Management Consultant Team of Chapel Hill, North Carolina. As Director of Special Projects at St. Joseph's Hospital, St. Paul, Minnesota, she functioned as a problem-solving facilitator. Through her work in hospitals as a health care consultant, she has provided problem solvers with the people-centered PRESEARCH framework which converts unwieldy problems to manageable solutions.

She received her nursing diploma from Presbyterian Hospital School of Nursing, Charlotte, North Carolina. She completed the two-year independent study program in patient care administration at the University of Minnesota. Her bachelor of science and master of public health degrees were conferred by the University of Minnesota. The culmination of her academic pursuits was made possible in a large part by her having been chosen in 1977 as a Fellow in the prestigious Bush Leadership Fellows program. She is a member of Sigma Theta Tau and Phi Kappa Phi. She is the author of *Help with Career Planning: A Workbook for Nurses.*